The Double Diamond

A novel

By

Cotton Ward

Aunt Delma —
I hope this isn't
a poor companion
to the good books and
art in your house.
Cotton

1stBooks - rev. 05/22/01

For Zoe, Zachary, Cassie

Author's Note

Someone has spoken of an existential moment all people grow to. Mine came while standing in a river, and though my words at the time—I think I said them aloud—were no more profound than "That water keeps flowing and flowing," it must have baggaged me in some way, for I do not wish to be false to rivers. Therefore, in this work of fiction the rivers are true according to subtle name changes, and not to miles and compass points.

BOOK ONE

Cotton Ward

1

Tom Bird was hamstrung.

The horses needed hay. They were out in the pasture pawing, but they weren't getting much. The snow, thawing by day and freezing at night, was mostly ice on ice. Tom Bird's pickup wouldn't run, and he had neither the money to fix the pickup nor to buy hay. He could go to the creek and chip cottonwood bark as the Indians did, but surely that diet was too spare for thoroughbreds.

Bird was patching a stock tank and still thinking on the matter when his sister drove up. Her name was Sally and she was checking on him. Because it had taken him thirty years of buckarooing to accumulate any kind of capital and then had blown it "on those fool racehorses," she considered him addled in the big things in life. He in turn thought her useless in everyday tasks and was glad her husband had figured life out and bought into a car dealership that made it big. Bird didn't see how she could get by without a purse.

Sally got out of the Buick and asked if the coffee was on. She was a tall, straight woman, with sharp nose and chin, and dark hair beginning to get silver points.

"Fresh out," Bird said. "How about towing my truck to town?"

She cast an eye at the rusting carcass. "To the dump?"

"I bought that pickup from Hondo Motors," he reminded her.

"Sixteen years ago," she reminded him.

They chained up and eased through the ruts of his driveway. On the freshly-graded county road, Sally drove like hell, throwing a blizzard of gravel onto the pickup's grill and windshield. Bird tried to honk but the horn didn't work. For a mile he waved at her, sometimes flinching when a single rock swelled huge in the flightpath leading to his head. He waited for her to glance just once in the rearview mirror but she didn't, and with gritted teeth he rode out the barrage until they hit the pavement at the lumber mill. The windshield had a dozen fresh chips.

At Jensen's Garage, Bird asked his sister to wait in the car. In the early years of Hondo Motors, Sally made people pay their bills. She'd learned toughness but nothing about cars. Bird flat feared the sisterly help. He explained, "When you point to the motor and say, 'What's that thingie,' it costs me an extra fifty dollars."

"What am I supposed to say?"

"It's not your choice of words. If you called it a thingamajig or thingabob or whatchamacallit or doodad, I don't think it would be much better."

"Okay. Just remember. Frank Jensen is a greedy man."

3

Bird took the keys inside and told Jensen to fix it. He grabbed a cup of coffee for Sally.

"Thanks, Sis," he said as he handed the styrofoam cup through the window.

"I suppose you're going to Alforcas." It was a bar that coerced rough men to be civil.

"For a while. Maybe fishing if Frank gets it fixed early enough."

Drinking, Sally understood. Many people were fond of that. But fishing in November snow flurries made sense only to her brother. He carried a duffel bag of rod, vest, and waders everywhere. When the two of them went to East Los Angeles for an uncle's funeral, he fished an aqueduct while Latino kids stood on the access road and riffed on the loco fisherman. When people in these parts spoke of "the fishing cowboy," listeners understood.

"I'll take you fishing now to the Big Timber," Sally said.

Bird grabbed his duffel from the front seat of the pickup. The Big Timber wasn't his first choice, but it was nearby and maybe not too late to catch a brown trout coming up from the reservoir to spawn.

"And I'll bring you back if I get a mess of fish to fry," Sally added.

She did not say idle things and Bird decided to creel a few if he could. Like most women, she thought it folly for a fisherman to return from the river smug and happy and empty-handed.

The snow that had been moving about the peaks slid down the timbered slopes and onto the sagebrush flats, where the county road meandered toward the cottonwoods of the Big Timber. The snow was so fine that it both rose and fell in the light gusts, more like gnats than bits of ice. Rigging up, Bird had to fight the notion he was inhaling bugs. Sally had the car heater on and a book out when he followed a trail through the undergrowth to the river.

The Big Timber begins at ten thousand feet and is, by elevation, halfway to the sea in forty miles, though it travels 900 more before its waters reach the Pacific. The high prairie which is halfway to sea is a short run, for a dam blocks the canyon where it used to exit the high country onto the farmlands of the Shoshone River plain. The water still flows, but the river is not the same; it is a desert river, with more mud and less rocks, and when it comes together with its sister, the Little Timber, it loses even its name because a Frenchman got sick and called the river he drank from Bad Water. In November the Big Timber ran low and the freestone glides were holes for small rainbow, but Bird, still thinking about late-spawning brown trout, walked a mile downstream and began fishing where the current made a long run against a cut bank just above the canyon of the reservoir.

He first tried the current seam near him, raising one small rainbow on an olive caddis. To fish the far seam he changed from the dry fly to a big brown and olive nymph. At the head of the drift, he had two bumps which he took to be darting fingerlings, and then the universe paused. He struck hard and fast. The rod bent, fast to an anchor. Then the fish rolled on the surface and he saw it was a rainbow, a silver female, four, maybe five pounds. The fish shot deep and downstream, tearing off all the fly line and twenty yards of backing before it jumped straight up on its tail. Bird had a deep parabola of line submerged in the water and he thought, I cannot land him, while he stripped in line and splashed downstream on moss-slippery stones in thigh-deep water, watching as the fish made two more spectacular shivering jumps against the same cursed slack, still stripping and thinking, I will lose him, as the fish went to more porpoising jumps before submerging to sull in the deepest, heaviest current, allowing Tom Bird to come up tight.

He flipped the long loop of recovered line ashore and looked around for a beaching spot. The fish started shaking its head and Bird floundered downstream to change the angle of the pull. The fish responded by making another run, this time at him, and he was again madly stripping in line. Though he knew the fish had not tired, he guided it toward some slackwater where the trout might be beached. The fish, relenting, rose into mutual view and tore off in a run that burned Bird's fingers where he held the line. He worked the fish in for another short run, and several more, before it began to list. The fish came in heavy on a taut line and bowed rod, and when Bird felt the friction of the fish on stones, he gave one last tug, dropped the rod, and jumped to scoop the trout onto the dry stones and squatted in readiness to tackle it should its flop be toward water. He picked it up. The line had busted in the scoop. That was always a chancey moment.

"You are seven pounds," he said after he rapped the head and placed the fish on sandgrass. "Beautiful."

All his life when he had caught a truly big fish in a good way, he quit fishing. Lighting a cigarette, he sat on the bank beside the fish and relived it on the stream. He reviewed the take, the roll, the long run finishing in three shivering catapults, the moment of head-shaking which even now in his memory was a bad time.

"Beautiful fish do not sull and shake their heads," he admonished. "Yes, big fish do. But to be big and beautiful..."

He was using the word beautiful a lot, but it was a short word for all he had in his head. Though he rarely remembered where he last laid his gloves, he could recall a cinematic narrative of every big fish he'd caught, along with those he'd hooked and lost. Ten years from now he would come upon the cut bank and would tingle in his flesh as the trout took and ran again.

He broke down his rod and carried the big silver trout by the gills to the car, laying it on the spare tire in the trunk. Sally was off somewhere. He honked the horn and she came back with a little bouquet of aspen and maple leaves. It was her highest praise to count enough steaks to feed her family, including Bird.

Out on the highway, Sally said, "I suppose at Alforcas you can find out about Katie's boy."

"Yes," he said. Katie was a longtime Alforcas barmaid who had gone away to the Mayo Clinic and died.

After a silence, Sally said, "She was the most immoderate selector of men I ever saw."

"Yes," Bird said again. Late in the night, if Katie was in mind to, she kissed and rubbed the targeted man between drink orders.

"What's to become of the boy?"

"I imagine Al will take him. That would be the best thing. He has been raised by the Alforcas."

"Why such a slut?" Sally mused.

The word jarred Bird. Though he knew Sally meant no ill, he would still have rebuked her if Katie were living. But now that Katie was dead, it did seem to be the salient mystery of her life.

Sally steered into the gravel parking lot of Alforcas. "Dinner's at eight. Call me if they don't get your pickup fixed."

As he was getting out, she accelerated a bit to make him hop free of the car, and drove away satisfied that her possession of rod and waders would bring her unsociable brother to dinner. Probably he would have come anyway—he was less the hermit since she had quit trying to stick a woman in his life.

Tom Bird bought a whiskey from Al's wife, Bea. He told himself he would have three, which meant four because he never counted the one just before going out the door. He drank the first two alone by the window. The snow, still light and gusty, began to make a cover on the highway. A truck rolled by, full of bawling cattle. In came a noisy bunch from Quinn's next door. Working cowboys, all of them: but their horses grew fat and their shovels grew dull; in the spring they herded two hundred cows up the highway to their allotment and in the fall brought them down to eat the hay they'd spent the summer hauling. The last haying crew Bird had been on he was sixteen and doing what his father told him.

Al came in with Katie's boy. They both had on stocking caps and mittens when they entered, but in a flurry the boy shed these and ran to the far wall and looked at the Union Pacific calendar. With his finger he traced the days of November till he came to the nineteenth.

Al stamped the snow from his boots and said, "Tyree's counting on the calendar."

The boy, who was six, sat down at Bird's table.

"Tom, is that whiskey?" Tyree said in evenly clipped words, lisping slightly on "whiskey."

"It is." Bird slid the glass away from the boy, who, like most boys, liked a draught of beer, but unlike most boys, could not distinguish the foamy amber

6

beer from the unpalatable whiskey: Tyree had to ask. It was one of the things that made people think him not-too-bright. "I'll get you a glass of water if you're thirsty."

"I am thirsty," said Tyree in his mechanical voice.

While Bird was getting the water, the cowboys weren't saying much so he asked if they knew of any colts needing broke.

They thought a bit and then one said, "You might try the Double Diamond."

Bird's gaze darted to the man's face to see if he meant anything by the remark. The day he picked up his saddle and bits from the Double Diamond after thirty years there, he was in the Alforcas when a fellow learned the news and said, "Hell, I thought you was *branded* Double Diamond." Bird hit him so fast he forgot to unclasp the small tumbler he was holding and consequently made a mess of his hand and the fellow's chin. For Bird, it was the only time he'd slugged a man, and just as he learned not to kick a horse by breaking a toe, he was taught by a lacerated hand not to hit men. However, the potent recklessness had quieted the suggestions he had a brand on his ass. And this man had meant nothing.

"I don't know," another mused. "She's selling out."

Bird moved down the bar to where Al stood wreathed in cigar smoke. "That true about the Double Diamond?"

"So I've heard. But I can't imagine the Double Diamond in financial distress. Maybe Eleanor is just ready for palm trees and ocean breezes."

"Yes," Bird agreed. "There's forty-five hundred cows bought and paid for on the best range in the country. She's not losing money."

Tyree had a skyscraper stack of plastic-wrapped crackers on the table when Bird brought him the water. Bird delofted the pile and carried the basket of crackers back to the bar.

"What's to become of the boy?" he asked Al.

"I don't know. Katie had family in Texas and California. But she wants the boy to stay in town."

"With who?"

"As usual, Katie never got around to thinking practical on it."

The saloonkeeper was a worldly man with a patient manner and tired wisdom. A graduate of Stanford, he'd been a highly-paid geologist for oil companies on three continents, somewhere along the way losing the zeal for his job and retiring at 50 to buy a marginal bar in the northern Rockies. Ten years in town had not changed him; he was a glum yet charitable man somewhat baffled by the irrational antics of his neighbors. He had come to see destiny as malignant and sought to cheat it by not desiring much of anything. This monkish mind had a twist peculiar in the West: he would not run a tab nor pour drinks on the house. It was tiresome to dun people for money or listen to broke big-spenders ask if it was time yet for the house to act hospitable. Katie, who came with the Alforcas purchase (she had let him know), managed a private tab for three months before Al found out and paid her off, forbidding it further. She quit the Alforcas then— and quit twenty times more over the next eight years. There was always a reason, and Katie always left town to look for something better, but when her money was gone she came back. After the boy was born, the Alforcas was clearly, in Frost's line, "the place where, when you have to go there, they have to take you in." Katie continued to quit periodically, but Al took to calling the episodes vacations and paid her for them, so the boy would have clothes and toys like other boys.

"Tom, why don't you take him home for a couple of days. He needs to romp and work. This hanging out in a bar all day is no good."

"Do you think he wants to go?"

"I think he will."

"I'll ask him. Does he understand about his mom?"

"He asked me this morning if she was still dead."

Several times Bird had asked himself the same thing. Al had shipped her body back and Bird had moved it to her final place, but sometimes he just forgot.

Tyree climbed out of the chair, drawn by the pulsing lights of the jukebox. He poked a finger around the grimy bottom, where he'd once found a quarter. A man and wife at the table next to the jukebox gave the boy a coin and asked him to punch some numbers. Even a small boy could know he was being told to get lost, but Tyree drifted back after pushing buttons. These people were saying the same things he heard in a taco stand in Denver. *When I was out a-ridin' one dark and wintry day*, sang the juke. They didn't look the same but they had the same bad hearts. The big music hid their words *their eyes were wild, their tongues were out, their flanks all streaked with sweat* but their gestures told him. It was the same at the taco stand in Denver, where she said, Goddamn it, I'm hungry too, did you think I wasn't hungry? did you think I don't eat, you big pig, you're always swiping my food and I'm fed up with it. And he, You goddamn slut, if you don't shut up and sit down I'm going to take your children and pound them into tiny charms for a gypsy's bracelet except for one which I will skin and have stuffed for my wall—. And she, You're nuts! you're crazy! And he, More today than yesterday.

Tyree, edging closer to the excited babble *Cowboy, change your ways or with us you will ride* did become an object of annoyance for a second time.

The man gave him a withering look. "Get along, kid. You're nosy."

Bird came along to shoo the boy away. Katie had not taught him to behave. No need—Tyree was sweet. Despite others' fears the boy was touched, she had never worried about him, certain that sweetness would do for him what it had done for her.

"Tyree, do you want to spend a couple days with me and the horses?"

Having been twice chastised, the boy now chastised with an angry, "Yes."

A flurry erupted at the couple's table and the man was striding to the door when the woman called out, "Are you going to fix the roof?"

"Yes," he said, swinging around. "Yes, I can fix it. I've got two boxes of shotgun shells that will fix it up proper."

He went out and the people in the bar looked at Joan, wondering why she didn't get up and go protect her roof. After they resumed contemplating their own mysteries, Bird went to her table.

"Ma'am," he said, "I can fix a roof."

Christ, Joan thought, *do they have a fucking starting gun in this town?* She looked up at Tom Bird and said, "Good for you."

"For forty dollars. Or a ton of hay, if you have it."

She slapped her hands on the table. "Do you realize I just split from my husband?"

"I thought that's what it was."

Joan leaned back in her chair, fueled with adrenalin. She was looking to rough someone up, and Bird had stepped into it. "You should get a medal," she pronounced.

The boy came up and tried to lift Bird's wallet. "Not now," Bird said. "I'm talking business." He turned back to Joan. "It'll rain some yet, I'm thinking." Tyree again slipped a hand into Bird's hip pocket. Bird looked sharply at the boy. "Didn't I say?"

The boy backed away and said, "I'm giving you money." He flashed a quarter, fished from beneath the juke.

"Still, you must do what I say."

Though Bird had never cuffed him, Tyree figured he someday would and that it would come hard. He stayed out of reach until the woman said, "The boy is scared of you."

"Enough," Bird said. "I'm gonna have another drink at the bar. You let me know about the roof."

Joan picked up her coat and purse and laid them on her lap, thinking of where she would go. She was hot and thrilled and sick and empty. Her husband had brought her here to start a new life in the northern Rockies, but the old life pursued and now he was gone. A point of injustice: she hated the place, but he who had yearned for it was packing to leave it while she had seven months to go on a teaching contract and a leaky roof.

Joan would come to understand that he had tired less of the area than the area had tired of him. A developer with a fast record, he was deep into the pockets of every bank and lumber yard and supplier around. Joan would come to wonder at the sudden impatience of so many well-drillers and hardware stores and concrete plants. She would observe in mute reproach the thievery by unpaid workers of, first, tools...and then finally any unattached items around the house. Their appreciation of the inviolate inside of the house would not be shared by a bank, and she would marvel at the ease with which the bank took possession of the house with its repaired roof. She would think back to how she had started the final argument in the Alforcas bar by asking her husband, "How's business?"

2

On Thanksgiving Day Joan put a turkey in the oven and contemplated what it would be like to sit down alone and eat a whole damn turkey. A cool drizzle outside led her to think of the roof—and of the cowboy with the little boy who had offered to fix it.

Joan drove to Sales grocery and bought a frozen pumpkin pie. She spoke to it as it lay on the check-out counter: "I am truly making a desperate effort and the least you could do is look palatable."

The checker, not a linguist, was offended. "Look, I'm here on Thanksgiving Day so you can buy that little pie. You should be grateful that someone will sacrifice so you can buy that cute pie for your family—"

"Are you saying I can't bake?" The easy familiarity of the Rockies routinely wore Joan to exhaustion thinking how to reply. With nerves twitching like tiny flames through sparse grass, Joan looked at the too-small face-mask stuffed in a snarled globe of frizzled blonde hair. She thought, I cannot parry.

"Sacrificing the Macy's Parade with my husband and kids isn't good enough, you want me to be cheerful like I was some robot—"

"Automaton," Joan interjected, the small flames leaping from blade to blade. Words gushed from the woman, as unintelligible to Joan as a foreign language. The automaton's wires had crossed; electricity was jumping circuits. The globe of hair was amok. Through it all, Joan was aware she needed to accommodate herself to society. And if she could accommodate, robots could assimilate. Might even thrive as the newest minority group. Special bars. Excise taxes on the extra arms. It could all be rational.

"Do you know where the fishing cowboy lives?" Joan asked in desperation.

"Sure," the clerk said, stuffing the pie in the sack, mollified by the opportunity to do another service. "Up Mill Creek."

"How do I drive?"

"None too good, I hear." The clerk chuckled at her joke and Joan forced a smile to keep the automaton cooperative. "Just turn right at the light, go past the mill and stay on that road until you see a new red barn by a little log house. It's about ten miles."

"Thanks."

"Hey," the clerk called when Joan was at the door. "Don't forget your pie."

Joan swept up the sack.

"Personally," said the checker, "I like Betty Crocker pies."

Her nerves still sparking, Joan sat in the car and thought through what she was going to do. She dug out a pad and pencil from her purse to make a list. The list contained two items: FISHING COWBOY and ROOF. It was too paltry to comprise a day so she added reminders to start the turkey and buy a pie. Making lists was an absurd pretense of purpose. That the advent of the practice roughly coincided with her son Ricky's death was something of which she had long been aware. Her husband never did make the connection.

"What are you always making those lists for?" he had asked when they still lived in Phoenix. "You don't do half of it."

"It gives me direction."

They were drinking coffee on the patio in the brilliant light of an Arizona morning in June. The house was up on a mesa and they could see a good part of the city snarled in traffic on the way to work. Swimming pools on the terraces below gleamed like blue eggs.

"What you ought to do," her husband said, scanning the newspaper, "is get yourself a boyfriend."

"I'll put it on my list."

"Says here building permits in Phoenix are down ten percent from last year. I wonder why I can't get anyone to work past noon, if the boom's ending."

"Mitchell, it's been a hundred and ten for a week."

"Do people melt?"

Joan put down her pad. "Why do you say I should get a boyfriend?"

"Keep you from harassing the crew."

"I take them iced tea and lemonade. They like it."

"They like having a pretty woman in a loincloth give them an excuse to sit down."

Joan felt like persisting about the boyfriend suggestion. She had always found her husband somewhat unfathomable and still thought, ludicrously, that somehow she had not pursued the avenues to understanding. "Wouldn't you be mad if I had a boyfriend?"

"Probably shoot you both, if circumstances were right. Interest rates are down. Maybe this town's overbuilt."

A year later Mitchell concluded that definitely was the case and they headed north to partake of the Sun Valley boom. For a reason Joan no longer remembered, they settled in Bannock instead and went broke.

On the Forest Service road she came upon the cowboy and the boy driving a band of horses at a gallop. Pea gravel from their hooves showered her car. The cowboy rode up the flank and lined the herd out and waved Joan by, but she lagged back, struck by the splendor and ease of the horses and horsemen. Bird headed the leaders, slowed them to a lope, then forced a mincing jog. He again waved her through and this time she pulled up alongside him.

She leaned across the seat and cranked down the window. "Are you still willing to fix a roof?"

"Today, I suppose."

"I've got a turkey in the oven and no one but myself to eat it."

Bird trotted ahead to swing the boss mare, who had been having other thoughts, into the lane into his place. Joan stayed back to drive beside the boy who was whistling like a machine. She asked how he was doing but he just smiled and whistled at the herd of sorrels and bays who had left him and were trotting into the home pasture. His mount wheeled into the lane and ran to the barn. When Joan pulled up, Bird was helping the boy off.

"My butt hurts," the boy said.

"See? I told you herding would teach you something." Bird turned to Joan. "Some outfitters left some hay. There's enough for another day if the elk don't find it. I got less desire to fix a roof, now."

The sharpness of his tone puzzled Joan, so different from the languid affability that he had shown in the bar. It wasn't really anger—impatience, maybe. She was shifting to leave when she saw the boy pull tail hairs and weave them into a strand. With a professional eye, she watched his concentration and his quick fingers: teachers at the elementary school thought him retarded but probably educable. When Bird came back from the tack shed—though not a large man, he had carried both heavy saddles in the crook of one arm—the boy had a tightly woven rope thicker than a pencil and as long as his arm.

"That's amazing." She pointed at the rope.

"He's worked at it the whole ride. I think he ought to ride backward so he can get at the tail better." Bird clucked his tongue and the saddlehorses headed through the gate, the boy still clinging to one's tail. "I'm a bit ashamed. You invite us to dinner and I'm still thinking about thirty dollars. I've got to go up the hill and call coyotes."

"I didn't mean to pay you with dinner. Thirty dollars is fine." She told him where she lived. "Come if you want. Thanksgiving is no time to be alone."

"Well, I got chores," Bird said, newly abashed by the woman's frank plea.

After the woman left, Bird pulled on his gloves and looked around for the work that needed to be done. The horses, tired and full, were lying in the snow. Low clouds hid the ridgetops but the rain had washed the ice from the trees, and the hillside mosaic of gold tamaracks and dark firs were bright against the snow on the ground. A dozen magpies drifted up from the creek brush and settled again.

"Coyotes forty dollars a pelt," he murmured.

Bird had become quite destitute. He had forty acres of grass, seven bred mares, no job, no cash, no credit. He had two young steers hung in the pump house and would not starve, but he needed hay for the horses, and also gas to go fishing; the creek on his place held no trout larger than a pound. Years ago— before he settled permanently on the Double Diamond—he had often been broke, but never destitute: then having a saddle and a slicker was enough to take care of the inner man. A financial crisis was new, and it stumped him.

13

Plainly he had to sell a horse. But when he walked out to the field to decide upon which mare, he was worse stumped. How to know which mare did not have the fast colt in her? He liked something about all of them. His original choice to sell was a five-year-old bay, first-time bred, winner of six in a row at the bush tracks of Utah and Wyoming. That wasn't much claim by itself, but Bird had seen her run twice and she had plenty of heart. Even when she bowed a tendon in her last race, the jockey could not pull her up until she passed the other horses long after the wire.

"Hell's bells," Bird said. "There ain't no chores to do."

He went to the pickup and honked the horn. The boy came running out of the house, tugging on his coat.

"Can I ride in back?"

"You ain't a duck," Bird said. "Get in the cab."

On the way to town, Bird realized he had not sat across the table from a woman, besides his sister, since Katie had gone off. Rounding the bend at the mill, he had to swerve to avoid hitting Bobby Coles, who was taking a leak in the road. Bobby hollered and waved. Bird, seeing Bobby's car at the locked mill gates, stopped and backed up, thinking Bobby had car trouble.

"What the hell happened?" Bobby said, wiping the slush from his beard that had sprayed from the pickup as it careened around him. "We on strike?"

It took a few seconds for Bird to figure things out. "Today's Thanksgiving, Bobby."

Bobby Coles was a good-looking man in his early thirties who had once worked for Bird on the Double Diamond before being lured by the regular hours at the mill and the concomittant regular hours to chase women, mostly unsuccessfully, in the neighboring towns. Most nights he spent on somebody's floor and had a wristwatch with an alarm that got him up to drive, sometimes a hundred miles, to work. Apparently the watch didn't have a calendar.

"Well, hell's bells," Bobby said. "What am I going to do now?"

The parallelism to his own phrasing and resignation induced Bird to invite him to Joan's house for turkey. "She seemed like she wouldn't mind the company," Bird said.

"I guess I will," Bobby said. "I got in with them cocaine boys in Jackson again last night. Reckon I'd be lucky to find twelve cents in the upholstery."

"Why do you do that?" Bird asked, meaning not only the cocaine but Jackson itself, about as far a drive as most folks would want to take for a summer vacation.

"Ain't nothing better to do." He walked around to the passenger door and nudged the boy. "Howdy, Tyree. Scoot over."

The boy grabbed the seat. "You sit in the middle, Bobby. I have to watch for dogs. Tom almost hit one."

Bobby asked, "Does he think I was a dog?"

14

"Another dog," Tyree answered, still clinging to the seat.

"Well, he's likely to hit anything, ain't he?" To Bobby Coles, avoiding men peeing in the road was like avoiding chuckholes, hardly cause for swerving.

"Let him have his way," Bird said. "He loses sight of dogs running out to chase the pickup and thinks I've run 'em over."

Bobby climbed over the boy and spent the drive tapping a rhythm on the dash with the stubs of two fingers he'd left in the green chain a year back. Probably after a night with the cocaine boys, Bird reflected. He didn't know why he liked Bobby. He'd been a no-account hand who thought the best way to get trout was with an electrical stunning device like what Fish and Game used to survey the population of a stream. And now he had included Bobby in an invitation he himself was accepting out of lassitude.

Joan did not mind the additional guest, however. She settled them before the televised football game with mugs of hot cider. It felt good to have a household of men. She had always preferred their company to women.

Joan was an attractive woman. Though not particularly pretty as a child, age had graced her with a rough-edged beauty. She had straw-blonde hair, chemically altered from its natural barnwood brown; fine olive skin lightly wrinkled around the mouth; wide alert eyes that she never shadowed—even a touch made her look glossy, and though she daily decried the thin marbling of lard on her thighs, she was solid and athletic. The gentle aging was coupled with a solicitous but dignified mien that made men imagine a future as a lord.

Before the men had drunk the cider, Bobby Coles had fallen for her.

Bird saw it right away. Joan saw it, too, and while it lifted her spirits, it was a complication that aroused her nerves. And she was plenty nervous already, what with men skulking around after dark gleaning debts of her husband who had flat disappeared from earth. Two days ago she had tried to have a nervous breakdown—she got more nervous, but not broke down in any way she could detect. When Bird, finishing his cider, asked her if she might show him the leak, she was glad to escape Bobby Coles' compliments.

She showed him the soaked towels under an archway. "Don't you like football, Mr. Bird?" She had called the other man "Bobby" right away.

"Nah, I never played it."

Bird had grown up on the eastern Wyoming prairie, where winters made basketball the state sport, especially of towns too small to field a football or baseball team. Bird had no interest in any game but basketball. Since his youth his possibles always included a ball and hoop. When he rode up to a new outfit with these items lashed to his bedroll and a fishing rod slung beneath a stirrup, the predictable greeting was, "Why, we got us a *sportsman*," that being a derogatory term at the time. During his long stay on the Double Diamond it became a tradition for the hands to give him a new hoop at Christmas to replace the one under the bunkhouse eave. Bird once hired a six-foot-six black man because he thought it would be fun to play ball with him. He even bought a pair of expensive gym shoes in anticipation. The man turned out to be a fine hand but a slow and fumbling player. Bird didn't need the shoes, because he could go around the man in his boots.

Bird thought about basketball and the Double Diamond and Eleanor Goodnight while he patched the vent flashing that was allowing water under the shingles. It was not a big job, and he had progressed just far enough in his thinking to wonder why Eleanor Goodnight was selling out, but not far enough to form a speculation. It was an incredible thing to him. Western ranches, like English estates, retain their identity with an indifference to actual ownership. A cow boss feels an indebtedness to the cattle and the land rather than to the owner, which might be a West German industrialist or a syndicate of tax-sheltering doctors. Eleanor Goodnight, however, *was* the Double Diamond. She had lived on it, she had mostly run it, and she had married for it.

"Are there really such things as skeletons?" Tyree asked Bird when he came inside. Bobby had said certainly, and scared him.

"Yes," illuminated Bobby. "But they don't come alive and jump around. They're inside you."

This alarmed Tyree more than anything Bobby might have said. A skeleton inside you was worse than those who rattled at the windows.

Bird intervened. "It holds your muscles up. Feel your cheek. That's your skeleton."

"Mandible," Bobby provided.

"Or that bone in the middle of your chest."

"Sternum," Bobby said.

"Feel your knee—"

"Patela."

Tyree was feeling these places, scared by what he was finding. Joan called the boy to her. Men were so comically inept with children. Joan gave him the hug and no-such-thing assurance he wanted.

They watched the football game for a while, even Tyree. Joan and Bird and the boy saw a bunch of brown and white shirts milling like maddened cattle around a synthetic pasture, while Bobby, better versed, observed, "If they'd just break a coupla them guys' legs, we'd be okay." Bird thought that strategy was against the rules, but he didn't really know.

"Tom, do you have a match?" Tyree asked, rising.

"Yes. What do you aim to do with it?"

"I passed gas."

Bird was stupified. Bobby Coles shoved a pillow in front of his face and said, "He wants to make a methane explosion."

Joan explained, "His teacher is Mrs. Blicke, who resolves that particular unpleasantry by smelling out the offender and lighting a match over his desk to mask the odor."

Bobby said, "If she did that where I work, the fucking roof would blow off the mill." Ashamed of his coarseness, he tried to salvage his character with a serious insight. "I always liked the smell of match smoke. Woulda ruined me to have a teacher like that." Bird's sudden laugh prompted him to expound. "A kid who don't like match smoke might get cramps." Having made this astute foray into the business of American education, Bobby turned back to the television. "Redskins ain't beat the Cowboys since 1876."

His mention of the year Custer got his glorious comeuppance surprised Joan. "Have you read of the Battle at Greasy Grass, Bobby?"

"No, Stewart Goodnight told me. If Benteen had been where Reno was, there wouldn't have been a massacre."

"Massacre," Joan said lightly. Some might call it a victory. In tow of her boom-prospecting husband, Joan had lived in Chiricauha land and Piegan land—and places in between: Crow, Arapaho, Ute, Navaho, and more...finding everywhere a spirit that issued from sage and pine and rock.

"Reno was a 'confused coward,' Mr. Goodnight said. Right, Tom?" When Bird looked at him like he was a busy parrot, Bobby added, "The Dawes Act, 1887. I learned my lessons, Joan."

The idea that a thirty-year-old man who made pilgrimages to Jackson and Aspen and Sun Valley to blow his paycheck had learned any lesson at all gripped Bird in self-absorbed laughter. Bobby grew suspicious of Bird's uncommon glee and thought he had a rival. He sulked. Joan put out a plate of celery, pickles, and carrots. Raised in a house of men, she forestalled crises with men by feeding them. Both her husbands had gone fat and dieted, and both had, instead of eating, gone on to crises without her.

While waiting for the various alarms of the oven timers—a stove which her husband claimed had more dials than a fucking jet cockpit—Joan taught Tyree to play Hearts. On the second hand, Tyree grabbed one of his fanned cards, scooted to the fireplace where he threw the card in. The Queen of Spades curled and crinkled, emitting a blue flame.

"There," Tyree said. "Now nobody will get stung."

Tyree left the supper table to go to the bathroom. When the door closed, Joan said, "He is so literal. He's more like a little man than a boy."

This was five minutes after Tyree had said a grace that caused Bobby, an aposteothastic Catholic, to cross himself: "Dear Lord, bless our food and kill Satan and don't let Bobby eat everything."

Two days later two men and a woman came walking up on foot to Bird's place. Their rented Pinto had become a Roman candle a ways up the highway. Bird, seeing the smoke, saddled a mare and rode out to meet the men in scorched suits and the woman wailing about her seared hair. They had legal papers granting guardianship of the boy of to one Jason Abo, maternal uncle.

Bird drove them and Tyree to the bus station. While Bird made inquiries of the clerk in the cage, the woman rushed up.

"He just took off," the woman said.

"I know where he is," Bird said and walked across the street to the Alforcas, where Tyree was in the darkest corner by the magazine rack, holding his knees.

"I won't let you take him," Bird told the woman. "Not until I see this Abo fella."

The trio brandished the papers. Bird grabbed the boy and drove home. Al mollified the delegation by insinuating he had a handwritten note which he would introduce to probate. The three took turns on the pay phone. Within a week the town knew that Jason Abo was a half-brother to Katie and a vice-president of Western Pipe and Steel, the conglomerate that had bought the Double Diamond.

3

Jason Abo, after a dawdling week of passionless baccarat play in Reno, chartered Red Dillon and his twin-engine Cessna for the flight to the Double Diamond. Before long Abo was at the controls, learning to fly while Red Dillon mixed highballs and reminisced about his days in the Alaskan bush before persnickety regulators hounded him out for being imprudent.

"I think that's it," Red motioned to a peanut-shaped valley of yellow grass among snowy peaks and dark-pine hillsides. "Buzz them sheep off the strip and then I'll land it."

Abo thrust the joystick and stomped on the right rudder, violently careening the plane. Red dropped his drink. Abo jerked the joystick and put on the left rudder and the plane still sailed away from his control. Pouring another drink, Red gently coached Abo into arresting the descent. The plane wobbled to equilibrium and Abo, his heart in his throat, yelled, "Those are cows!" He had come to doubt Red Dillon.

After landing, Abo threw his bags on the airstrip, muttering about the shuddering plane that wanted to nose-dive to the ground. Red was gargling mouthwash. "Yeah, they don't fly real good on edge like that." He added, "When in doubt, apply power," and went off to find someone with the keys to the fuel tank.

Abe meandered up the slope to the buildings. There was a modern house, a shop, a mammoth hay roof on sixty-foot poles, several barns linked by pole corrals. Seeing a cowboy walking across the lot, Abo hallooed him and, remembering Red Dillon's parting advice, said, "I'm Jason Abo. My company owns this place."

The cowboy, 17, gave Abo the look-over and, as he reported later in town, saw "a pretty boy in a jogging suit with a gold necklace and, the topper, a gold earring." When Abo rented a car from Hondo Motors, he was similarly described by the salesman and hence recognized as the pretty boy by a listener at Alforcas. A clerk at the new modern Safeway grocery said pretty boy bought nine magazines and wanted to pay with a credit card. The trader—he was a pawnbroker but he called himself a trader—said Pretty Boy had traded his earring and necklace for cash and "it weren't no plate, either." Though Abo would not again wear this jewelry, the sobriquet would stick, and Pretty Boy became a mark of recognition much like the fishing cowboy, a distinction that stood in stead for real familiarity. The name Pretty Boy would lose its unmanly connotation and come to provoke awe at one man's ability to make excess work.

For a week Abo was repeatedly hours behind locating his ward. At first he thought it was a deliberate shuffling on the part of the townspeople, but came to realize the indefiniteness of these people was a fact, like the fact that the boy checked in regularly at the Alforcas. He quit chasing Tom Bird and Bobby Coles and Sally Honstead and settled in at the Alforcas to wait for the boy.

He spent that time on the pay phone, trying to find out who his underlings were in this new division of Wester Pipe and Steel. Plainly they weren't at the ranch—all he saw there was a foreman named Stanger who meant to drink whiskey until someone put some cows on the place, and a bunch of cowboys who figured the jig was up and drifted on to other jobs. After a week on the phone, he still did not know how his division was staffed nor what its resources were. He concluded that he had been hasty accepting the position, that what he judged a lateral transfer to mitigate in-house enmity was more of a banishment, for the same reason. Selling his gold to the fat pawnbroker was really the last straw—he needed the money to feed the pay phone, as his AT&T credit card, rather than being reassigned to this new phantasmic corporate division, had been canceled. He was in mind to shoot someone.

This had been a steady problem for Abo. At forty, he could rightly expect to wield more clout; he was smart, and his father had been one of the inside people who had ridden the firm's growth from a California oil-drilling outfit to a huge acquisitive company that built birdhouses in Seoul and made condoms in Ohio. But his predilection to shot people, though expeditious, was not viewed in general by his colleagues as accepted business practice, a consensus skewed somewhat by the preponderance of whom had been intended victims. Abo was a talented man, but he was capricious, went the corporate sentiment, very capricious.

Only once had Abo actually wielded a gun, when he visited a consultant's home. Abo had his girlfriend's .32 and asked the consultant, a weekend target shooter, to show him how the gun worked.

"You know guns," Abo said. "How do you get a thingie in the barrel?"

The consultant, reluctant to disclose the operation, poured Jason a big drink.

Abo, fiddling with the gun, said, "You bought Alamo Oil under me, and though oil sliding to ten dollars a barrel might not have been foreseen, I still hold you culpable. I cut a very nice deal for Alamo, but *you* told me to get it. Recant or die."

The consultant, one of the inside people, almost an uncle to Abo, waved diffidently. "It's a good day to die, Jason. Smog's gonna be bad tomorrow. The heart, please. My wife wouldn't like a splattered head. Her father had a closed casket and she still sees him on the stairs sometimes at night."

"Okay, show me how to work this weapon or recant."

"I won't recant."

"Where's your heart, if you got one?"

"Oh, I lost my heart when I was sixteen. She was a typing teacher, fresh out of college." The consultant got up to make more drinks. "You have to suck on the muzzle to make the gun work, Jason."

Abo said he was doing that.

"Now pull the trigger to load it. The barometric difference between the clip and your closed mouth will chamber the round."

Abo went home and shot all four tires on his Volvo. The quasi Dutch uncle, in thinking him too stupid to follow a comic book, had improvised a devious engineering of his death. He felt grossly demeaned. And he had once sat on the man's knee and played cowboy!

As Abo stood by the surrogate victim in his posh neighborhood, where gunshots usually meant a foreshortened divorce procedure, a taxi rolled by with Roberta Flack on the radio. Abo sprinted after the taxi for two blocks and caught the midpoint of the song. "Just drive," he said.

Abo prowled his haunts for congenial business contacts, then prowled for an idea, and finally prowled simply to meet some sense of successful termination. At dawn he was outside an L.A. dive combating drunkenness by military-pressing a parking meter he stole off a pickup piled with them. He felt vulnerable. The disastrous performance of Alamo promised to be a big fall for him, and he had lately been given reason to doubt his father's ability, even willingness, to save him.

He had ventured out from Western before: he had even grown moderately wealthy setting up a company that insured small municipalities until people caught on that their dear little towns were insured and began to sue the shit out of said towns.

"Who is to answer for all these fucking tort claims?" he roared to his secretary after a meeting with his principals, where Chapter 11 had been the topic of discussion.

"You mean who is to retort?"

"I mean who is to blame, whom do we shoot? Shoot a couple of these fuckers who get their heads stuck in jail bars or get run over by a road grader and this nonsense will cease!"

The secretary was pretty sure all this noise about shooting was sexual, and she tendered her devotion by supplying a name from her mean-street past. That name was the last gambit of Abo's prowling.

Sobered by his workout pressing parking meters, Abo went inside to meet the garrulous hood. A firehose shooting Pine-Sol would not have hurt the building nor the line of morning drinkers.

"Fifty to burn, two hundred to kill," the man said with a braggart's nonchalance.

"In that case," Abo said, "I have somebody I want you to burn."

Abo sipped a brandy while the other soliloquied. Abo felt compelled to administer a whipping to a deserved cur, as one would to an ill-mannered dog in the owner's absence—merely fulfilling an obligation—but the hood didn't seem to be socially trained well enough to benefit from it.

Finance this snake or spare the fiend? Jason made an easy decision. He hoped that in the final reckoning the fiend would learn how gainful was the time taken to jounce a little boy on his knee.

In the ensuing months, Abo grew humble. He tried not to fawn, but he might have been accused of that when Western purchased the Double Diamond, one of the largest cattle ranches in the Rockies, with neither coal to strip nor oil to tap. Starting afresh gave him back his determination and anger. When told he wouldn't need the headquarters office due a vice-president because the cow factory had plenty of buildings, he had the first inkling of exile and vowed to be a Grant at Galena, biding his time until glory called.

When news of Katie's death came, the interplay of a bank, a corporation, and his father became obvious: the old man had maintained surreptitious contact with Katie. In Abo's memory Katie was like a second cousin who dropped by once a year and everyone relearned names. His one vivid picture of her was sitting on the long courthouse steps in Austin. He was nine or ten; she was a woman, wearing a leather flight jacket and Levis. The sun was high and sugar ants were so thick they made a moving rope along the crack by his feet. Katie asked who he was choosing to live with. Dad, he said.

"Probably best," she said. "I'll pick Mom to balance things. It hardly matters, since I'm a month short of twenty-one, but it'll make her feel better."

He remembered it was nice sitting on the warm cascade of steps with Katie. And then, when they were summoned inside, Katie's words, "It's hard to believe people can fight so"—which turned out to be her farewell, as he never saw her after she left the courthouse with her sobbing mother. A last minute *Next of kin* disclosure on hospital records brought him to her, obliquely.

Finally, Abo's routine stop at the Alforcas was rewarded. "He's here," Al said, "but you'll have to talk to Tom Bird before you see him."

"Where is Mr. Bird?" Abo politely inquired.

"I couldn't say."

"Was he the cow boss on the Double Diamond?"

"Forever."

Al went off to his chores. A patron pointed out the tinted street window. "He's getting gas at Rudy's right now."

Abo sprinted down the street. He recognized the paunchy cowboy, introduced himself, and asked for a meeting about the boy and ranching in general over the best whiskey the Alforcas could provide.

"Not today," Bird answered. "The sun is warm and I'm going fishing."

Abo remembered his times in the fast runs of Feather River, which had been, when not delightful, at least trouble-free. "Let me run across the street and buy a rod from that cheat. I'll go with you."

Abo saw a nod and dashed to the pawn shop. He had a rod and reel on the counter when Bird came in and told the trader, "Give him those waders of mine. I'll stand for it."

As they walked out, Bird said, "I always liked those Seal-Dris. They have fourteen patches and you can't suffer to get wet in winter, but they're too good to sit on a shelf."

On the highway, Abo said, "I think I ought to see my nephew."

"Probably."

Uncertainly, Abo added, "Katie was my half-sister."

"I know."

A cattle semi hurtled past. Abo raised the driver on Bird's CB, channel nine, and talked prices and mileage and market, meandering close to a deal.

"Todd?" Abo said after they exchanged phone numbers.

"You bet," came the crackled reply.

"If you're one of those pea-brains who jackknife on the freeway and back up cars into the next state, you can forget it."

Abo hung the mike. "I did not know Katie well," he said to Bird. "She was older and away to college when I was young. And then she was just away."

"Katie was a hard person to pin down, all right."

Out on the prairie between the timbered mountains and the greasewood lava hills, tumbleweeds flounced across the highway.

"I hope this wind dies down," Abo said after a while. "I'm a poor wind-caster."

Abo got his wish, for the north wind sailed blithely over the canyon of the Sur Fork below the reservoir.

The Sur Fork is a beautiful river, flowing clear and cold against basalt cliffs and around islands of cottonwoods. Runs and pools and riffles abound, and so do insects; the trout, wild and heavy and sometimes long, were not ravenous in winter but Bird had enjoyed some fine dry-fly fishing with ice jagged on the river's edge. This day, however, was one of those when the river just said no.

The first time they met after splitting up, Bird told Abo to try a heavy nymph to bounce the bottom, the second time he suggested a wild and gaudy and habit-shaking streamer or a mouse or anything else that wasn't practical, the third time he said, "I broke down my rod."

Abo had been ready to quit two hours earlier. But inspiration now struck him. He said, "On the Siletz River in Oregon I moved steelhead out of the pools so I could catch them with a fly rod by throwing rocks."

Bird followed Abo up a twenty-foot escarpment overlooming a deep run through boulders. Abo chucked rock after rock, and Bird saw several darts in the shallow of the far bank. Then a big fish moved upstream slowly in the shallow water and wafted into deep heavy current at the head of the hole. Abo astonished Bird with a cackle and a crouch and a quick volley of fresh ammo into the run the fish had just assumed. The trout moved upstream, faster this time, into a smaller hole undercutting cottonwood roots. Upstream were shallow ripples the breadth of the river, into which the trout did not swim.

"You cast," said Abo, handing over his rod. "I've just been flailing the water all day."

Bird slid down the defile, pulled off his waders, and swam across, a thing he did not like to do in winter.

He could see the trout as he cast. On Abo's rod was a Mickey Finn, a black-and-silver Darth-Vader Oakland-Raider monstrosity, and Bird directed it to drift on the far side of the trout. When the fly approached the trout, Bird stripped sharply and actually managed to bump the rainbow on the nose. The trout moved away from the fly and then, as an afterthought, wheeled to smash the fly, having had quite enough of hassles and willing to expend some energy in vengeance.

Bird was amazed at this redemption of a fishless day and just didn't know what to say other than he had not fished that way before.

They drove to Bannock in virtual silence.

"Where do you want out?" Bird asked, slowing down at Burgerville where teenagers used to rove thick enough to trample out the weeds in the lot. Now they rented videotapes and wore paths in home carpet.

"How about my nephew?"

"He's at a friend's place."

"That's where I want out."

"You're entitled."

Joan's house was up on a bluff a quarter-mile and a hundred thousand dollars below Sally. Bird disliked the winding climb; Abo, however, felt like he was seeing his end of town. The houses demurely tucked in the pines had garages instead of chicken coops. It elated him to be in the vicinity of people who had enough money to not be dull, if they so chose.

His elation was further spirited by the sight of a beautiful woman running out to greet them, and then tempered by her violent brandishing of a newspaper.

"See here!" she panted. "This house, with my name right there for the world to see, is to be sold at sheriff's auction two weeks from Monday!" She did not show the paper to either of her guests but read the incredible message again herself.

"You must have received notice," Bird said.

Joan shrieked, "My husband's desk is full of nasty letters about everything we owned or pretended to own. I've got to go chapter deep-six, or whatever."

"I can help you there," Abo said as he looked around for the child. "Where's the boy?"

Bird introduced the two.

"Oh, well," Joan said. "Sally has him."

Exasperated, Abo said, "This business has tried my forbearance. I've worn this Christ-like serenity about people's manners for a while now, and it doesn't fit. It's all come unraveled. Tell me where to find the boy! I'm the scourge of scuttlebutts and in a mood to scuttle some butt. Where is the goddamn boy?"

"Don't get in a huff," Joan cautioned. "Sally lives just up the road. You're awful rash. Not like Katie at all."

"Kinda like Katie," Bird said. "He throws rocks at fish. Come on, I'll take you to Sally's."

Abo had nowhere to dump his anger and complied.

Sally's house was on a wooded knoll across a small but year-round creek. Lavished in oak, it was the most handsome house in town; the special luxuries like an outdoors Jacuzzi and a two-story redwood deck made it legendary. Bird and Abo found Bob Honstead, Sally's husband, reading the paper in the hot tub. He greeted them with his natural humor and said, "That fish you caught in the Big Timber was a mermaid, size nine. I've been having unnatural dreams about her being in the hot tub with me."

"She isn't still in there cooking, I hope," said Bird. "We got one today that's quite a bit smaller but she's still open to good cooking."

"That's my life, unsatisfactory compromises."

The two of them used to fish the Sur Fork on Sunday mornings while Sally went to church. Besides the river having big trout, the drive back had two small-town taverns that could be, in Bob's phrase, "uproared." Those trips had waned and ceased. Bob was a man to keep score when fishing, as in all else. However, Bob competed against men rather than the river, , and consequently was nearly always outfished. Now he uproared the taverns after he too went to church and did his fishing on charters out of Oregon for tuna and king salmon.

Sally came outside and wordlessly unfurled a white cloth: Bird saw, first, a large blue trout and, second, *his* trout, in detail so fine it made an illusory relief.

"Japanese *kyokatu*," Sally said, handing Bird the sheet. Bird would hang that sheet in his kitchen and would often peruse the fins and scales and gills in wonder that the fish still lived.

The boy came outside then, dragging a small blanket and sucking his thumb, a thing Bird had never seen him do. Bird held his introduction as Abo moved steadily towards the child.

"Are you Katie's son?" His voice was hushed.

The boy recoiled. "Some boys suck their thumbs."

"Men, too." He hunkered down and stuck out a hand. "I'm your uncle."

"Mom says uncles are nice."

The boy slapped the man's hand and Sally sent the two of them off to the kitchen.

25

Sally brought drinks outside. Having heard the boy blurt that Tom was fixing a roof and selling a mare to get money for whiskey and cokes at Alforcas, Sally said she wanted to buy twenty-five percent of Bird's horses.

Bob did a comic downing of his drink. "I don't even play the stock market. Gambling gives me the willies."

"Bob, those mares of his are in foal to a son of Northern Dancer, the only son of Northern Dancer between the Mississippi and California. And you're not gambling—I am."

"This is a community property state," he protested feebly, knowing that Sally would poison him before divorcing him and so the division of spoils was moot. Rather than hear again about the moribund Utah mink farm he had bought, he listened to his wife outline the necessary contract and made only editorial comment.

Abo and the boy came outside. Tyree, who made easy alliances, had a finger hooked in Abo's belt loop.

"Tom, can you drive us to my car?" Abo tousled the boy's hair.

The adults searched the boy's face for meaning.

Sally asked, "Where are you staying, Mr. Abo?"

"The Bannock Hotel, I guess."

"Do you have any books for the boy? Any stuffed animals? Are you prepared in any way for a child?"

"I just saw the kid an hour ago!"

"Which only attests to your inefficiency and lack of devotion."

Abo fidgeted with an irritation that parlayed itself into a rage against a town of self-righteous conspirators. "Are you mountain folks all in-bred? Is that the deal?"

"You need guidance, Mr. Abo," Sally chided. She grabbed Tyree's coat off the chair and unfurled it with a shake. "I'm going to give you that guidance. The boy has had a large home and may not be ready for a closed one. We'll stay at my brother's house. I'll grab my toothbrush and be right with you."

They were cramped in the pickup cab on the ride down the bluff. Bird felt he ought to placate Abo, but the gathering dusk made him think of chores. Rounding a bend, he saw Joan on the roadside kicking a pine cone. She flagged them down.

"The bastards just repossessed my BMW," she said through the passenger window. "I can't stay here."

Abo stoically took in the situation. "Get in, lady. I'll just hang onto the rear bumper and get dragged to wherever I'm being dragged to."

What Abo would remember best about meeting these two women was the villainous shame of insincerely kissing the boy goodnight while sincerity

26

suffused his soul. He was scrutinizing his actions, watching himself as the women watched him. He was a marionette struggling feebly against a higher will.

The Double Diamond dispersal auction was held on a blustery day with charcoal clouds scudding low, heavy as water. A hundred years of equipment and sundry ranch tools drew a large crowd. The yard at the number-one house was crammed with two acres of tractors and wagons and balers, brand-new swathers and rusty horse-driven cutters and rakes, chutes and cider presses, collars and harness and double-fire roping saddles, tools and tarps, fence posts and rolls of wire, two thousand ton of hay. Bird was overwhelmed by the accumulation and the milling crowd. He walked out to a bare knoll behind the equipment shed. The crackle of the auctioneer testing his mike from a flatbed trailer was behind him and he was looking out at the place where he'd spent most of his life.

"Tom, I thought you'd be here." Eleanor wore a leather jacket to break the wind and Bird thought she looked cold. "This is so much the end it's liberating in a way."

"I saw Walker's saddle."

"You probably think I should put that fucking saddle in my bed and wonder what life would have been had you not drowned him."

"I do wonder," Bird said. Eleanor was a wiry woman and she sure looked cold in that unlined jacket.

"Probably about the same. I'd still be a widow with a dead ranch."

Bird looked out over the snow-covered pastures. Yellow grass poked through between drifted ridges of snow. Ponderosas grew tall on the foothills and firs crowded the mountain slopes. There were fifty thousand acres of deeded land and ninety thousand acres of lease running from the Little Timber to the Cayuse River, with more than a dozen creek drainages feeding those two rivers. When Bird was boss, the most cows he ever lost in a summer was nine.

Bird said, "Do you suppose the new owners know how to run a cattle operation?"

"They will if you go back." She smiled secretly, looking past the valley at the mountains where the granite peaks were blown free of snow. "I know you quit because of Stewart dying."

"Why'd you quit?"

"This summer I had dinner in San Francisco with my banker. He said the bank could loan on the cows. It had come to that."

Eleanor heard, though she tried not to, the auctioneer conduct the first bidding. The ranch was too vast to be profitable. It required too many hands, too many buildings, too much equipment. She thought it possible that a hard-working man, even in the face of tax-sheltering competitors, might still manage a profit from a small ranch. Her husband Stewart had never been a lover of hard work.

"I've heard that you have a house full of women and children."

"It does make a houseful," Bird said.

"Let's take a drive to the old place. I don't want to stay here."

The old place, now known as house number two, was on Bruin Creek at the west end of the valley. The house itself had been patched and buttressed in a utilitarian way and was home to foreman Jim Stanger. The heavy plank corrals, blistered by weather, were occasionally used, but no one any longer tried to forestall time's lethal play with the rest of the lot. They drove past the decrepit smokehouse and coops and sheds to the rear of the lot, parking beneath the hay derrick. A coyote padding four hundred yards away stopped to eye the truck, then sprinted off like a telegram. As they stepped out, pigeons swept out of the old busted barn, made a great buckshot circle over the pasture, and returned to light on the few remaining curled shingles.

"Stewart lost touch with the ranch after we moved up to the airstrip. Looking forever at the business angle never let him see the ranch as it was. Me, I could always come down here and see it again." She looked again at the great skeletal barn. "God, we were a busy place when it was all right here."

"Where will you be living now, Eleanor?" Bird asked.

She started for the pickup. "I think I'll go to Arizona for the winter. I'm a director for Western. That'll occupy me about one week a year—and for the other fifty-one I don't have a plan. I've been too long brooding about leaving the place. It's time to leave. I'm going to go home, take a nap, and start packing."

When Bird dropped her off, she held the car door open for a long time, smelling a sprig of sagebrush that had been caught in the door. She said, "I'd like to see you in that house of women and children. I'll bet you're uneasy as hell. Goodbye, Tom."

Bird thought about her parting comment on the way home. In truth, he was uneasy. He felt like he was getting a drink out of a fire hydrant. There didn't seem to be enough coffee cups or bedding, and Sally was always running off to town to buy such things as well as mountains of groceries that couldn't be stored on the wall of shelves where Bird kept things.

Abo was uncomfortable, too, but he had to be present in the house frequently enough to pass the little tests Sally arranged. These made him a little indignant, but his claim on the boy was so clearly a technicality in the presence of better claims that he submitted. He was moving things into house three at the airstrip, but this task was lengthy since his girlfriend had fortified herself in his L.A. condo and would not relinquish anything except the most personal of toiletries. Furnishing a house from scratch was quite beyond him. He made a list: a clock, a philodendron, a deer rack, a toilet bowl brush, canned peaches, etc. He set out one day to buy some of these things but got no further than the plant, which he gave away to a woman in a cafe who said she'd locate an encyclopedia salesman for him.

Joan too was in an incomplete process of moving. For her, the complication was she had not enough money to get into an apartment. Sally had got her a Buick from Hondo Motors entirely on credit; no one else, however, was willing to grant any slack at all to a known bankrupt. A man who managed a nice complex near her school made her a fancy Polynesian fruit drink in a plastic cup and explained how if he let her in, it would take him six months to get her out. He told her this from a recliner in the office. "And I am just about the laziest person to ever live," he said, aiming the TV remote. "This situation is okay if I watch out for the extra nuisance. When you finish your drink, would you mind taking the cup to the dumpster rather than use the can in here." His tone was self-congratulatory. "Little things add up fast enough. I don't need any big thing like a deadbeat protected by the courts."

Sally was nominally living with her husband, but tending the affairs of so many people kept her coming back to the Bird place. Bobby Coles, in love with Joan, made the house one of his regular stopovers; since the floors were pretty much taken, he slept in his truck at first, but as the days grew shorter and whiter and the northers swept down, he began stealing inside to claim a vacant corner.

As ever in the high latitudes, people made winter camp.

4

The air was arctic in clarity and bite, and when it stirred it made a man feel naked. Bird's thermometer showed thirty-eight degrees below zero, and after chores he, like dozens of others, drove to town and gave his reading at the Alforcas over as many cups of coffee as he could stand. There was nothing to do, with it so cold. You fed and thawed out pipes and tried not to burn down your house or barn. Then you idled away the day talking about how tough it was. About the best thing that could happen to you was you could claim the coldest place in the area. Such a silly distinction actually drove some men to lie.

"Lot warmer here in town," Bird lied while taking off his coat. In a cold spell like this, the coldest air sloughed off the mountains and settled in the lowest part of the valley where the town sat.

"It sure is," said Julio Delatorriente, rolling his wheelchair closer to the woodstove. The group, mostly men, included the fat plumber who, while deer-hunting the previous fall, snapped off the safety while his finger was inside the trigger guard, reducing Julio to wheels.

"Only if your poozle is in town," said the plumber. "And mine ain't. She said she wanted a cutting horse. A Canadian cowboy with a cutting horse stopped for gas and drove off with her. He put her in the other stall of the trailer. I guess he didn't want conversation."

"No one exactly laments her departure, Phil," Al said from his relaxed but studious position behind the bar. "Throw another log on the fire."

"*I* do," said the plumber.

"No, you don't," Al said. "She never was yours and about made you crazy. As for the cutting horse, Tracy had as great a desire for my boat or Julio's welder."

The plumber rose and held out his cup. "Put some whiskey in my coffee, Al."

"That's why I tell the truth," Al said, pouring. "It's good for business."

Al showed Bird a postcard. On the front was a saguaro cactus and on the back a short inscription: *Phoenix is too damn nice to be healthy. Write me about Tom and the women.*

"What should I tell her?"

"Nothing to tell."

Abo came in, poured coffee and joined Bird. "I took your sister home. She says I'm fit to raise Tyree."

"No one really plans to cut loose, Jason. Katie's first wish was to have the Alforcas be the boy's home. I think at the end she must have fretted about money."

"Tom, can I get a direct answer to a direct question. What's the deal here with everyone about Tyree?"

Bird gulped the dregs and poured a refill. "Katie," he answered.

Abo said, "Tyree has more connections than a Sicilian. Damn, it's cold. Does this town have a health club?"

"We have a clinic with a doctor."

"I mean racquetball courts and jacuzzis and eucalyptus steam rooms."

"Nope. It don't."

Abo thought about that for awhile. "I don't think much of a town without a health club. Where do people get a workout?"

"Well, a lot of people just work."

"Exercise increases your vitality," Abo pointed out.

"Might," Bird allowed. "But all that running around might leave people too tuckered to work."

That spring Abo would build the High Valley Racquet and Gym Club by creating a syndicate of most of the prosperous people in town. By doing so, he left few people with money enough to buy subscriptions. In six months the investors had tired of feeding the club and dissolved the syndicate. Abo personally bought back the building from a disgruntled bank, invited the former investors to become paying members and thereby had a profitable amenity of civilization in Bannock.

Al brought Abo's mail and Abo retired to a table to go through it. Among the blather of internal memos was a terse message from his father saying that a congressional committee investigating the failed Big Sur Savings and Loan had found interest in a large purchase of junk bonds issued by Abo's insurance company.

Abo trashed the stack of paper and ordered a whiskey. He was not in a mind to drink, but he was feeling reckless and knew that his recklessness was more acceptable socially if he had whiskey on his breath. He began to generate rage. Why should it be repugnant that people in an insolvent enterprise escape, themselves, solvent. That was victory. This is the Age of Reagan! Turn the foxes into the hen house and have the taxpayers replenish the chickens. It is morally and economically uplifting to the commonweal to rise above the commoners and stomp them—it models for all the avenue to emulate and inspires the will to do so, for revenge. A man can cup his hands and hold a full drink of water—spread the fingers to quench the thirsty plebians and does it trickle down? No, it falls uselessly on the ground.

Oh, Abo was metaphorical. He rushed to the phone and rang up Henry Beems, a congressman from Oklahoma. They exchanged pleasantries like two wary dogs greeting one another.

"I've got some heat here that I could do without," Abo said, the first to quit the smelling. "What'd we elect you for, if not to stop persecution of this type?"

31

"Jason, you're not my constituent. Call your Congressman."

"None of that. I paid for my rights. If that doesn't impress you, consider that I might shoot your ass and leave you to bloat in the Potomac."

"Your violent tendencies do not advance your case," Beems said. "I'd recommend that you don't display them when you talk to your Congressman."

"Is that the way it's going to be?" Abo was uncertain.

Beems fell into a detached rhetoric. "It is incumbent upon me to do what is right for the citizens of my district and of this nation, not pander to the base whims of people who lavishly contributed to my campaign finances." There was an audible click that left Abo disheartened. "Thanks, Jason. That was a right tidy moral divorce."

"Isn't that illegal, taping this?"

"Not at all. I truly would like to help and I'd rather not cast aspersions on you, but if Ethics probes I will give my full cooperation. Hell, that little speech will sanctify me. Here's hoping you're in as big a jam as you think. It's been nice talking to you."

"Beems?"

"Yes?"

"I can still afford a plane ticket to D.C."

"That's nice. It'd save the federal marshals some paperwork."

They hung up simultaneously.

Abo strode over to Bird. "Tom, can you show me the ranch and explain what I ought to do? I'll put you on the payroll a day. I need to get settled into this ranch or I'll be working on a truck farm at Leavenworth."

"I've got time. But it's too cold to work a horse hard. If it warms up to zero we can ride some of it and I can tell you some of it."

"Tell me when it gets zero."

Abo propped up firewood to make a pallet by the stove and fell asleep. Bird drove to the school to leave a message for Joan to care for Tyree. When he came back, Abo was still asleep, the sun was unclouded, the air still, the Alforcas thermometer at ten below and rising. He prodded Abo awake and they drove out and mounted the best of the motley remaining Double Diamond pravvy.

They rode a mile at a walk so the horses would not sweat. Then they trotted five miles to the mouth of a basin two miles in diameter. Sagebrush poked through the snow and up on the ridge were chapparal and mammoth solitary ponderosas. Water bubbled through holes in the ice of a small creek.

"Best grass around," Bird said. "I put as many cows and calves here as early as I can. The calves get a good start. Then you just generally disperse them on the forest. The Forest Service has numbers per allotment. Trust them. They got those figures from me." Abo's white Arab had turned around to face home, or the warm Barbary shore. Bird said, "Saw that horse around and job him with your heels."

"This pony is dissing me," Abo said.

"In drought years, don't milk your AUM's. Feed hay sooner rather than exhaust the grass. Take care of the grass and it will take care of you."

Bird swung his horse westward in a trot. Abo's horse tried again to turn home and Abo sawed and jobbed and the little Mediterranean dreamer galloped after his mate, slipping and flailing, until it caught up and fell into a trot, which did not please Abo since his buttocks screamed each part of the two-beat gait, unable to copy Bird's rhythm of sloshing rather than bouncing.

Two hours later they came to a mountain. Abo had come to know the distinction between mountains and hills. This was a mountain. It usurped the sky, rising through miles of dense timber to a treeless rocky spire. Cayuse River, pinched between ragged jutting ice, swept in a canyon on the western flank.

"This can be bad," Bird said. "Cows drift up the mountain and over. When they get over, they're in the Sur Fork drainage. An early storm will start them drifting down the Sur Fork. They might get trapped in the canyon, or above it, unable to get to water. Always have enough old cows here to start home the right way."

Migrating elk had broken a single-file trail coming down the mountain. Bird and Abo rode the trail up through the dark timber onto the broken country of rock knobs and meadows and pockets of fir, country as vast as a sea, snowbound and hushed. Skirting the high side of a thicket, Bird reined up and pointed downhill. Abo saw the head of a cow elk above the brush. Soon there were a score of heads, all bodiless and motionless and staring at them.

"This bunch will be in Double Diamond hay in a few days," Bird said. "Keep the good hay near the house. They climb on stacks. What they don't eat, they trample. Fish and Game will sometimes help out, but it's best to regulate what and where they eat."

"Charity," Abo said.

"I never thought so," Bird said. "Just wisdom to protect what you need and regulate the inevitable."

Wisdom, Abo reflected should litigate against this cold ride. He recalled a man of wisdom. His name was Gentry Wilson, the selection of a head-hunting firm specifically told to find a marketing man from Time, Inc. In the interview, Wilson said age had given him wisdom. Abo erupted, "Wisdom! That's not our trade. I don't need a doctor of philosophy. I need a master of flimflam. I want a man who can bamboozle a squirrel out of his last acorn in February." The man replied, "Wisdom has taught me I am fated for hell and to get my compensation in the mortal life." Abo hired him.

"Tom, let's go back," Abo wisely suggested. "I'm freezing."

As they turned the horses, a few elk began drifting off, then some broke, and there was a resounding crash of brush as the herd fled.

They rode back with a desultory banter and then a weary silence. Abo found that if he did not think of being cold he was less so. One's mind slips in early hypothermia, and for a while Abo thought of this and was again beset by shivering and acute pain in his extremities. They stopped to build a fire and were relieved, but in the saddle again Abo was cold as ever. Bird, more acclimated, suffered but did not fret like Abo. A fool hen beneath the fronds of a spreading fir raised its head, then ducked it again and puffed out its feathers. Killing this accommodating grouse with the third throw of a stick, Bird said, "You get cold when you're hungry." He built a fire and dressed the bird.

Warm and full-bellied, Abo said he was drowsy and asked Bird not to let him freeze should he doze off.

"Your body knows cold," Bird said. "You will roll over and shiver and grab sleep a minute at a time."

"Then why do people fall asleep and freeze?"

"They freeze to death, not sleep to death."

Abo was lying in the snow, curled around the fire, when Bird urged him to mount, the number-one house still too distant to be had by dark. During the dinner stop, the horses had foraged unsuccessfully and were now devoid of zest; winter-trained to endure bleak futures, they plodded on, their faces white with ice from the condensed streams of their breath.

To avoid gates, Bird took the route back along the flanks of the hills rather than through the valley pasture. As darkness fell, Abo discovered another ill-charm. Unseen branches the horse passed under whacked him in the face. He dropped the reins and covered his face with his arms; when a quarter-moon rose to bring gray to the blackness he saw Bird doing the same.

"Are we going the right way?" Abo sought reassurance, imagining unpiloted horses going where they whither.

"This'n don't think so," Bird said. "But he operates by compass, not a map. That's a thing to learn. Horses are good at directions, but not infallible." The horses suddenly grew invigorated and went into a trot and soon the yard light of number-one hove lonely below the canopy of stars. "Stewart Goodnight and I were caught in a spring blizzard on War Eagle and couldn't see. I told him to let old Dan have his head to get us back to camp. He kept reining, so I rode up and jerked off the headstall. 'Now we'll go home,' I said, and we did. Another time I got lost up Willow Creek and the horse was, too. He skittered around and ran one way then the other, worse lost than me. I put the saddle over me and spent the night."

Abo watched that bottomland star as they rode. He had known such distance only on the sea. Finally the star became a planet and a ranch and a house. They rode to an empty corral.

Bird asked, "Is this information doing you any good?"

Abo's face muscles did not work so he grunted. Inwardly he pledged not to seek knowledge he would not need, as he ever foreswore a like trip. Abo finally chawed out, "Tom, can you help me off? My hips are so sore I can't lift a foot out of the stirrup."

"Flat cannot," said Bird. "Maybe you could topple off, but you sure can't lift a foot." He slipped Abo's foot free and dropped it two inches and held it for the dismount. "You've learned something, something invaluable to a ranch owner."

"Did we do this for class awareness?" Abo squawked, slipping off the saddle like a skin of water. "Christ, Tom, I had that class in college!"

"It was your idea," Bird said.

That, Abo acknowledged as he found his legs, was a lesson most acute.

They loosened the cinches and left the saddles on for warmth and fed a few flakes of hay. Double Diamond foreman Jim Stanger had seen them ride up and had the coffee on.

Stanger was a tough, smart hand, age 36. Tall and stony-faced, he had a gruffness underpinned by absolute confidence in what he knew. Career hands and summer boys heard his voice in their heads, in his absence, like the men of the *Iliad* heard gods. He was laconic like Bird, but without Bird's politeness.

Revived by coffee and sardines and bread and whiskey, Abo said, "Quit the patronizing, Stanger. I'm no cowman. I'm a manager of information. I tried to get information of a kind today and didn't like it and didn't think it helped much. Tom's whimsy is excused; he isn't on the payroll." Stanger yawned. Abo continued: "I want Omaha feeder prices, carrying capacity of range, average weight gain, slaughter prices, current calf prices, expenses of all kinds—" Abo paused to think of what else.

"For that," Stanger said, "I guess you'd need an accountant."

"Practice not being insubordinate, Stanger. You're indispensable now; I'll grant you that. Pour yourself a big whiskey there and come to work."

"I'm going to bed."

Abo whipped out a Browning 9 mm. and fired the clip at the floor between his feet. He shouted, "Does that say I'm serious?"

Bird looked at the chewed wood and linoleum. "Jason, he has a legal lease here. That one hole is big enough for a mouse to get through." Tom rolled the ejected brass with his boot: all had a jagged crack from head to mouth. "You can either throw that gun in the creek or put it on your wall. It's no good to shoot."

"I just bought this from the trader!"

"He's not a very good person to buy from. Are you two going to fight?"

"Does he want to?" Stanger directed this question to Bird, convinced that any reply from Abo was unreliable.

Bird said, "I don't know."

"Don't you understand?" Abo said in a weary tone. "There are things to be done. Sorry about your legally leased floor—thought it was mine. Which it will be, soon as your lease runs up. When exactly is that, anyway?"

"It goes with the job. You can fire me any time."

"You're fired."

"Tom, I believe he does want to fight. I'm going to stomp him."

Which he did, after a very long time. Bird admired the perseverance of Stanger doing it, and that of Abo for having it done to him. Furthermore, while Abo was getting the worst of it before he rallied, he was in reach of the knife used to open the sardine tins yet did not go for it. Also, he was careful of the furniture. He did not bite or gouge. In every way, he was surprisingly decorous in the brawl.

Winter was hard on Tyree. He was a boy, unaware of the past and future, did not know that time could exist three places. In a rare crying jag he might blurt that he wanted his mother. But he did not understand consciously the steady longing for Katie. Al and Bird and Bobby Coles and many others saw it clearly in the boy, but like the boy were not aware of it in themselves.

School was also trying. Tyree, so very inventive in accommodating what he knew to what he learned, could not answer correctly at school: school was somebody else's invention. When the children played games at school, Tyree did not play to their liking—did not play to win nor according to the rules—and was only included in the games at a teacher's urging. He was not brash yet did undermine the teacher with his natural insousiance.

Consequently he was generally left to his own ways.

It was the same at his various homes. Bird liked him and called him Segundo when they did chores but did not know how to nurture. Joan's nurturing was conventional, alien to a boy who craved Katie's unorthodox way of treating the boy as an adult. Sally was aloof and matriarchal. Jason came closest to connecting before he became enlightened of child-rearing by the women—then he grew wary and manipulative. Al truly loved the boy but was so imbued with weary reserve that the other pseudo-parents judged Tyree could not thrive there with such utter lack of stimulation: Al just took walks and dispensed liquor. Tyree spent much time in the bar playing with the colored drink straws, counting and sorting and hiding them, always taking a handful on their walks so he could match colors with leaves and rocks and painted things, because matching pleased his friend Al so.

5

The mares grew heavy with foal. The snow melted in patches but there was still no grass, and the mares hung around the mangers between feedings, chewing on wood fences. Deer hung around in the osiers along the creek all day, waiting out their fat reserves. One warm day Tom Bird rode a barren mare into the hills and followed a bear's tracks to its den in the apex of two fallen pines. The bear, probably a sow with new cubs, had ventured out less than a hundred yards. Still, it was a sign. Soon there was a trace of green along the roadside, then in the fields, and it was over. They had all survived on the Bird place.

A mare nickered to her baby inside. Tom brought her into the barn for foaling. She kept nickering, muzzling her flank, but her teats did not wax and so Bird turned her out after two days of dry feeding. The next morning a black colt stood at her side.

He found the afterbirth and laid it out to see if all was expelled: a blue sac the color and outline of a deer carcass, connected by a purple cord to a red and white pile of blood and tissue. While iodining the colt's navel, he appraised its conformation.

"He's straight," he told his sister that afternoon.

"A baby? What color?"

Women always ask the color, he thought. There were many things to ask, but they always first asked the color. Colors meant more to them. Some men were good with colors, but a lot of them weren't entirely men, either.

"Mostly black now," he answered, "but he'll be gray later."

The horse would actually be white at age seven, short and stout, a speed-burner that worked its way up to stakes races at Longacres, where it jumped the rail, went caterwampus across the infield into the lake and drowned.

"Anyways," Sally said, "I hope he's got black hooves. I remember how Papa hated white hooves."

And Bird went back home, thinking colts may be red or black, straight or crooked, large or small, pretty or jug-headed, balanced or gangly; they might sway daylong in the stall or paw huge holes where one does not want holes; some have recurrent bucks, others an impulsive kick; in his short time with racehorses—augmented by a life with cowhorses, pack horses, wild horses, harness horses, trail horses—he had learned to care for none of these things and wished only for a little bit of intelligence and a game heart.

More foals came. A young mare struggled in her first birth. With calves, one slipped a rope over the front feet and assisted with a pull, but a horse's legs were its worth and asked delicate treatment. Bird worked the membrane free of the colt's nostrils, let the mare further expel the head and front legs, then worked his arm under the brisket and slipped the colt out. Mother and baby, both exhausted, required an hour before they could stand.

This colt grew strong and in a few days was broke to lead, like the other babies. On a cold day in March, Bird answered the summons of free time as always, with a fishing rod.

He went to Crooked Creek, a spring creek that was open to fishing year-round. From a long seep on Paddy Mountain where it founted, it was for many miles a meadow creek, sporadically dammed by beaver, issuing from that gentleness into a dark thorny entanglement that cascaded two mile down to Cayuse River. This thorny cascade is where Bird usually fished: the pleasure of shooting flies in seams of frothy, boulder-strewn water for small trout was enough to overcome the daunting horrors of casting. Driving the parallel two-track road, he idly watched for a place to enter the brush as he drank a thermos of coffee; unintentionally he arrived at the confluence of the creek with the Cayuse River.

The Cayuse was a favorite, the trout strong like fast-water trout must be, though rarely exceeding fourteen inches. Now its water ran muddy next to that of the creek: the demarcation between brown and blue currents was neat and protracted. Though the Cayuse was closed, Bird saw that he could clearly fish the water of the creek inside the Cayuse's banks for a hundred yards or so.

He walked downstream until the waters could be said to have nearly mingled. Here the river came out of a long shallow run and, narrowing, bucked up against a bank of trees. Low branches, partially submerged, shivered in the current. He waded across the lip of the shallows, where the water fell as though over a pole into the pool. The first two steps were deeper than he expected. The third dropped him into the hole. He fell like a man through a haystack or through a snowdrift, no stumbling, just a vertical plunge. Borne downstream, he held his arms like outriggers and groped with his feet for the bottom. In the deepest part of the pool, nearing the sweepers, he struck out swimming for the far bank. Before he could afford chest waders, he often swam, but then he always protected his cigarettes and his flies. He discovered both losses after dumping his waders.

He had only the fly on his rod, a number-ten hare's ear, and he was cold. He did not expect to fish long. He fished the hole thoroughly and finally came up tight against a small trout. Stripping in, he found largesse: protruding from the trout's mouth was a sculpin, too large to be ingested. The sculpin is a mottled-green minnow of about two inches, rather like a catfish in miniature. It is a poor swimmer and hugs the bottom under rocks. To trout, it is a delicacy, rarely captured and cause to abandon caution, like oats to a horse or wine to a man. Bird found a tangle of monofilament in a bush and used a portion to tie the sculpin to his fly, another to tie small stones to his leader. Bouncing the sculpin on the bottom destroyed the high-water lethargy of the trout; Bird brought in fish after fish until the sculpin was stripped clean.

Bird considered himself a big-fish fisherman, but in truth he communed with rivers: the sculpin ranked with any trout he had landed. He drove home thinking of the many purported sculpin imitations, such as the muddler minnow, which caught fish because they also resembled a grasshopper or a stonefly or some edible alien. The real thing had given him incredible fishing in adverse conditions. Bird had designed and tied twenty-five sculpins, and he was still designing the twenty-sixth in his mind when he pulled into the lane and saw Eleanor Goodnight leaning against his front gate.

"Hello, Tom. Been swimming?"

He was damp but warmed by the hard-working Ford heater. "I read your postcard. You said Arizona was too hot."

"Probably just right, now that I'm back here shivering. But it's pointless. If I was going to leave, I should have done it when I was seventeen. Do you have room for a guest? There was a snowslide somewhere up north and the motels are all filled with travelers."

Bird was slow to take this in. Some of his dream scenarios were close to this—always with a twist as odd as he supplied now: "Everyone's moved out."

"Then there's room?"

"Everyone left," Bird persisted.

"I understand you, Tom. But I'm not going to bunk in the barn because of timidity and propriety. You would, and probably will. But it really is fine for you to make me a cup of coffee and lend me a room. We might even say things to one another. We used to know how to speak to one another. When Walker died, we stopped trying. And then we just plain forgot how. Lord, that was thirty-some years. When did Walker drown, Tom?"

"It was 1949."

"Yes," Eleanor murmured, turning up the collar of her jacket. "Yes, it was."

Tom showed her the colts, which were of some interest to her. Their sire had spent the previous spring at the Double Diamond. Hap Meeks, a friend and sometime business partner of Stewart's, had purchased the unraced son of Northern Dancer in Florida and lodged the stud at the ranch while he arranged syndication to racing interests in Washington State. Eleanor knew little about racing but enough about Hap to know he had come out of the deal with substantially more than he went in.

Eleanor followed him while he did the chores. Inside the barn welled a rich nostalgic smell of hay and horse and saddle leather. For a time they watched the horses boss and bluff around the hay and then walked out to the yard. The sun had slipped behind the ridge, leaving two red streaks like the wake of a boat. She told him about the fantastic sunsets of the southern desert; he listened, saying little—was this what she meant by talking?

Inside the house Bird put on coffee. Eleanor had eaten in town, so Bird fried himself a steak. He got out the cribbage board and they played a few hands. It grew late. Bird made up the bed in the spare room. They retired.

Slipping out of his wet clothes and under a dry blanket should have been a great comfort to Tom. It always was. His habit was to use the daylight to work, the dark to sleep. But now he lay in his bed half-turned to look out the windowpane at the smudged stars, the current of memory flowing muddy alongside the clear stream of the present, the two gradually mingling to become one water and one time in the spring of 1949.

Walker Goodnight, at twenty-one, was as pretty a hand as one might ever see. Tom Bird, a year his junior, was also a pretty hand, and their friendship had a competitive twist extending to the affections of Eleanor Knutsen, daughter of the Norwegian who owned the Bannock lumber mill.

Eleanor spent her early years in near squalor but with a bourgeois veneer so necessary to Europe's dispossessed. Her father, though an expert sawyer, was a Wobbly and didn't stay at any job long. Later he acquired a modest sum of capital from Norway and bought the Bannock mill, an abandoned casualty of the Depression. War came again, a curious godsend, and the Knutsen family prospered. Amid rising fortune, Eleanor's mother tried to inject reserve and elegance into the household, but by then Eleanor was an American girl, vivacious and unpretentious. She swirled through school dances and town fairs, disdained the parlor for walks along the river where her father's men bounced nimbly across floating booms, clawing logs tight to the boom with peavey poles. The rough-hewn lumberjacks, in town for winter, would sweep off their hats and struggle for a greeting without invectives when she passed on the street. The young cowboys bought her sodas with a stunning politeness, and two well-off widowers measured her and were pleased.

At eighteen Eleanor was marriageable not only by circumstance, but also by inclination. She resisted her mother's plan for her to go East for a refined schooling; why leave her home that she knew? What was it she did not have here? Where else were men like Tom Bird and Walker Goodnight?

Once a month she drove to Bruin, a hamlet of Forest Service buildings and miners' shanties, to stay with a girlfriend, daughter of a USFS district ranger. The Goodnight ranch became a one-night stopover coming and going, the whole family much taken with her and the two young men ardently in love.

In January and February of 1949, snow came so continually she could not make this trip. Snow fell behind the snowplow, plowing became impossible, and the road to Bruin was blocked for six weeks.

Neither electricity nor telephone ran to Bruin, so after two weeks a dozen men tried to ride the forty miles with a packstring. The snow was up to a horse's shoulders, and the men with big horses took turns forging a trail. The last snow had been heavy and wet, leaving a top resilient crust that horses sometimes had to lunge through. It was a wearying effort for men and horses, and to no avail, for they were stopped at the last summit before Bruin where snow was eight feet deep, composed of stratas of crust and powder, so that horses became stuck and had to be hauled back by rope or rolled sideways to be freed.

When this party returned, the thirty residents of Bruin had not been heard from for three weeks. Eleanor, anxious for her friend, got up an expedition of the two young cowboys and her father, who knew snowshoes. They rode to the summit, and Gustav Knutsen went in the last ten miles on snowshoes, returning with the observation that everybody was lying around like overfed Roman senators and that he would have stayed himself if news hadn't been expected of him.

Spring came late. The snow settled and iced over, and gradually waned beneath a steady drizzle. In late March the road to Bruin was finally plowed to a packed snow floor. Eleanor set out on her trip, reaching the Goodnight place at dusk. She was driving her father's new International pickup, the box loaded with tree-rounds for traction, but still nearly spun out in bogs of slush in low sunlit spots. She would have made the Goodnight place had she not met Tom and Walker on horses. They had ridden to a rise a mile from the ranch to await her, and Eleanor had stopped short of that rise to say hello and then could not advance.

The men looped their ropes on the bumper; the horses lunged and skittered on the ice; the pickup, in sliding, sought a deeper hole.

Tom sided his big dun next to the door. "Climb up, Eleanor. Walker will get your bags."

"Don't do it," Walker said. "That horse of Tom's isn't fit to carry a sheep camp. This'n singlefoots. Feels like you're in a rocking chair."

"Nothing doing," Eleanor said, climbing out. "You boys get off and help dig out this pickup. I'm not leaving it to get smashed by another car."·

The two men looked chagrined.

"There's room to get around," Tom said.

Walked added, "In the morning when it's froze we can drive it right over."

Eleanor's silence had vigor and command.

Tom said, "I'll go back and bring up a team."

"Malarkey." Eleanor waded over the plow drift and began breaking off limbs to throw under the tires.

The men were obliged to help; with steady shovel work and what limbs as could be had, they paved a two-track route to the top of the rise. Though they went at the work ambitiously, Eleanor could see they did not like it. Eleanor would come to see that hour of work and banter in sun and snow as a cresting of the divide between idyllic youth and maturity, the idyll ending in the brief solitude of the drive to the ranch when she decided whom to marry.

Eleanor was shooed out of the kitchen by Mary Goodnight tending the buckaroos' supper over a mammoth coal-burning stove. She walked the lot to the barn where the cowboys were putting up the horses. Though Eleanor did not like to ride, she liked seeing the crowded corrals of the Double Diamond, a hundred and fifty horses with all the colors of an artist's palette: blacks, browns, whites, grays, bays, sorrels, red roans, blue roans, buckskins, red buckskins, zebra duns, paints, Appaloosas, palominos, mouse duns. The Double Diamond's policy was ten horses per hand. Though Walker and Tom under her playful interrogation had admitted to regularly using only four of their allotted ten, both defended the dire necessity of having ten. When she came upon them, they were out in the corrals divvying up the string of a buckaroo who had recently quit.

"Consider, Tom," Walker was saying, "that if you take Wire Cut he'll be wasted. He's a heeling horse. The last time you caught heels it was your own, dancing with Eleanor."

"I can catch heels," Tom avowed. "And if you take McGruder"—like many of their horses, the big buckskin was named after the person they got him from—"you'll get thrown and I'll have to nail you together again." A year ago Walker broke his upper arm in a fall; Bird splinted it with cut latigos and twenty-penny nails. "He's cold-back and you're so groggy in the morning after a night dreaming evil harm to my Eleanor...I'd need a horse bigger'n McGruder just to carry the durn nails."

The men, seeing Eleanor, were embarrassed. She slipped inside the corral and the men rubbed some of the dirt off their faces.

While the three of them chatted, Bird stealthily moved Chance, Walker's best horse, toward the gate; he opened the gate and busied himself with his slicker while the horse meandered out. To Eleanor, Tom appeared to slap at the horse to restrain it, but Walker correctly saw it being hightailed onto the prairie. The gelding, proud cut, galloped out to a herd of barren mares a half mile away.

Walker threw his saddle on McGruder—exacting this small revenge—and rode after. In no mind to tarry, Walker raced McGruder and thus unwisely started the mares. He was an hour turning them and getting a rope on Chance.

In that time Bird found himself riding an expanding awareness that the fault truly was in the stars. From where they stood in the lots he could look out upon two hundred square miles which, in every way but one, was his realm. And that exception made insignificant his self-made codes and laws. Soon the grass would be up and people on the ranch would glow with the sight of fat cows—it was the religion of the country—but Bird wondered if he again would be moved by that spirit which, in the end, produced the Goodnight bank account. He was the prince of cowboys, but the kingdom paled beside the one measured in miles and compass degrees from the brass cap of a certain township.

He learned this at the brink of a proposal. Pride intervened and would not allow him to make it.

He was lying on his back in the bunkhouse when Walker came in. Eleanor had gone to the house. All the hands had washed up and were outside smoking, waiting to be called to eat. Walker washed and dug out his good clothes. He said he planned to propose after supper.

"I don't want to beat you to it," Walker said, polishing a boot near the stove. "You propose too and we'll give her time to study on it. She might marry someone else, you know."

Bird, wrenched into wisdom, saw that Walker could take his things up to the house and tell him what to do. Walker would not do that, and Bird would not be a vassal anyway, but it was a fact.

"I done proposed," he said. "She said no. It wasn't exactly that way, but close enough. I'm not coming to supper."

Walker Goodnight looked at Bird a long time. "I'll bring you something," he said. From the door he said: "I'll tell them Prince threw a shoe."

"Prince didn't throw a shoe."

"Cryin' out loud, Tom, you don't miss a meal even when you're hungover!"

"Nobody needs to know why."

Walker came in very late with a smuggled slice of pumpkin pie. He delivered it to Bird with a whisper and went to bed. Bird ate and, with food in his belly, dozed off.

But the sleeve of care did not unravel in his sleep.

This is a beautiful place, Tom. They say that Mr. Goodnight won the biggest ranch in the state in a horse race.

It was not true. He bought up neighbors with less water and more debt in their inevitable bad years.

It's amazing that Mrs. Goodnight can cook every day for so many people.

Her father's camp cooks did it for more and hungrier men, hard-working lumberjacks out in cold weather needing plenty of fuel.

I don't know if I want to do that. I think I'd rather pitch hay than cook. Walker says you'd be the best cow boss that ever swung a rope. Wouldn't that be exciting, the three of us working this place?

It never was.

Just looking at those piney hills makes me tingle. It must be the most beautiful place on earth.

The Creator made those piney hills without lines of demarcation.

Walker is a good man, Tom.

That he was, the best Bird ever knew.

The morning after Eleanor left, old man Goodnight, already besieged with an infirmity the doctors could not identify but would kill him nonetheless in a year, saw that a band of horses was missing. They were thirty head he'd bought last fall, and because hay rations had been meagre the latter half of the hard winter, Goodnight figured they had pulled out for their old winter range in Squaw Valley. He jostled Tom and Walker awake and told them what he thought.

"The range is *fenced*," Goodnight said with aplomb undiminished in the fifteen years since the Taylor Act divided the range. "They'll get up in the high country and be stuck."

The boys walked outside and were amazed at the warmth. A chinook was blowing out of the southwest; roofs were raining water; puddles and ponds dotted the snow. Walker slipped and fell.

"A few more hours of this," Walker said as he stood, slinging water off his coat before it soaked in, "they can eat last year's grass."

"I can't say how a horse thinks," Goodnight said, "but I *can* say he has no imagination. They'll go to Hell just because they've been there before. Some of those mares are getting close. Bring 'em back." Goodnight turned for the house. "And watch those creeks," he called back. "It is mighty warm."

The men roped out sharp-shod horses and rode out north toward Squaw Valley. The dawn sky was overcast and plumes of mist curled out of the draws. Slush from the horses' hooves sopped their pantlegs, but they felt very fine, seduced by the chinook, the jingle of spurs, creak of leather, huffing horses. Because of the rapid melt, the trail became hard to follow. Along late morning they lost it entirely and had contrary views on what draw the horses might have followed.

"I'll ride up to Rabbit Springs," Bird said as they scanned the ridges of several drainages leading roughly north to the Squaw Creek country. A warm drizzle had commenced. Rivulets were running everywhere, every draw a river system in miniature, cutting canyons in the snow.

"Where should I ride, Tom?"

"Walker, if you look out in that snowfield you can understand every canyon you've seen. The world must be a new place, else all the big rivers would be in canyons at sea level. The water would fall off the mountains in cataracts into sea-level sloughs and there wouldn't be any trout fishing." He paused to lick the cigarette he was rolling. "And if I live long enough to see all that, I may hear another fool question like I just heard. She said yes, didn't she?"

"She wants to be married in June, Tom. Will you be the best man?"

"Always was. Let's meet at the fence on the saddle above Chipmunk Spring."

Neither man saw any sign of horses. They continued to ride north, splitting and rendezvousing. The slushy hillsides wore a horse out, even these two,

Walker's Squealer and Bird's Prince, the hardiest of the remuda. Snow balled in the horseshoes and had to be frequently cleaned. In late afternoon they came within sight of chimney smoke from Al Brandt's cabin below Nigger Rock.

"Let's rest the horses and get a bite to eat," Walker said.

Besides running a few cows on the public domain, Al trapped, and now he had the hams of a fox on the butcher block.

"How do you like your fox, boys?"

"I think we'd better try boiled," Bird said.

Al had run his traplines that morning but had not seen any horses. He did not think horses would go up into the high country to cross the divide but after hearing about the boys' ride allowed it was a possibility. Walker told about a bunch of Goodnight horses that were sold to a Canadian outfit one fall and were back by late spring.

"Did I tell you about that, Tom?"

"You did. I studied on it. They crossed the Continental Divide. What pass do you think they used? I'd like to know. People sure picked a lot of passes and I wonder if a bunch of going-home horses picked a good one or not."

They went outside and tightened the cinches. Walker said Squealer was going to buck. The horse had acquired his name as a colt being halter-broke: he would stand for the halter being put on but as soon as the pressure touched his poll he would squeal and throw himself, and he did this for two weeks, whereas most colts were broke to lead in an hour. Though he had become a tough, thinking horse, his defiant nature needed outlet from time to time. Bird asked if Walker wanted him to snub the horse. Walker said by now he could diagram the horse's fits, and Bird busied himself with his own rigging until Al yelled, "Pick him up, Tom, he's clinching."

Walker rode the unmanageable horse around behind the cabin. By the time Bird rode to pick them up, Squealer had thrown a front shoe, lost somewhere beneath the snow.

This concerned them. The snow had largely become water on ice. Al looked around for old shoes, but they were outside under the ice, and Al didn't know exactly where.

They found they were able to travel well enough if Bird led, allowing Squealer to get purchase on the chipped ice. The sun was getting low when they gave up and started home. They planned to get fresh mounts and go back to Al's cabin that night. Wherever the horses were, they would remain there to feed into late morning.

At dusk they came to a seasonal creek, roiling and turbulent and overflowing its banks. Bird's mount went across easily. Walker's horse kept slipping on the bottom ice beneath the shoulder-high torrent and balked. Bird rode back across and they went downstream to a better crossing.

Again Bird rode across. Squealer, not balking this time, followed into the heaviest current, went down in the hind end and rolled beneath the water. Bird spurred downstream and when horse and rider came up he threw his lariat across Walker's saddle.

The horse was still scrambling and the rope was lying across the saddle, but Walker appeared dazed, both hands on the horn, his hatted head bent, frozen. For a moment there was equilibrium in the man, the rope, and the scrambling horse— then a greater moment of collapse where Bird saw the necessity and impossibility of retrieving and throwing again to rope Walker. The horse rolled again and Walker did not come up.

The riderless Squealer clambered ashore downstream but Walker was not found until a day later, caught in a sumac bush a half-mile below the crossing.

After proper mourning Eleanor married Jake Toole, a mine owner in Prairie City, twice her age. Two years later she divorced him for being stupid and then married Stewart Goodnight, younger brother of Walker. Stewart soon learned she did not love him, but he believed the fading memory of Walker would cease compromising his own claims, which it did after a time, and they were happy.

Some years later Tom Bird pointed out to his sister the little snow-fed gully and said, "All I had to do was rope him."

7

Eleanor spent many days looking at houses to buy in Bannock. Nothing suited her. Oh, the bathrooms had water enough, and the kitchens had modern appliances, and there were shade trees and some bedraggled flower gardens. But nothing spoke to her, said this was it, the place of your tomorrows. She was resolute in buying a house but in a quandary about what and where and why. One weekend she rolled over to Sun Valley to be feted by a real estate woman with a list of posh estates to view. Eleanor had not been to the valley since the Double Diamond had leased some hay ground on Gold Creek some fifteen years before. Unprepared for the glut of wealth that had stolen into the valley, she brutalized the agent. Two million dollars for a house! Was I to exchange a herd of seven thousand cows for a place to read and sleep? That lifetime of work for a fancy driveway and central vacuuming? The town itself seemed alien, a blizzard of million-dollar homes blown north and south, people in stores chatting bicycles and carbohydrates, a clerk who fawned over her because she did not berate him for ringing a sale wrong. When did the frolic of a ski resort implode to a madness of possession? Nothing made sense. If the rich wanted to rub shoulders, why the acres of unused buffering, the stone fences, the locked gates? At the bed-and-breakfast inn where she stayed, the boarders talked brand names and real estate until Eleanor nearly bawled at the conjured image of Stewart stomping in with his latest manure-smudged portfolios; it would have spoiled his mind to know that his life's direction was to have his schemes pay off so that he might, at some point, play. Now, after three years of settling Stewart's schemes and finding herself in possession solely of the herd's sale proceeds, a tidy sum to be sure, Eleanor arrived alone at the end: she had dollars and days to play.

During this driftless time, she thought often of children. Stewart's sterility now seemed the bane of her life. On that thawing day at Bruin Creek, it had all been so clear: she and Walker and Tom Bird and ensuing generations of Goodnights bound to the prettiest place on earth. After Stewart was tested, she had considered going to Tom Bird. Tom was proud, but men were weak; he would rationalize and take on guilt and scramble other emotions, and still not understand much inside his own head. Eleanor would have been pleased with Bird's seed, just as pleased with Stewart as father. But both men would have seen and known. Eleanor was nearly selfish enough to inflict that double-barrel cruelty save for further selfishness: she truly did love the Double Diamond, and her clout, and did not want either compromised by other ties.

She went on long walks from the inn, grappling with her unease. Ice-dams formed and broke loose on the river. Swallows pestered houses for nesting sites. Sage flowered on the hills, and in sunned-up flower beds tulips budded. One day spring asserted itself so sharply with its green song that she understood what disquieted her: it was spring and she wasn't pulling calves. Calving *was* ranching; that was the payoff; to feel the season without the glory of herd growth made her feel purposeless.

Understanding this made her gutsy. She could make anything, do anything. She could look forward to a healthy twenty years and do any damn thing she pleased. She had money. She needn't waste a minute. She could travel or disport or start a business or even go down to the Alforcas and prove what pikers they all were.

She had freedom. Having choices was a novelty that had vexed her, making her feel useless and irresponsible. The seasons had always ruled her. These ghost calves broke the bond and she was free as a lama.

She ate dinner and played a few hands of solitaire, not wishing to feel rushed nor desperate, though she was. At dark she phoned Hap Meeks and told him she would be there shortly. And then she arranged for a cab with a polite, intelligent driver to be at her hotel at 7 a.m., this cab from the nearest large airport 160 miles distant.

Yes, she was showing off to herself, proving a point, but it was also good to stock up on politeness and intelligence before visiting Hap Meeks.

She was walking down the Spokane concourse when a boy of about twelve ran up and said, "Lady, follow me to Mr. Meeks."

They went to the lounge where Hap was sucking ice from a water glass. He gave the boy a dollar.

"How are you, Eleanor?"

"Right as rain."

They walked out and two other kids came running up with a chorus of I-saw-her-first. They recognized Hap and pulled up.

"Sorry, kids, she's done been found," Hap said. To Eleanor he explained, "I've got half the kids in this terminal bounty-hunting you. Fifty kids hired, I pay only one. Proves a point of business—piece-work."

Hap was a solidly-built man of fifty, with dark hair needing cut and a moustache needing fertilizer. He wore dark glasses and a blue suit. He was a vain, happy, restless man, with much impulse and scant responsibility. Toting her bags, he said, "Airport motel?"

"Romantic," Eleanor said.

"There's a Denny's next door."

"Stellar."

They drove south through the Palouse country to visit Hap's friends. Hap talked steadily, less to tell Eleanor something than to occupy his time. The rolling plains of winter wheat and fallow ground spread like a rumpled quilt beneath a flat sky.

"They grow good subsidy here," Eleanor said. There were miles between houses. "What kind of people live here?"

"All kinds," said Hap, who would know.

"Looks like a good place to go broke and be glad."

"It ain't so bad. All those four-wheel-drive center-pivot tractors out on them peas and wheat sure do get someone to Hawaii for scenery." That too he would know.

Hap's friends lived on the bank of the Snake River in dry cheatgrass and sagebrush country. They had a private boat dock and a garage submerged in the water. On the gangplank, Hap punched a remote control to open the garage door to reveal a wafer-thin fiberglass speedboat and a sturdy aluminum jet boat.

"What about high water?" Eleanor asked, looking at the boats in the garage.

"This river's so dammed it's plumb forgot what high water is," Hap told her.

As more guests arrived, they went on rides in the speedboat. On the last trip in before dinner, Hap, who was on the dock, activated the door to close while the boat was running in to moor. The driver was slow to cut the motor. Though the impact was not great, the door was flimsy; several feet of the bow pierced through, wedging the boat so that it could not be backed clear. Eleanor felt ashamed of her friend, but Hap thought it a perfect frolic and worked with great zest with hammer and crowbar and saw to extricate the boat.

Returning to the city to her hotel, Eleanor remarked as odd the boat-owner's lack of anger over Hap's prank.

"'Tain't odd," Hap said. "He's my broker, and no genius; he can't afford to get mad."

"That's cruel."

"He got rich being nice at parties. Right now he is ecstatic thinking how my two hundred dollars of guilt will be parlayed into thousands in commissions."

She looked at Hap's square-rigged face profiled by a trailing car's headlights. "Your folks do tire me," she said and curled against the door to sleep.

Daily, Hap squired her around the business cabal of Spokane, trying languidly to get into her pants and fervently into her pockets. She enjoyed the meetings and also enjoyed the time alone after shooing Hap away to tend to his affairs. On the evening before her return, Hap drove her to the orchard country where stood the son of Northern Dancer who had spent last spring on the Double Diamond. In his iron corral the stud lorded, thick of neck and whinnying mightily to his mares in the barns around him. The farm was a polished, modern facility with a neat geometry of paddocks, stalls, sheds, hot walkers, pens and track, with horses and people passing hither and yon: shoers and muckers and exercise boys and owners.

"That cowboy get colts all right?" Hap asked.

"I saw several."

"Come look at my colt."

As they walked, Hap told of how he came into possession of the stud. The horse had various leg ailments, not so severe to keep him from training but recurrent enough to forestall his racing debut until he was four, at which point the owners decided to retire him to the breeding shed, since the Northern Dancer line had become the foremost in the world. But he checked sterile. No mares caught. A vet told him this story in a Florida bar and theorized that the bute the horse had been training on was still affecting his potency. Intrigued, Hap bought a mare and submitted her to the stud through the summer. When she preg-checked in, he bought the stud cheaply and took him west.

Hap drew up at a stall. "And here's the boy out of that mare. He's young for a two-year-old, bred in August after everyone else abandoned the stud. He's a July colt. I lied and said June 30. But for a July colt he's a sculpture. Folks here are awfully high on him."

The bay colt stood broadside with neck curved to watch the visitors, idly pawing the feed corner where the evening hay would appear. He had the bright outset eyes the Goodnight men sought: *good vision, good horse,* they proclaimed. Eleanor felt strangely cold and tight in the chest. This spoke to her.

"How much?" she whispered.

"Is he worth? Oh, I'd guess twenty-five thousand. Dam's a Princequillo mare, old but a stakes producer. Hard to say, though."

"I'll buy him at twenty."

Hap chewed a hay straw, thinking. "You know, I don't have twenty thousand lying around. It kind of ties a man up without some quick cash. You get the check and I'll get the papers."

"I need to talk to someone about delivering him."

"It's on me, Eleanor. I'm going to go downtown, find me a foreclosure and a friendly bank and make me a quarter million on your twenty thousand."

The result of this colt landing in Bird's hands was Jason Abo got a primer in handling horses. Though the horse was broke, he had broke skittish, according to Bird, who proceeded to start from scratch. Abo, who often brought Tyree to the Bird place, witnessed the transformation. In thirty days, the colt stood with dropped reins, dodged to face recalcitrant cattle, trailed placidly in the mountains.

"I didn't know race horses did all that," Abo told Bird.

"He goes along with what I want. I can't say if he wants to, or thinks he has to, or can no longer make decisions."

Now, Abo had ridden horses, but generally thought them a nuisance. Backpacking in the Sangre de Cristos, he had wagered and won a hundred dollars outpacing a pack string four miles from trailhead to lake. It made him feel superior. But the feeling waned as he saw the two-year-old transformed. He got a notion. He wanted a horse!

It is something of a western mandate that a man selling a horse must arrange for the buyer to be unhappy after the purchase. Being known as a good horse trader is high praise. This quaint tradition is mantained by people who are otherwise scrupulously honest. The man who sold Abo a horse would drive across the state to return a hundred-dollar bill accidentally left on the table, yet he smugly sold Abo a pretty bay who had to be thrown to shoe, was night-blind, ran away when one dismounted, and cribbed with a ferocity that tore corral planks off the posts.

Abo took this complaint to Tom Bird.

"Are you going to run cows?" Bird asked. He was annoyed by the lateness of the year.

"I intend to."

"Get your checkbook and let's go."

They drove south out of the hills and past the prairie of hay fields to the dry country of arroyos and mesas. Tucked against a cliff, miles from anywhere, was an old Airstream trailer, the bottom lined with straw bales for insulation. A few plank sheds and a round breaking corral of woven brush were behind the trailer. At the bottom of the cliff a little green delta fanned out from an open artesian well. Sixty or so horses drifted about, grazing on what appeared to Abo to be bare dirt.

A pair of mixed-breed cow dogs shot from the barn, ecstatic to have a car to bring to bay. Jim Reeser came behind them wiping his hands on his shirt. He was a friendly big-boned man of forty, with sun-blackened hands and neck and face below the white band where his hat sat ("lots of chrome," his wife periodically admired when he stripped for bed).

They shook hands and Bird explained their mission.

"Well, gol-damn, I do have horses to sell. How about a cold drink?"

Reese took a tin pail off a post and filled it from the well-faucet. He limped some and had a pain in his gut, which he kneaded with his fingers as he drank.

He passed the pail to Bird. "This business sure do make an old man out of a young one pretty quick. I might hold together till my kids can do the rough riding, or I might not."

Abo had understood the offer of a drink to mean something other than water; after a sip of sulfur his desire for something else soared. "Do you have a beverage that comes in a bottle?"

"My wife makes a fine currant wine."

Reese led them to a root cellar, flung back the plank hatch and backed down a ladder. The floor was a bed of sawdust and blocks of ice chopped from the spring. When Reese climbed back up with the gallon jug, Abo saw in a corner a hung carcass.

"Is that a horse?" he asked.

"I was meat-hungry and he had too much buck," explained Reese, handing the jug to Abo.

Abo swirled the wine in the jug, studying. He uncorked and drank.

Bird and Reese smoked and talked of the land, of the changes that are noticed in miniscule and therefore debatable: the dryness, the weeds, the bugs, the birds and critters on the upswing or inexplicably diminishing.

Abo set aside the wine. Frequently involved with poisons, he embraced Aristotle's credo of moderation in all things, at least when purveyors were unknown. "Let's buy horses," he said, without much confidence, and started off to the single strand of barbed wire enclosing the horse herd on eighty acres of scrub. The wire was irregularly strung on sagebrush and rocks and a rare post sunk half-heartedly.

Tom Bird said, "I'd buy them before I looked at them."

Abo turned back. "Is he going to tell me about them? Am I going to have to hear about the horse capable of everything but slicing cheese? Tom, I'm going to point to the first dozen I see and hope I get skinned on only eleven." He went back to the wire and shaded his eyes to see the far members of the bunch.

Bird pointed out to Reese a flock of sage chickens that flew over the butte and settled on the road to dust.

"What do you suppose he wants?" Reese asked Bird.

"The best cow horse you have under a thousand dollars. Five that can herd and have had a rope swung over them. Maybe one good roping horse. Two long horses. Three green-brokes with promise. All geldings."

From a shirt pocket, Reese brought out his bookkeeping pad. He figured. Abo hollered for them to come mark his selections.

"Exactly what I had picked for you," said Reese after he was shown. "Fifty-two hundred dollars."

Abo had suspicions but was suddenly loath to dicker. He authorized investments of tens of millions, not this pittance!

When the horses were delivered, Abo did not recognize any of them. Jim Reese told him about the individuals and led up the best of the string: "This is one fine pony for a grade horse." And Abo, in a short time, wholeheartedly agreed.

In his search for corporate redemption, Abo had examined many ways for quick profiteering—from subdividing portions for vacation cabins to selling the tracts of timber. Now his efforts were all toward running cattle. He rode long days, enduring chafed thighs, stiff knees and hips. He patched fence, learned where to salt and how to vaccinate. He completed a tidy requisition for money to buy cows and forwarded it by mail. Phone queries gainsayed that the proposal was somewhere, all right. During this time Abo installed a fax machine in the ranch and so pestered vice-president Thomas Furman with missives that his own machine began to ooze handwritten notes.

Such as:

Abo, when do you plan to generate income? Furman.

Abo sent a message explaining that he needed cows and was in the process of procuring same.

Fax: *I mean, to justify expenses like this transmission.*

Again Abo referred to his detailed prospectus about the cattle business.

Fax: *What have you been doing all winter? Furman.*

Abo got Furman on the phone. "Fixing fence!" he barked. "I've been fixing fence."

"Ah, Jason, I can't really picture that. I mean, really. Get it straightened out up there. Say, do you want to team up with me for the golf game?"

"What game?"

"Maui next week." Furman interpreted the long silence. "I thought all division chiefs were meeting. Pity. You're the only scratch golfer in the company. Well, straighten it out up there, won't you. Call me when you hit town."

Abo called his father and explained the absurd condition of the Double Diamond.

"Furman's coasting. Through shithouse luck, he's riding a bigtime winner. I'll intervene. You'll get the funds."

"Fine. I start buying tomorrow."

"How's the boy? He getting three squares?" Like many children of the Depression, the senior Abo thought regular meals was the crux of child-rearing.

"He doesn't go hungry," Abo said.

"I ought to see him sometime."

"Might be an idea."

"Your mother's first husband, Katie's father, was a Russian aristocrat, driven out by the Bolshies when he was a boy. He was quite old when he married your mom, still spoke of pilots as aviators and got miffed when American peasants making fifteen dollars an hour addressed him. He died possessing a few old photographs of his father with the czar and a couple of suits bought him by your mother. He never did quite get the drift. Jason, don't expect too much."

At the end of May, Abo's cows rolled up in a parade of semis, the silver trailers scoured green with manure outside the slats. The job of putting them on the range promised to be one of some days. Since school was out, he asked Joan Collins to stay at the house and watch the boy. Needing money, she agreed. With a liberal dispensing of wages, Abo got together a branding crew and saw the stock dispersed in a pell-mell fashion. On a Sunday morning after this was done, he had time for a shave and a leisurely breakfast, followed by a drink. He joined Joan on the porch. Tyree was down at the creek sloughs, hunting tadpoles.

"I'm impotent," he said.

"Good. You won't be disappointed then." She shifted her chair to take the sun glare off the magazine she was reading.

"I hope it isn't permanent. But it's been in effect for a year or so."

"I'm no doctor."

"I just think it's dishonest to allow false expectations."

"You're innocent. I didn't have none."

Abo finished his drink amid a whirl of uncertainties. So far the northern Rockies had been more stressful than idyllic. By this time the cocaine boys were filing into the Grecian Horse absolutely unprepared for the next moment, and here he was drinking Stanger's cheap whiskey and feeling blue. He went into the house and poured the last of the whiskey in his glass.

"I'm impotent," he told Joan again on the porch.

"Still?"

Eleanor bought a new box Jeep. Unlike the old ranch Willys, this thing called a Jeep looked and rode like a car. She made a fair sweep through the army surplus store and Jack's Sport Shop, buying camping gear to cover every contingency and whim; most of it, she got stuffed into the Jeep. After stopping at Tom Bird's place to see the colt, she picked up Jigs at a Crooked Creek ranch and drove to Cayuse River to camp.

Jigs was a blue heeler, a pet of Eleanor's whom she felt impelled to leave with a neighbor when she sold out, because he was also a dog who needed to work. He was not a slavish dog but a dutiful one. Though he would jump to herd cattle for a stranger, he would also stay with her until given the permission to do so. Over the next few days, he provided—besides company—security, growling at camp visitors when he had suspicions. Upon his instinctual judgement, Eleanor kept her eye on the visitor and her mind on the .30-.30 in the tent.

Eleanor spent the time agreeably. The campsite was good, on flat grassy ground in the shade of ponderosas, with firewood on the hillsides and the good clean water of the Cayuse a few steps away. She had more than the necessities. It was fine to read through the stack of Western reports, take cold dips and hot sponge baths and think.

One day Tom Bird came riding over the south ridge, trailing three pack horses. He brought the string down the steep slope slowly, switchbacking and stopping at the bad places to see that every horse stepped properly. He was halfway down the hill when Eleanor recognized him. She and Jiggs walked to meet him as he crossed the river, the string tied halter-to-tail with shoelaces, a tether that would break before a horse sent its trouble or ill manners down the line.

"Are you bringing me supplies, Tom?" she said.

"I brought mostly old straw and sandbags. I'm seeing if maybe I have the horses to guide. Did you know you must have a license before you can hire your outfit to a hunter? I've been thinking about that and wondering why." He had suspected where she might be camped, but he was surprised she was so settled in: two tents, a lean-to, tables and benches. "Eleanor, I hate to make biscuits for one. I'll hobble these and cook up dinner, if you're hungry."

"Did you ever learn to cook biscuits without burning the bottom?"

"Yes, I did learn. I turn them over and burn the top instead." He swung off and started untying canvas manties. "Looks like you have a nice camp. I'll put these ponies on the hill across the road."

"Bring your oven to my camp, Tom."

In a short time he had the packs off, the horses hobbled, and the one manty with gear open. He grabbed the sourdough, the Dutch oven, rod and waders.

He did not fish that evening. While dinner cooked, he was shown through Eleanor's extraordinary camp; a highlight he hadn't seen from the hillside was a folding aluminum kitchen that had everything in the right place and was bigger than his cupboard and shelves and sink at home. After eating, they built up the fire and made coffee. The sun fell early from their ridge-squeezed portion of sky; the mountain chill descended. Bird faded with the light and left Eleanor's camp when the stars grew dense.

"Tom," she called after him. "If you intend to fish tomorrow, I brought a pole and would like to go along." She heard a hearty acceptance from the dark and yelled, "Wake me."

Then she banked the fire and went to bed, very pleased. Bird, on the other hand, found the night so wonderful that lying in bed he was made forlorn by thoughts of Katie, not Eleanor.

In the morning they drove to the end of the road. Bird hoofed it to the canyon of the Cayuse to fish upstream while Eleanor fished downstream from the Jeep. In the canyon the river was a baffle of current defined by boulders, frothing white except for the marbled swirling eddies behind rocks which held fish if sand had not drifted in. When feeding, the trout were in the tail of the eddy and could be caught; when not feeding, they held the bottom around the boulder and infrequently succumbed to trickery. The water was still a milky green but low enough to offset that; the fish had their eyes on; Bird got into fish. They did not dart like creek rainbows but rose smoothly like a bubble, with exposed backs, to intercept the fly, as big-river trout do, even though the river was not big. Bird lost himself in the river, continuing to fish down the canyon, and also lost himself in time, not thinking until mid-afternoon of miles and hours and Eleanor. He scampered upstream on boulders as though feinting in basketball, until he was winded, then trod and trotted to the edge of his endurance, thinking, "Good Lord, I'm jogging," a wonder that seemed to give him strength.

When he came upon Eleanor, she was bent under a chokecherry bush, side-arming a grasshopper against the upstream bank. It was a bad place for fishermen but a good place for fish, and she landed three before the commotion killed the hole. To Bird, watching discreetly, it seemed like her thoughts were right but her rhythm had hitches that foiled her intent.

"How did you do?" she asked when he neared.

"Fine," he said. "I fished a caddis, but the fish took them as grasshoppers, I'm thinking."

"It's too early for grasshoppers. Why do the fish take them?"

"Why do they take a real grasshopper, the first one? I'll get the beer."

The beer was cached around the next bend; by the time he fetched it, Eleanor was lying on her back, hat over her eyes.

She heard him and sat up. "A beer would be nice."

He handed her a can and pointed to his bulging creel slung on a broken branch. "On this river I keep them at thirteen inches. The river can't rightly grow trout bigger. Do you want them to eat?"

"Let me see them." He brought her the creel and she looked at the fish piled in a bed of damp grass. "I last ate fried trout at a San Francisco restaurant when my banker said he'd loan on the cows. It was not good, as I recall."

"Some things don't help the digestion any," he said.

"I would like these trout."

Bird could see that negotiating the rocks and current and brush had tired her. "Do you want to rest some before we go?"

"Yes. I'll drink another beer and rest."

"Eleanor, you fish well."

She laughed and lay back down, shading her face with her hat as before. "I learned to fish watching you one day in this canyon. I was on one of those knolls about halfway up the ridge."

"You were on that one there," Bird said, looking at a rocky knob that collected three narrow draws and made one broad one.

She lifted her hat to see. "You saw me?"

"I saw Two Bits."

"Ah, Two Bits," she sighed. "She was put down in 1953."

Bird tried to think how everything was then. Salmon ran in this river, before the dams; they came up in the low water and cleared redds and were very hard to catch but easy to spear, and plentiful enough to fill the larders of everyone who hadn't an aversion to the softness of their spent flesh.

Bird said, "I'll go get the car if you want to nap."

"That's a fine idea."

"Do you want to take a long nap—I can fish a couple of holes."

"Fish," she ordered, then chuckled. "What holes do you think I flubbed?"

"Couldn't say. They change through the seasons. Hope you did, though." He gathered his tackle and looked up at the knob. "You were there all morning. You must have napped then, too."

"Nope," she said softly, her hat further muffling a drowsy voice. "I watched you four, five hours. I saw what you did. I'd only been just married to Stewart and it felt peculiar, watching you. But I was curious about that fishing. You're right, it was Two Bits. She was a good one. It doesn't seem like so long ago, now." She lifted her hat and eyed him. "I could study things pretty good then. I don't think I flubbed too many holes."

Bird fished long, not lost in the water as before, but deliberate, and was late joining the shuttle to camp. The horses, over time, had figured out hobbles and were feeding high on the west ridge. No movie stars, they did not come when whistled. It was dark when Bird had them gathered and packed.

Eleanor brought him a sandwich. "Are you really going to guide with racehorses?"

"I'm still studying on what that fee is for," Bird said. "I know it is possible that I will lose a horse. Naturally that would be the best mare—only I aim to leave the best mare home."

Eleanor bid goodbye and lingered there in the dark, listening to the pack spring splash across the river, scrabble up the skirt of shale rock and for a long time maneuver up the hill behind the fainting jingle of the bell on the lead pack horse. It amused her: Tom was training the lineage of lavish expense and meticulous selection to the mundane bell of a plodding pack string. The chill, the quiet, the loneness settled on her. When she could no longer hear the bell, she thought, A man is in the mountains, without apprehension or hurry, a man who does not carry water on the saddle, who will stuff his pockets with matches and call that camp gear, who on the trail will watch the horses rather than look for elk...and yet would guide.

Despondent about Joan's rigorous interpretation of her job, Abo linked up with Bobby Coles for an all-night foray through the mountain web of cocaine. It was ridiculous: miles of barren highway, the houses with nobody home, the hassles for scores, the roadside bars where women ate the beer cans after finishing the contents. At dawn, driving back from town, determined to go on a purifying 10-kilometer run, Abo heard a terrific lowing from the Crooked Creek pasture. He stopped the truck. The cattle were by an island of timber beyond the creek, bawling up a storm. He drove through a nearby gate toward the cattle.

Crossing the creek, he saw recent tire-tracks. In the herd of fifty or so pairs, roughly half the cows were bawling for absent calves.

Abo looked at the tire-tracks, the square of chewed-up earth, the trampled hay. "I've been rustled," he said aloud. To be rustled was an odd notion: Abo shook away the fabled conjurings of gunfire and stampede, and looked closely at the tire tread.

He followed it north on the Forest Service road. At every fork he stopped and found the tracks, saved from total obliteration by later traffic because of the truck's width. The trail went over Coyote Wells to a county road, thence to the state highway, where manure showed direction.

Abo sped to the Bannock sheriff's office. Long past feeling ridiculous, Abo told the sheriff, "Someone rustled twenty-five of my calves and they went thataway."

The sheriff, rather than vaulting into his car, repeated everything told him before he jotted the facts down on an incident report, all while Abo stewed about thataway becoming the farther by the minute. (What to do? Bird later explained to Abo. When Bird was a lad, cattle had to be trailed to railheads and rustlers lived short lives. With trucks, rustling was a lucrative enterprise.) Luckily for Abo, the crime gained stature when three other ranches were hit the next week. He was able to cajole the state cattlemen's association into posting a modest reward, which he amplified tenfold in barroom talk for those who did not or could not read. It is true he took the matter personally, and it is also true that Abo had not deciphered the rancher's work day and so fell easily into the old work habits of fury. In the northerly towns within driving distance he strolled into bars and said to whomever was present, "Some bastard around here is rustling, and there is fame and fortune to the sharpie that says who. I'm from the Bureau and I'm gonna tap phones and look at bank accounts until I find the dirty villain, if someone doesn't beat me to the reward." Mostly the patrons cast a weary bland eye that did not indicate whether they liked or disliked rustlers, so at times Abo lingered to sling around drinks and saw in such free-spending sprees that patrons came to realize that rustling was indeed misbehaving. And so he held hope that morality might be tweaked.

Greed was actually the case, for Abo received a phone call suggesting that two brothers named Silva up by Snowbird had rapidly acquired a herd of weanlings. "This is Hank," the caller said. "It ain't my name, but it is to you if they turn out to be the ones. I'll call about the money."

At Snowbird Abo got directions. The Silva brothers lived up a creek canyon on a strip of grassland overloomed by talus slopes of sparse brush. The land, as well as a prefab house squeezed between the slope and the creek willows at the end of a rutted road, were come by honestly, and neither brother could say who had first tired of ordinary ambition and spurred the acquisition of the calves thick on their small crescent of pasture, so thick that Jason Abo had to slap rumps to forge a passage as he walked up the lane from the padlocked gate where he left his car. The brothers were loading metal interlocking panels into the stock trailer, discussing how they were to feed their burgeoning herd even as they prepared to add to it, and when they saw Abo, both men thought of manacles and shame. Vulnerable to inference anyway, they recognized in Abo an outraged fidelity to possession. The older brother, with a sudden clarity about the ultimate responsibility of the enterprise, said, "If there's any killing to be done, you have to do it."

The younger Silva had killed before, but at the behest of his country; with no practice in premeditation, his thinking went awry and left him mute while Abo said from the far side of a single-strand electric fence, "I got drunk and sold some calves. It must have been to you since I saw my calves up the road. The question is, Do I get paid for them?"

The younger Silva said, "Yes."

"Gosh ah-mighty good. Send the check." Abo vamoosed.

The Silva brothers watched him go. The elder Silva said, "Let's scatter these cocksuckers."

When the law arrived in late afternoon, the calves were gone; the brothers might have withstood the scrutiny if not for the twilight arrival of drifting-home weanlings: a hundred bawling calves coming down the creek, stranded on the bluffs, strewn along the public road. Still, the beef was not in their actual possession, granting them opportunity to proclaim innocence with a semblance of hope of being believed, since they had reputable day jobs and were generally well thought of. Out on bail, they again saw the advantage of a missing Jason Abo, whose testimony was the frame supporting dozens of damning corroborations, but finally adjudicated their conscience by reconciling themselves to a lot of TV.

On sentencing day, the younger Silva told the judge, "Everyone advised me to not buy cattle with borrowed money. I took that advice."

Thereafter Abo kept an eye on the cattle by the roads. He bought one of the new off-road toys, a four-wheel cart with a motorcycle engine, and outfitted it with bags, slings, spray tank, and PVC sheaths. Thus he was able to transport shovel, twenty gallons of 2-4-D thistle-killer, a vet kit, beverage cooler, rifle, and a Fish and Game tranquilizing gun, with assortment of hypodermic darts, which was his answer to the cowboy's lariat: when Abo wanted to immobilize a cow, he rode up behind the animal, shouldered the gun, and let fly at the hind quarter. In practicing this art, Abo killed two heifers with incorrect dosage. He maintained overnight they were merely in heavy sedation but coyotes disputed his reckoning and by morning the point was moot.

Clearly this was not the ultimate cowboy outfit. Abo's hired hands were three boys who had left school at sixteen because it was too hard. They knew something about horses and cattle but could not do much beyond what they were told. This was troublesome. For one thing, Abo did not know all to tell. For another, he was not always around to give orders: when done with a task, the boys found shade and awaited further assignments. So Abo went to the fishing cowboy with an offer.

Bird declined. He had done his time in another's employ.

"Tom, I'm talking stock options. I'm talking pension. Membership in the High Valley Gym Club and a good parking space."

Bird allowed those were dandy things, but he had been getting by without them and would try a little while yet. However, he was available for day jobs, perhaps. And, he added as parting advice, the Double Diamond was woefully undermanned. "If you prevent the loss of six cows or gain an additional pound per animal, you cover a buckaroo's yearly wages. You're not getting the irrigating done. Fences need to be rode. A man should be on the mountain to tend that herd; we used to have a trailer for him; I don't know if it was sold in the auction or not. You need to intermingle bulls yet keep them from serious fighting. You need to keep records. Mostly you need more eyes. You need to know what is happening."

That Abo knew better than most, having been in many chemical forms of doubt. "I've got in mind a day job," he said. "Go hire what I need and tell them what to do."

"I'll do that. It may take two days."

"Take three!" Abo sang. He wrote out a check. "And find, if you can, a secretary that can do things like write checks and otherwise run the show. In every business you'll find a secretary who truly knows what is going on. I need one more than anybody."

Bird found all but the last, the factotum. The men descended on the ranch with tack and hungry bellies. Abo was unprepared for the onslaught: bunkhouses needed to be cleaned, cooks hired, provisions bought, logistics arranged for men and food coming together. He was overwhelmed, desperate for the administrator by proxy, an able secretary. Joan was still watching the boy for pay. Abo offered her a promotion.

"I'm not trained," she told him.

"You're smart. That's enough. I can't hold two jobs."

"And what is your other job?" Joan asked. "Just wondering."

"It's whimsical, my job. I can't be bogged down."

Joan mused, "You would like me to be a baby-sitter, a concubine, and a gal Friday. Might as well be married."

"I can do that," Abo said. "I don't do lawns or always come home. But I'll buy you the best clothes."

"Jesus. You're making a proposal."

"No, I'm not. I'm responding to yours."

"I was being facetious."

"Ah, Freud spoiled that line."

Later they sat on the porch after sunset, eating TV dinners in the fading light.

Abo said, "Think how romantic it is—like an arranged marriage in the old country. A marriage of convenience, what better motive? As far as love, hell, I'm in love this moment."

"But, Jason, I don't love *you.*"

"No woman ever truly has," Abo said between bites. "I won't mind."

8

Bird had three days' wages in his pocket: money for gas and something more. He sliced up the last of the hung beef, soaked it in spices, and jerked it in the hot summer sun. He filled the pickup with oats and tack, loaded the snorting colt and a barren mare in the trailer. Then he called on the Double Diamond to see if Segundo could accompany him on a month-long swing through small tracks in the western states.

Abo's approval came automatic; he had been thinking enrichment along the lines of summer camps, though he himself had detested going to camp until he reached puberty and learned the trails to the girls' camp.

"It will be good for the boy," Abo said. "Hanging around me all summer has got to be dreary. I'm a dullard as far as children go. I don't make slingshots or buy milkshakes or watch TV. When do you want to go?"

"I'm ready now."

"Tyree's out back with Joan. We'd better ask the priestess."

The priestess had vexed a tangle of roses and lilacs and raspberries into order; she and the boy stood sweating among vanquished brushpiles, their shears still snapping alongside their legs.

Abo said, "Lord, it's a yard. It looks like the carnage of Odysseus' suitors. You could flay out the eleventh floor while I the loyal swineherd barred the elevator. Oh man, literature do inspire." He gathered some spears and piled them. "Tom's going racing a month and wants to take the boy."

"That was the plan," Joan said.

"Gather him a lot of clothes," said Bird.

Abo and the boy left to do that. Bird told Joan, "My horses will do fine on grass. But look out your window when you drive by, please."

"What makes you think I'll drive by?"

"That man is wondering whether he loves you. I figure you're about the same."

Joan stooped and slung some pebbles at a feral cat sneaking into the yard, a black puff of fur on a starved skeleton. The cat yowled and bounced off in a stiff-legged hop, then crouched and wailed in fear and menace.

"He is repugnant," Joan said. "Speaking of the cat." She hooked an arm in Bird's and started for the back door. "I just don't know, Tom. I like this town a lot better now that my husband's gone. And I'm not sure if it's being free of him in particular, or being free of a husband in general."

"He didn't sound like much, what I heard in the bar that night."

"Tom, I have twice married, both times the result of love in a tailspin. I'd like to approach a third union more analytically. Why haven't you married?"

The Double Diamond

"They either married out from under me or weren't the marrying kind."

Segundo came outside dragging a packed duffel bag, his coat pockets stuffed with candy bars. The horses were stamping in the trailer. Goodbyes were said and Joan walked alongside the truck with her spiel of motherly cautions until Tom hit the next gear. She watched the dust plume of the truck. Abo stood nearby, uncharacteristically silent.

"I guess I'll go visit my family," she said.

That night she gave analysis a last try and etched on her list pad a flow chart that didn't flow straight, nor did it branch into discernible tributaries, but flooded. Her pad, like always, spoke of the hollows of time. She packed a suitcase.

On the road Bird watched Cassiopia and the Big Dipper spin a clock towards dawn; when the light began seeping back, they were in a Utah valley. Bird parked in a creekside turnout and put the horses on a knoll across the creek and started breakfast. The colt became entangled in the picket rope a few times, and needed unwinding, but Bird was pleased with the horse's calm study of the matter. He rigged a rod and shook Segundo awake.

After Joan left to visit a sister in Wisconsin, Abo spent some days riding among cattle hock-deep in grass and imagined himself working. He had become used to the gentle reprimands of the schoolteacher, the humor of the boy. Those things like lotus had dulled and lulled him. Now freed, he was again afire, eyeing a mark. But, alas, as a town, Bannock crawled. Raising cattle and overseeing a placid Gym Club was joltless, pinned to slow rhythms of people shedding fat and bovines acquiring it. Abo's needle was still pointed to the eleventh floor.

On the plane ride to headquarters he pored over company reports. He was not an effective reader of numbers but the jargon alerted him: major changes in stupefying obfuscation amid dazzling delight. Something was shaking, and the incredulous thing was no one had sought his advice or alliance.

He learned the rumors. Cash-heavy, Western was ripe for a takeover. A trade magazine said so. Responding to rumor like flies to dung, raiders gathered with coercions of mergers, leveraged buyouts, greenmail, buy-backs. White knights were solicited. The clerks and shop foremen knew these things, but Abo's old associates hadn't a thing to tell him. He was indeed out of the loop. Even his father stayed aloof: "It's sensitive, son, very sensitive." They did not talk further of the matter. Abo did not wish to know if his father were an accomplice to something sordid. His father was his conscience, a hard-working cocksure man who would browbeat and use his fists and take bread from a street waif, so devoted to fair play he was a remorseless bully. For Abo, that star of conscience was distant and had many permutations, but it was fixed, a thing of

63

gravity and direction when his own mind roved into the dubious beyond; he needed the ethics of a square-shooter who could nobly ruin a man or a town.

Abo took the Gideon Bible from his hotel room and read about some righteous wrath on the flight back to the Double Diamond.

When Abo drove into Bannock he had been awake twenty-four hours, forty-eight hours wearing his blue pinstripe suit, which still looked darned good, he judged, as he drove past the Alforcas to a dive called Ronnie Rocket. Letting his eyes adjust to the gloom, he surveyed the barnacles and pool-players, and loudly announced, "There's a lot of pretty women here. But the men I see are all pikers, wage-earners, with good hearts and empty wallets. Anybody who prefers a full wallet and empty heart, come round while I drink my glass of milk." The crowd was stupified, up to the very minute Abo raised a glass of milk, and then there was some grumbling. "I know some of you ladies are devoted to your escort," Abo continued. "Naturally. But in a crowd this size someone must have doubts."

At this the men rushed him. Abo grabbed a chair and fended them off, calling for the first taker to slip behind him out the door. The women rooted for him. The Tybalt of Ronnie Rocket leaped across a table and was crowned by a chairleg and the effusive flow of blood common to head wounds made everyone stop to see if his brains weren't following. A stocky red-haired red-bearded man said, "I ain't got no woman either," and invited Abo to see a movie down the street.

The man was a Viking with tattooed arms, a Vietnam vet who told Abo how he still hit the ground when a car backfired. The film was *Apocalypse Now,* and hardly had the credits rolled when the vet bolted from his seat and shouted, "Those aren't gooks! Them's *Filipinos!"*

The appalled vet gave further lessons in verisimilitude. Abo dozed through much of the movie and afterwards tagged along with the vet on a vague mission to score. The vet's name was Al, as in (Abo was told), "Al kick your ass." They meandered through Bannock's warren of millworkers' houses. A sign on a Path of God church told Abo PUT YOUR WILL INTO NEUTRAL AND LET GOD SHIFT THE GEARS. Another sign on a railway car on a siding said DO NOT HUMP THIS CAR.

No sirree bob.

Such succinct lectures. He followed Al-Kick-Your-Ass until he felt free enough to drop the surname and call him just Al. A barking dog got Al to howling. Abo said don't hump that car and Al said he hadn't really thought along those lines yet. Up a dead-end gravel street they came upon an old bungalow with a weedless garden of peppers, tomatoes, and beans. Neon pulsed behind curtains, red and orange and blue beating like a heart on this street of staid yellow windows. Al rapped on the front door and it fell open. A dozen stoners sat on the floor, their heads glowing.

"How about that," Al said.

"I don't think I want any," Abo said, awed. "I've got to work tomorrow."

Abo woke with his head packed with glass balls and gauze. He sat up and re-introduced himself to the world. He was on a tarp, covered by his suit jacket, walled in by pine trees. A web of frost was on the grass. Through the trees, a few rods away, was a camp.

That is not my tent, he realized. He was making progress. He stood and slipped on his jacket.

Abo followed the sound of trickling water into a draw and splashed his face and drank. What in the tarnation, he thought. He really wasn't very curious. He noted that his suit had sure held up nice.

He climbed to gain a view and looked out over the Map Rock pasture where the old cows had been thrown in with a Limosine bull. Reconnoitering further, he found his car on an overgrown dead-end logging road behind a rusty yellow Toyota. A black-bearded man was making a fire beside the tent.

"The breakfast man," said Blackbeard as Abo approached.

Abo remembered insisting that trespassers fix breakfast.

Blackbeard sliced curls of kindling with a hunting knife. "You sure are one noisy motherfucker."

Another man came shirtless out of the tent, a muscular blonde half Blackbeard's age. Two steps from the tent flap he pissed, a breach of camp decorum that breakfast seemed unlikely, now, to mollify.

"It's the camp crasher," the young man said, slicking back his hair and stretching. His hair was corn-gold, and with his taut beefy build and copper tan he looked like Thor in the funnybooks. "You know them camp robbers? Big white and gray birds with a long tail?"

"Gray jays," Abo said. He didn't want breakfast at all.

"You shoo them from camp," said Thor, "they hop away and come right back. You throw a stick at them, they fly up into a tree and wait until your back is turned and come back. You shoot them, they don't come back."

"The symbolism is fallacious," Abo said. "I own this particular camp."

"It's National Forest," Blackbeard said, still slicing tinder.

"Up the ridge a mile, it is."

Thor sloshed some gasoline from a five-gallon military can into a metal cup and threw it on the wood beneath Blackbeard's nose. "You always think you're fucking Jim Bridger," he said as he flipped a match. Flames blossomed with a *whoof.*

"Waste of gas," said Blackbeard.

Thor warmed his hands. "We're set up here. We're homeless people. We're in the news every night. You wouldn't give us grief when we're down on our luck."

"I would indeed. Your luck's still bad." Abo knew their camp was doing no harm, but they had not been civil last night and this morning's undertone of threat was extreme bad manners. He was slowly coming to want an elevation of associates: these picayune predators he kept company with were infringing on his ability to flock with the real worthwhile predators now stalking Western. This situation tested his resolve. "I'm sorry, but you'll have to go."

Blackbeard said, "Last night you wanted to dine with us."

"That was before I heard the camp robber story. You gotta git."

Thor set a coffee pot on the fire and pulled out a good burning truncheon. The action surprised Abo. He had worded the threat with an ample supply of bluster, as Westerners are prone to do, so that it could be dismissed by responding in kind, yet still retain its meaning. They were evidently indifferent to this nuance and now his options were narrowing. He looked around for a bigger stick. The sun was fully over the mountains and the warming earth exhaled a blanket of thin mist. The burning sage odor of the campfire hung low in the chill air. The smoke or the mist or something else swirled in Abo's head; water flooded his mouth. "Is that what it's gonna be?" he said.

"Screw it," said Blackbeard. "There ain't nothin' special about this place. But don't you go runnin' to call the police or the posse or whatever you got in this place.

"No law," Abo said and turned to go.

Abo could not get the nurses to give him enough morphine. Every four hours when the drug arrived he informed the nurse, with imagined lucidity, that he had a high tolerance for drugs and a low tolerance for pain, and they simply *must* be humane and triple his dosage. The trifle they gave him edged him towards sleep but did not get him there, and, unable to move without his nerves becoming paralyzing filaments of lightning, he contemplated a future of psychiatric care to go along with a physician's and an orthodontist's: he had cracked ribs, a broken collar bone, a missing incisor, bruises from the hip up. He spent two days in Intensive Care until a doctor said, "There should be internal bleeding, but there isn't," making Abo feel like a malingerer in the serious place of electronic and human monitoring. They shipped him off to the ward of the can't-be-helped and already-saved. Inadequately doped, Abo finagled the cart so he could see the spikes of his heartbeat. He rang for nurses and showed them irregularities and asked for morphine. One nurse told him, "Too much morphine and that bumpy line you don't like would be flat as a table." Abo replied, "It'd be flat before now if I didn't know myself how to dose." The anticipating and witness of his heartbeats was a meter of future psychiatric salvage efforts.

Three days after being pummeled by the trespassers he felt well enough to seethe. He relived the treachery: conceding a stalemate of honor over the harmless camp, he had bid adieu and was assaulted from behind by, not Thor, but Blackbeard, brandishing not a stick, but a rock the size of a football, and it was a late scurrying sound that caused Abo to begin to turn and thus receive the rock on his shoulder rather than head and though he was dimly aware of some kicking after he went down and nothing thereafter he knew brilliantly that the big blonde menace had stepped in to avert murder. The gratitude Abo felt towards Thor was paid in fancy by being spared the horrible atrocities reserved for Blackbeard. Oh, to run Blackbeard down in the four-wheeler, tranquilizing dart at hand. Tranquilized, Blackbeard would face a smorgasbord of fates.

In another two days Abo left the hospital with a fistful of Tylenols with which to ameliorate tremendous shooting pains when he moved his right arm or leaned forward. When the pain shot through his side while he drove home he quailed, wailed, and bawled. A mockery! A farce! Squirt guns on a four-alarm fire! Strangely, the drive *to* the hospital had been more difficult than painful, all sensation swallowed up by a desperate intent to make it to his destination and survive.

He glanced at where the bastards' camp had been as he drove past and marveled at how many times he had been in bad city neighborhoods at bad times and never been mugged until on that idyllic piney hill; the bastards had lifted his wallet amid the rush of packing camp.

He stopped at the oversize ranch mailbox and raked the pile into the car with a brave sweep of the arm. Pain shot. He closed his eyes. Sweat beaded on his upper lip. He fought nausea and waited out the storm. Mail was scattered on his lap, the floor, the seat, in the crevice by the door. He unfurled the *Wall Street Journal* on the wheel as he drove the lane, scanning the stories, navigating with nary an upward glance, like a homing pigeon, thinking it amazing that the mountains of inconsequence were a half-day late in news of the frantic trading of an Atlantic island—...when he saw it! He braked hard, skidding on the gravel into a wire fence: the homing-pigeon sense was defunct with all his attention riveted on the item that said the SEC had suspended trading of Western Pipe and Steel. It had been thirty years since Western had sold pipe or steel and there it was, this name in print declared worse than rotten by an SEC which had gone to sleep since William O. Douglas had exercised real thought in the post. The item gave only the fact of suspension, no cause, not even a speculative paragraph. Abo could not imagine a scenario that would lure this era's SEC to *see* hanky-panky, much less rouse to act.

Abo sped to the house, running through names of people further east who would have a later edition of the *Journal.* By the time he got to the phone he had many names in mind but not a clue where his fucking book of phone numbers was. That's what six months in the mountains did to you. Isolated, snowed-in, horizons-girded, you turned into a *rock!* He rushed about, seeking a hint. Where would a rational man put it? That was not a great lead.

In the condo of an aggrieved ex-lover with an attorney on retainer was his goddamn rolodex! Would she look up a frigging name for him? Yes, she might. There was that much love.

Jenny answered out of breath, and Abo visualized her emaciated aerobic-freak figure squeezed in spandex. He asked her to look up some names and she more or less thought it quaint of him to ask favors when they had so many other things to discuss..."except that my lawyer has advised me not to talk to you, but rather to refer you to him, and I would be happy to supply you with *his* number, but you already have it, and besides my pulse has just dropped below 120 and so I must, literally, run. *Ciao.*"

At the click Abo impulsively flung the phone. Pain! He slumped to the floor, holding his head still and eyes closed. Medical barbarism! Romantic treachery! Corporate chicanery! And he was a mess, truly a mess, spilling tears and groping for the couch and wanting mainly to be whisked from existence for a little while.

Which he accomplished with twelve hours of fidgeting sleep. When he awoke he was less manic, almost cerebral. Chewing Tylenols, he put in a stint at the phone, but the wheels at Western were, predictably, neither in their offices nor homes. Strangely, that day's *Journal* had no follow-up, no elaboration. So he drove the Double Diamond, chatted with cowboys, communed with the west wind that rippled the grass and hummed in the trees; he was pacific yet resolute; patience was his counsel. When worry and desire began to make rumblings, he quelled all that with a simple mantra: "Cattle are looking good." The cattle were fine and he had a plan and patience was his sidekick.

So. The wind rushed and hummed the next day too and his father kept his usual barber appointment. The Armenian barber passed the phone.

"Hello, Dad," he said.

"Jason?"

"The wind here blows from the west and on Wednesday mornings Dad gets a barber-shave and a haircut. It's good to have these verities or I might feel quite a-sea."

There was a pause and Abo thought, God, if he hangs up like Jenny my serenity will quantum-leap to hysteria.

"Jason, you don't know what it is to lift your jugular to a straight-razor and close your eyes with utter bliss. That's success."

"Might you extend some of that trust you have in a ludicrous Turk-hating Armenian cretin to your son?" The vociferousness hurt his ribs. "Just a thought."

"It's all account of that cow queen on the Board. The company had too much cash to escape being raided. When we proposed a friendly takeover, she was adamant to prevent it."

"Morals, Dad. She didn't think it right to finance a buyout by saddling the company with debt which could only be paid by dismembering the company while its friendly raiders did some profitable skimming."

"Son, I don't know if it's right. Corporations that ponder morals we call corpse. Stockholders and management want returns now. We used to speculate about the company in the next generation. Now a five-year plan is an excursion into infinity. Loyalty is passe. I wish we could say we were proud of our product, that it improved people's lives, but mostly our widgets are unnecessary and aren't doing the planet any good. I budgeted a startup line for a product for under a million dollars and had to justify every nickel screw; marketing asked for twenty million dollars and nobody had a thing to say. It's a game you accept on its own terms if you want to be a player. I'm a player. When the players are banks, stockbrokers, execs, and rich white men, the Sermon on the Mount is irrelevant. I get up in the morning and go to work. The next day I do it again. Some days I don't do that, and they're called weekends and vacations. I had some children and I think about that and I think about dinner. Today I'm meat-hungry. Does having cattle about make you more, or less, keen on beefsteak?"

"Dad?" Abo was not at all sure about this man.

"The deal is this, son: Western Pipe and Steel had enough cash to buy all the shares, every flipping one of them. And it did. The company owns the company."

"Dad, that's ludicrous."

"Well, it's unprecedented."

"It's impossible! I have stock."

"The ESOP, you mean. That was in Westco, an insurance company essentially bankrupt, a condition largely brought about by its purchase of the Western pension. The Feds have hold of that; current speculation is that pensioneers will get, at best, twenty cents on the dollar. With the pension thing and some other troubles—well, it was a requiem, you understand. This was a close-held company and with the buyback authorization it was slick and simultaneous and computerized. That's it. Finis."

"Oh." Abo sucked in a breath, looking for an idea. This was too fantastic for a handgun. "Call up the White House. That's your boy."

"He wouldn't understand it if I explained it to him. Besides, Nancy won't let him near the California cronies since they started getting indicted." He added as an afterthought, "Not that I'm in that company, mind you."

"Boy oh boy."

"I wish I could have done something for you, and perhaps I still can, but frankly your winter's hibernation did not endear you to Schuberg and the rest."

"I fixed fence!"

"I know. It shows initiative, but it's labor. I don't know how this will shake out. Right now I'm a salaried employee of Western, about to retire like any man might to enjoy the fruits of his investment. Of course I do have some money, so if you should need help with the rent or groceries, don't hesitate to call." Silence. "Read your mail and don't drink before noon. So long, son."

Abo muttered a feeble goodbye, stunned by that parting advice which is exactly what his father told him upon his graduation from college. Then Abo was sure he would be legendary. And now he looked at the future and saw the Double Diamond on the market, the Vice-Presidency of Land Acquisition an anachronism, and himself offered a position as chief of shipping clerks and maybe something of more promise should he prove competence by making the transition smoothly.

Rent! Groceries!

He would be excused, this once, of not heeding his father's advice.

Eleanor heard about this amazing thing and flew to Washington to see a senator who had forsaken the family ranch for law school and political platitudes. He was a mama's boy and a hypocrite; yet he retained a deference to the bigwigs of his early years—like the Goodnight name—and so was nearly always useful. He was again. Through him she entered offices of decision-makers to cajole and lecture. In a few days the government decided that the current board of directors of Western Pipe and Steel would continue to function.

Having pressed for that decision, she was then greatly chagrined to find her fellow board members not so committed as she to baring skullduggery and regaining honor. The board chairman, philanthropist and heir of a candy-maker's fortune, voiced a consensus of all but Eleanor when he adjourned the meeting with these words: "It's a matter of metaphysics, I suppose. But a corporation is an entity, just as a person. Let the entity function."

The members shook hands and Eleanor followed the chairman to his car, hypothesizing this and that, what-ifs and how-abouts, just who was to weigh shenanigans against sound stewardship..."Who makes decisions, Mr. Hershey?"

He stood at his car enduring the tirade, a silver-haired pointy-chinned man in an impeccable suit and weary but serene with his impeccable morals. "Mrs. Goodnight," he said as he slid behind the wheel, "*we* do."

She watched him pull into traffic and then turned to the sidewalk and wondered aloud, "Then why didn't we?"

"Segundo, Utah doesn't like us."

It was Sunday afternoon and Bird had not been able to find a Catholic church in the phone book and was alarmed at the diminishing sheath of twenties in his wallet. Utah had no pari-mutuel racing, but some sons of Zion with the renegade spirit of Brigham Young raised fine horses and backed them feverishly in exhibition races. In the barren mare's first race, Bird made a paltry bet, watched his horse storm away from the pack and breeze to an early win, and then came to understand how clannish Utah racing was, as racing secretaries at the next two tracks on the circuit wrote creative conditions to bar his horse.

Up north through the desert farmlands of Idaho and Oregon...a sojourn of three-day meets three hundred miles apart, five-eighths tracks with tote boards on trailers and a stall being the rope that holds your horse to your trailer. The barren mare, his meal ticket, made her entry fees and some more, but Eleanor's colt was on a gentle road, exercising for wind, just he and the boy handling and riding so that new things were not scary. Time was measured by the colt's coming debut.

Backtracking to Cache Valley and on up to Wyoming's western slope and through South Pass with its ghostly stomp of Americans flooding to the Pacific, driving on and on, a reminiscing man and road-weary boy...to the Popo Agie.

The Popo Agie is now mainly a feeder of ditches irrigating hay fields, but the prairie was still evident, and above the water-checks and ditch-gates the river ran cold and pure through the willows. They found a turn-out, unloaded and watered the horses. In a short stretch of riffles upstream from the trailer, small fish were rising, and while Bird puzzled on arousing bigger fish the boy caught enough for a meal.

While the bacon-wrapped fish sizzled on the skillet over a small fire of cottonwood twigs, Tyree heard about the mountain rendezvous held on this river, of trappers who waded icy streams to set traps and thought life grand; of the far-roving partners living perilously in hostile country, and also of brigands plundering the Blackfeet. Bird tried to make the boy understand what it meant for two men to leave the Bear River in January and travel on foot fifteen-hundred miles to St. Louis to sign a note for supplies.

"Did you do that, Tom?"

"No." Bird handed the boy a fork to turn the fish. "But it's uplifting to know that some did."

They ate and loaded up and drove north. The boy curled on the seat and slept. The Wyoming desert gathered up more of the scenery until the world was a sea of scrub brush rippling in the heat beneath a sky more silver than blue. Forty years ago Bird turned tail on this rangeland and rode across the divide to the mountains and learned cowboying was mostly the same there except one needed a bigger horse. In his mind more than his eye he saw the high dry prairie where nothing could ever be found except by buzzard. And into the mind emerged as through dust his relentless father bidding leave that lifetime ago: "What do you expect to find?"

The other side of those mountains, is all he knew then. Over those mountains now befogged in summer haze, he had striven toward a future. Over those mountains—that great expedition! Hiring on and moving on; twenty miles, forty miles, guided by rumor and song, an aimless and mundane search for work that was also an exuberant and epic assault on destiny. Time may gild the dust and make gallant the drudgery, but still Bird reminisced upon that westward trek when all things were vibrant and good, when his heart beat strong and his mind rang clear; and how could he know, how could he know that when he could answer his father's leave-taking *I found it, I found Eleanor Knutsen* he would also begin to share his father's skepticism for the usefulness of discovery.

Racing in the bushes is analogous to minor league baseball: illogically hopeful, faintly addictive, with much low-rent travel. Two hours before Billings, Bird and the boy washed clothes in a creek and dried them fluttering from the side windows. They parked at the track too late to get a stall, so they walked the horses and tied them short to the trailer and put hay on the wheel fenders. Then they made a fire and cooked biscuits to eat with jerky. After supper they shifted gear from the pickup bed to the trailer and in the bed made a pallet with tarps and sleeping bags.

That was racing in the bushes.

Before retiring, Bird confirmed, in the moonless black, that a half mile away a neon cocktail glass spilled onto a busy highway, and asked the boy if he would like to limber his legs. In the bar, which was called the Jolly Dimes, jockeys and trainers and trackmen pursued a discussion of the next race day that was equally close to forming and fixing. What keeps it from being the latter is that the system is informal: necessary participants may not be present, or present conspirators not unanimous, or jockeys willing to help out are unable to control their mounts, or people imbibe too much and can't remember, or someone receives better advice before post time.

That would be the bushes.

From one of the patrons, Bird borrowed a conditions book, found a race for the mare the following Saturday and a debut for the colt on Sunday. When he returned the book, the man asked with a calculated nonchalance, "You got anything worth feeding?" Bird's negative was equally calculated, for he planned to get some traveling money on the colt. As he and the boy were leaving, they were detained by a short, lithe Indian in ranch clothes, dark like a Paiute but thin-featured like a Cheyenne. Scarcely sober, he mumbled that he could ride in this state but he couldn't drive and might he hitch a ride home? When told they were walking, the man said, "Oh, too drunk for that," and meandered back to the bar. When Bird studied the jockeys the next day at the faces, he found this man much the best. His name was Lloyd Stevens. He had soft hands and rode lightly and rhythmically and went through traffic on the inside with courage. Bird named him to both mounts.

In the paddock on race day, Bird boosted Stevens onto the mare, said the mare rated well, and had suspicions. Stevens toppled off the horse in the post parade and Bird, along the rail before the grandstand, heard one man say, "I thought Lloyd quit drinking," and heard his companion reply, "He quits when he's broke." Bird yelled at the remounted Stevens, asking if he was okay, heard *just-through-damn-starting-gate*, and then watched the jockey lurch against the neck on the first jump out of the gate and bounce off, the unweighted and knowledgeable mare subsequently heading the pack with ease.

Again, the bushes.

Stevens went off in glory in an ambulance, but the hospital declined to take on the challenge of detoxing him. The next morning Bird stepped up to a trailer and met at the door the jockey cradling his boots and helmet. Bird thought, He's still got a little pride.

"I want you to gallop a horse," Bird said.

"That's where I'm headed."

"Need a ride?"

"Thanks."

They drove to the barns. Horses on hot-walkers were steaming in the cool Montana morning. Bird confessed, "I don't have a horse to gallop. But I have a race this afternoon and I mean to keep an eye on you till then. This horse is special. And you can ride, partner."

"I can ride," the jockey said in a low sullen voice. "He says I can ride."

"You got the right to that laugh. But you don't drink very well."

The jockey paced away in his stooped, rapid way. Then he turned back, head up. "What horse I riding?"

Bird led the man to the stall where the sleek muscled colt indignantly nosed the empty feed bucket.

"Where that horse come from?"

"Good stock," Bird answered. He was by nature laconic, but the horseman's vernacular of omission of auxiliary verbs and disregard of tenses inspired him to a greater conservatism. "He run."

"Put my mount fee on him," the jockey said. He walked down the barn row, asking the world if any horses needed galloping. Bird kept tabs on him. The jockey rode two-dollar exercise rides until noon. Bird bought him lunch, saw him into the jockey quarters. There were two hours to the fifth race, a six-furlong race for maiden two-year-olds. Bird could do nothing for the colt but look at him. Bird mucked the mare's stall while Tyree sat on the mare with a halter and dangling lead rope. Tyree and the mare moved down the barn row. Bird looked away from the colt to see the boy and mare wander off, confronted at each stall by a horse's head, some nickering, lonesome-like, some charging with pinned ears, also lonesome. Bird was calmly moving alongside the opposite barn row to intercept the horse when he got help from several quarters and it became a general ruckus, with the horses on walkers kicking at the moon and the horses in stalls aroused. The mare with Tyree aboard remained placid, was caught easily and came back to Bird's barn to graze a wedge of grass by the water spigot while Tyree braided a quirt from tail hair and Bird leaned against a bunk of hay and dozed ten minutes. Upon awakening, he saw himself forked and thought, Is that my son?

Like other men of Bannock, he had made his calculations. Could he have failed to carry a one?

His arithmetic doubt faded. He was awake now. It was just the boy on horseback looking in on his dreams, and the dreamer looking out. Years ago Bird had been a consort of Katie's for nearly three months, since then a realist who did not resist when Katie said, "Come on, Tom, I'll make strawberry shortcake for breakfast." The numbers didn't jibe. Somehow Bird would have to accept—they would all have to accept—Tyree's uncertain parentage.

Tom Bird handed the boy the last handful of jerky and said, "Let's go get the little stud ready."

In the paddock, grain and excitement and youth mixed a frothy sweat from the colt's ears to his flanks. A little washing is not cause for concern, but this was beaver-wet. Bird boosted up the jockey Lloyd Stevens and said, "Get him relaxed if you can. Stand a minute by the far side and let him look. Don't hustle him out. Keep him checked until he's collected and going easy, and then on the backstretch go around the field in a rush. I don't want him to duel anyone. He's got such a nice stride that if he gets by, they'll have to pin their ears and dig while he's running for fun."

Prophecy is the currency of horse-racing: after each race the true prophets are recognized, rewarded, redeemed. Rarely, though, is a bettor's analysis or owner's boast as accurate in detail as Bird's parting words to Stevens. The colt came out slow, faced the flying dirt with nonchalance, stayed resolute through the bumping of young horses, then simply glided away to win by a romp.

"Segundo, we're flush," said Tom Bird, fingering the pack of ducats in his shirt pocket.

They cooled the horse, waiting for the urine test, and were back to cash in before the last race. Bird gave the boy some bills to buy whatever his heart commanded and himself walked to the paddock, intent on bolstering his account. He studied the circling horses, finding a myriad of flaws. Mostly this is unproductive handicapping: the eye is a terrible deceiver. He picked up a discarded form, delved shallowly into those arcane numbers, and finally resorted to looking at the horses' names.

It is a mystery of thoroughbred racing that good horses have good names. One explanation might be, as Earl Ward put it, "a good horse is a good color"— meaning that when you admire a horse you come to admire its color. Similarly, people familiar with a fine horse may regard its name as dashing and noble whereas a stranger finds it pedestrian. Another explanation might be that serious breeders do not bestow cute monikers on their foals. If neither of these explanations fully account for the phenomenon, there must be others, for a horse fits his name. Man O'War. Secretariat. Platers could sooner carry lightning than those names. War's Kid, The Boss—those are your cheap platers. And no horse could possibly bear the name of John Henry—with its connotations of strength, endurance, and pure ornery combativeness—better than John Henry. Bird did not embrace all this as dogma, but his attitude was colored by the fate of the first racehorse he had owned, a filly who was given him to resolve a debt and who, though talented and courageous, was accursed with the name Cozy Georgie and quite naturally caught the sniffles and died.

In the bushes a study of names is worthwhile, if only for its insight into humanity. Had Bird looked back at the day's card he would have seen Got The Runs, doomed by a simple *s* to be chicken-feed. He would have seen a thoroughbred obliquely threatened, Betterbefast Joe. He might have watched a quarterhorse race featuring The Dark Horse and The Other One, where he would have heard the announcer call *It's ole Slag Heap on top, with the other one second, and the dark horse third—and comin' up strong, that dark horse, I believe he's a-gonna win it, but here's the other one charging! But there's that dark horse! Aaaand...I think the other one got him.* Many suspicions about the place were confirmed.

Had Bird been able to look back over the years at a particular owner's stable, he would have seen Sam's Girl, Sam's Kid, Sam's Baby, Sam's Hope, etc., and so would not have placed his win money in this last race on Sam's Pride, because Sam probably did not have a whole lot, naming as he did; Sam was probably some daft old codger hanging round the barn in the moonlight, cooing to his broodmares.

Two things of note happened in this last race.

The first was some jockeys and perhaps some others accepted the opportunity to acquire traveling money. In the six furlong race, Sam's Pride was rated to absurdity, thirty lengths back into the first turn, and after the horse improbably caught the herd, the jock sawed at the reins throughout the stretch, finally getting the head high enough to shorten its stride and twisted to one side so it ran to the outside rail, thus narrowly escaping winning.

If in the bushes owners' silks were used, there would be some Jolly Rogers out there.

The second noteworthy thing was the bizarre snapping of both front cannons of the ten horse on the second stride out of the gate. Few people saw the race, for the horse lay squarely before the grandstand on this six-furlong track, pink-white shafts of bone jutting fully through the skin as the horse gamely tried to get under him what no longer existed. It was terrible to watch, these severed legs hinged only by hide and a struggling horse not yet accepting the fact. Seventy seconds elapsed from this spill to the race's conclusion, and at the moment the horses passed the finish line, the owner vaulted the rail and strode across the track, kneeled beside the fallen horse and began sawing at its throat with a pocketknife, which when accomplished did vividly demonstrate how much blood a horse had and how long a strong heart could issue it.

In the bushes things are done with dispatch.

But Bird did not concern himself with the humor and the pathos of the bushes. Foremost he knew he had a horse that no longer belonged there.

9

Tom Bird and Tyree left the prairie town of Billings and rolled west through Montana's north-south grid of timbered ranges and flat cow basins, crossed the Galatin and Madison and fetched up at dusk at a meadow on the high meandering Big Hole. With a bottom as uniform as a canal's, the entire river was holding water: no rock, no froth, no current-fingers, nothing but 1800 cubic-feet of water in a three-foot deep trough. It was not the fishing cowboy's type of river.

The fish of that river disagreed. They would not come up for dries, but they smashed gaudy streamers cast from mid-stream to the bank on fast strips. Bird caught a dozen over eighteen inches in two hours.

Money, big river trout, a fast horse. That was a happy night.

In the morning he called Eleanor and got her okay to run the colt in a futurity at the Elko, Nevada fair meet—yes, the bushes still, but a stakes race nonetheless—and since she could attend she could then conceive the horse's future. That race was three weeks away, the first of September, the clove of seasons in the Rockies.

They swung west through the Lolo Pass into the Pacific drainage, through the gorges of the Idaho batholith on in to Oregon. And along the way there were rivers to fish: the freestone Lochsa with a yellow-hued bottom and willing cutthroats; the Red River, nearly sterile; the Selway, fast and boulder-strewn and rich with small mountain trout; the Clearwater, the Imnaha, the Powder, the Burnt, the John Day, and the wonderful bucking Deschutes, where Bird saw flotillas of rafters uselessly casting dry flies over the busy backs of nymphing trout.

And so to Elko for a week of galloping and one three-furlong breeze for the horse. The boy and man, bunked in a motel for miners, learned to shake earwigs from their clothes before donning them.

Hap flew Eleanor to Elko in his Cessna. Though no great shakes as a pilot, Hap did have his IFR license: Instrument Flying Rating, according to the licensors; I-Follow-Roads, according to Hap, the licensee. They flew into the desert basin at dusk, joining the Friday night odyssey of miners and buckaroos carrying the wage money that sustained this many-faceted waterhole on the Humboldt.

Hap parked the rental car before the first bright lights he saw and was soon embroiled in a raucous crap game on a table that had been covered with green felt before he flapped in. Eleanor took the keys and drove out to the track.

She found the man and boy sitting on the tailgate, sharing a can of peaches. The three of them walked to the barns to look at the colt. There was nothing really to see; it was too dark. Eleanor stroked the colt's head.

"He needs to go to California," Bird said.

"You'll go?"

"No."

Eleanor sat on a hay bale by the tack shed and lightly kicked a feed bucket, like a child, for the sound. "I know you were in the picture when I bought the horse. It just wasn't a very clear picture." She reclined against the shed to look at the rising moon, a steady fount of melancholy for them with the colic. "But then it never is."

Tom Bird sensed her mood and had some kinship with it, though his discord was primarily the doldrums of a long trip. He was medicating for both when he suggested they leave Tyree with an Idaho couple who stabled nearby and who had befriended the boy, while the two of them made the cow town rue its licit gaming.

The prospect of diversion was good tonic; the bravura was better. They had a steak and a couple of whiskeys at a downtown eatery where the gossip was of jackpots and women who couldn't stay with a man. Then they went in a dawdling search of Hap Meeks.

Tom Bird had met the fellow Meeks a few times in connection with the Northern Dancer stud. Perhaps he disliked him more now that he was the squire of Eleanor, but even before that complexity he had thought the man at heart a waster and a poltroon. But after spending an hour at the scamp's elbow at an Elko craps table, Bird had to revise his judgement as harsh. It was Meeks' good luck as a craps-shooter that got him promoted to a dry-gulcher. The man was no absolute waste of skin, went Bird's reasoning, but not one to be trusted—a dry-gulcher all the way if the stakes were high enough. Still it was a promotion, and Bird with his fattened purse accepted with equanimity the departure of Hap and Eleanor to find hotel rooms.

The plural: rooms. How large the final letter loomed in Bird's mind as he nursed a whiskey at the casino bar. The other patrons, in refuge from the bustle and din, were as silent as if in church, a contemplative environment for a philosopher of the letter *s*. But decades were there, too. Physicist met philosopher, and possibilities were excluded. The past was a finished tale, the beauty of *once-upon-a-time* made ugly by *the-end*.

Tom bought an iced doughnut from a convenience store and used this to entice the boy from a pallet of blankets on the floor of his neighbors' Airstream.

The next day Eleanor was feeling fine as she walked up the wooden grandstand with Hap to watch the first race. Earlier a cloudburst had hurried over and now the sun was brilliant and everything glistened and smelled fresh and woody. She picked one horse from the post parade, another from the unreliable chart of past performances in the locally-printed program, and cashed a nice quinella when in the field of young quarterhorses all but her pair careened down the track like things being shot at.

Tom Bird joined them in the stands, troubled by what he had seen. "There seemed to be no herd mentality, only panic," he said as he stood before them, slapping his thigh with a rolled program. "Maybe I should scratch your horse."

"It was just one race, Tom." She had come a long way to watch the horse run.

"Eleanor, this is a good horse."

Hap was watching through binoculars the horses in the paddock and said, "Horses are great until proven bad."

Bird said nothing, but Hap Meeks lost his promotion. While what he said was true, it was a thing to say about your own horses and not someone else's.

Eleanor said, "Tell me what you're thinking, Tom."

"The horse is obedient. But this track is hard and has tight turns and rough horses. You must say yes or no."

"Will he win?" asked Eleanor.

"Yes."

"Oh, then he must absolutely run. Have you seen the program? There is no line about the Montana race."

Eleanor left and didn't come back for the next race and so Bird received Hap's woeful tale of the poker game he had haunted last night: "The worst is women. A novice *turista* might come in and drop twenty dollars, but the old broad that waits for aces and dozes between hands will stack up chips like skyscrapers"...and Bird wondered why one would not do what the old women do. Then Hap ended his tirade with the true source of his discontent: "Eleanor told me I'm bemusing. Not amusing, Tom. *Bemusing.* Is that rank or what?"

The gate opened and Bird watched the race before asking, "Why Eleanor?"

"She's five years older than me. The actuarial tables have us dying simultaneously in each other's arms."

Bird did not know if this was sarcasm or an honest factor. Hap was tanned, trim, handsome, wealthy, pining for the affections of a gray-haired cow woman. It didn't follow. It's true that when spouses die, the living often seek marriage with old friends, for stability and continuation; yet Hap Meeks was a man of means with the temperament to use that means to endear to him someone young, pretty, devoted, a trophy...and Eleanor, besides being none of those things, was tough and bitter. Only love could explain the irrationality.

On his way to prep the colt, Bird grabbed a styrofoam cup of coffee from the Lions Club hamburger stand. He met the boy at the backside gate and posed arithmetic problems while he drank the coffee. Bird doled out the agreed-upon price of a dime for each correct answer until the amount added up to the price of a hamburger. Tyree raced to the grandstand and Bird went to the stall. He heard Eleanor chanting *whoa* and looked over the bottom stall door to see her hanging onto the colt's halter with one hand and with the other smearing manure on the horse's rump. Unaware of his presence, she bent and grabbed another handful and daubed it on the flank. The colt's mane was deliberately ratted, as was the tail, which also had a fringe of clipped hairs at the base, the look of a wormy horse.

"What the hell," Bird said finally.

Eleanor turned and brushed back a strand of gray hair with a clean forearm. "I lost sixty-three dollars in this town."

Out of a bag she took an elastic wrap and some cotton padding and fashioned a swollen ankle on the colt's right foreleg. Then she brushed out some of the more obvious smears and cleaned the saddle and girth areas.

"I savvy," Bird said. Racing corrupted. He couldn't picture Eleanor Goodnight planting thistles in her pastures or culling good cows.

"I lost sixty-three dollars in this town," Eleanor said. "I'm putting fifty on the nose."

Eleanor had the colt the way she wanted it. Bird said, "That is your horse," and put on the halter and led the horse to the paddock. The ugly-looking horse joined in the sham by lathering up a dark foam, spinning around the lead-rope, kicking the plywood paddock box. Bird told the jockey just to hang on and that there was five bet to win for him, a crude insurance Bird always employed in the bushes.

At three minutes to post time, the odds on Eleanor's colt were fourteen to one. Four minutes later the two-dollar win ticket paid two dollars and twenty cents.

In the bushes, secrets are hard to keep.

After the urine test and coolout, Eleanor redeemed the hide and healed the ankle. Tom Bird sat against the tack shed and let the owner groom her horse. He calculated aloud that she had lost two dollars and fifty cents, counting the bet for the jock.

Eleanor straightened and banged the brush on the colt's back. "Don't tell me figures. I've dealt with figures for fifty-one years and I know exactly what figures now. I have sixty-five dollars and fifty cents to get back."

Nevada likes people with that attitude; determination to get even is a great but expensive virtue. Eleanor lost more money. The sum didn't amount to anything; she blew more on a cab. This she knew in reflection, after the horse had been hauled to California, Bird and the boy hauled to home, losing ducats were blowing off toward the Ruby Mountains, and she was stuck in a town with a

80

pilot and with the remembrance she had been churlish with Tom. Clearly, she needed purchase.

In her hotel room she consulted a bottle of tax-free Nevada whiskey about the whole Western mess. For many years she had dealt with the moneymen of San Francisco and elsewhere, and had found most congenial and forthright, but always she had known bastards skulked about. Born when bastard had meant bastard—disapproved of only by a prissy arched eyebrow—Eleanor now viewed the word through the bottom of a whiskey glass with a snarling connotation: illegitimate, craven, sneaky, as misanthropic as a feral dog.

And as the evening and bottle waned, she murmured, as punctuation to her thoughts, "Bastards."

She was, for the moment, whipped. Not only hog-tied and stifled with regard to Western, but just plain whipped. Sails folded. Drifting to the nursing home. This could not possibly go on.

With nightcap in hand, she turned on the television for news. There was a story about a girl who had turned in her parents for possession of drugs and police had found a large amount and the parents were sure to serve years in prison, and then a press conference of the President who cited the incident and said the girl must have loved her parents very, very much.

Eleanor sat numb.

Then she burned.

You cleave us but puff up our chests. You bastard. Have mercy have mercy have mercy. She could hardly conceive the enormity of the sin: feeling good for doing bad.

She could not sleep. This was despair. She lay in bed with fragmented thoughts. Treacherous whiskey! It must in fact be the tax that induces sleep. Count sheep, count taxes, count bastards. Despair!

She must have dozed. The digital clock read 2:38. She was awake, deciphering the clock, unraveling the antidote to despair: the country was too fractious to lockstep to ruin. Tyranny, have at the ACLU, the Urban League, B'nai B'rith, the National Wildlife Federation, the Sierra Club, the NRA, the VFW, the KKK, all the fanatical little state and city groups with a mission, all the lunatic letter-writers and linked-arm street criers. God bless the fanatic. Hail the single-minded. Stand for judicial review and jurists appointed for life. Unfurl the stars-and-stripes and burn it and unfurl it again.

Even that narrow-eyed pointy-headed moron's warped vision had cantankerous American passion. Purgatory awaited him, but perhaps it would be a short stretch. He didn't have political foes shot.

Before Tom Bird unbuckled the halter to let the mare free in his home pasture, he said, "You've got a thin coat. The mosquitos will hammer you."

Debilitated by hard race training, the hair was dry and fine and shedding at the touch.

In the morning the horse was dimpled on the chest, neck, and ribs, beyond reach of the tail. The bumps were big as thumbs and coherent as a golf ball. Horses can't think to be angry or be much distressed. They endure what they can't flee, untroubled by what-might-have-been.

10

When Joan Collins returned to Bannock, she found the town in an uproar debating the veracity of the high school principal and that of a ten-year-old boy. She didn't quite know what to think. Pederasty was simply unfathomable. But the sonofabitch had a zillion other faults, and she could not help feeling smug that the Pleaser had gotten to feel the backhands of the palms he had curried. In Joan's mind, guilty or not, the man was atoning for past sins (reference Old Testament) or meeting the irony of fate (Greeks).

A year ago, she had gone to a school board meeting in the high school auditorium. She hurried in precisely on time, dressed in white blouse and navy-blue skirt, properly coifed and tastefully bejeweled, utterly professional in appearance and demeanor, and saw, behind the front-row scattering of the usual Concerned Citizens, the entire male contingent of the Bannock coaching staff seated as a body four rows back, talking behind their hands. She thought, What the fuck? Teachers don't sit through the drone of board meetings. When her turn on the agenda came, she heard sniggering and understood this was a social event. She told the board the kids of the small logging town of Elk City were spending five hours a day on the bus, longer in winter, and that such a thing could be remedied by boarding, shorter week, branch school, a combination of these or something else this august body could devise...

The chairman said he was well aware of the logistics of the Elk City route. The man to his right was more pointed: just what the hell was she trying to accomplish? The man on the left wing poured a glass of water from a pitcher and tried to speak reason, but they were all men, and men had to be men before thinking of children.

Joan flared. "Probably none of you have been on a bus for a long time. It is neither educational nor enjoyable. I took a ten-hour ride on a Greyhound fifteen years ago and I liked to have died, and still haven't recovered. These children do that every two days. Think of what that means on a school bus. Twelve-hour days, these kids put in. Problems invite solutions. Thank you very much."

She turned her heels and strode down the aisle, aware of the coaches falling sideways, clutching one another, overcome with silent hilarity.

The next day the Pleaser came to her classroom door before first period and said she was suspended for three days, and that the assistant principal would take her classes (poor ever-so-loyal Gary giving her an almost insurrectionist shrug). For a time she glared. Then she accepted the vacation and promised to pay him dirt like he wouldn't believe if he tried to take any pay.

This was that kind of dirt all right, though unengineered by her.

She saw him at the hardware store after the allegation. He said the trouble would be resolved and departed—not the blustering, puffed-up vehemence she expected, but a deflated spiritless litany as he sidled by her in the paint aisle. It was no surprise when he resigned and rented out his house. It *was* a surprise when board member Harvey Wells, an electrician, stood on her doorstep and without waiting for an invitation inside said Gary would be the principal and she could take the assistant principalship.

"No one else with an administration endorsement?"

"A few. We want you."

The electrician's van was idling in the driveway and so she was content to negotiate on the step. "I never sought this job, so I can be candid. That suspension was a chickenshit trick and I don't want to work with a chickenshit group."

The electrician never flinched. "Well, at first we didn't all feel that way."

"Okay, I've got a couple of wimps that can maybe get strong."

"Mrs. Collins."

"And I'm obligated to sub for a colleague at a lookout through Labor Day. I'd like to think about it till then. Still offering?"

"Yes. Good day."

She called to him as he reached the van. "Mr. Wells. Any male that can be called a chickenshit wimp by a woman and not lose his senses must have something going for him."

"Wish you wouldn't make a habit of it, Mrs. Collins."

Joan Collins went to the Caroline lookout and Jason Abo heard about this thing. He stopped at Tom Bird's. The cowboy was gypping a colt about the round corral. When Abo straddled the top pole and unfolded a Forest Service map, the horse flared, fought the longe rope, and fell squirming on his back. He scrambled up and stood in a wall-eyed trembling skittishness as Bird clucked nonsense syllables and moved up the rope to the horse.

Abo said, "Sorry about that."

"Wasn't you," Bird said, patting the colt; "was him."

"Tom, my map says Trail 496 goes to Caroline lookout."

"It does."

"Is it all right for a man on a horse who thinks steadily about living until tomorrow?"

"I haven't been on it in a long time. Those trails have got damn little maintenance since the CCC boys went off to war. But I can't think of any place that could be bad. When supplies used to go that way, one sandy hillside was worrisome to packers, but I don't see problems for a single horse." Tom walked around his colt, lifting feet. "The 060 trail is shorter. It intersects the lookout trail at an old moonshiner's dugout. You can't miss it. Even so, it's a long trip."

Jason studied the map. He found 060 and asked, "How long?"

"A good five hours." He backed away from the horse and the horse followed him, allowing him to grab the lead rope. "You do know there's a road on the east side goes clean to the top."

"I know."

Bird unhaltered the colt and climbed over the fence. He drank from the hose, filled a bucket for the horse, tossed in a flake of hay, shook out a cigarette, and finally understood. "An overnight trip, isn't it?"

"Who can say? I would not want to be inhumane to the horse. Thanks for the info, Tom."

"The boy?"

"This town never stops. It's Al and your sister divvying him up now."

The next day Abo regretted his late start up 060. The day was hot, the west hills reefed with billowing white clouds likely to grow dark and angry. On the open hillsides a breeze cooled his sweat, but in the draws the muggy air squeezed him. For a Mississippian in these mountains, ninety degrees would not normally be hot, but on this day that person would feel his regular Gulf of Mexico skin, the air heavy and stifling like a skin of wet canvas in the sun. Deer flies appeared early to bedevil the horse. Little Pete constantly worked his tail and head and what muscles would quiver to shed the flies, and Abo helped out with his hat, but the attack was so relentless and the defense so futile both man and beast grew harried as the day plodded on. Abo exhausted his canteen, adding another torment; each brushy cutback gave false hope of finding a rivulet. He was too high for water. He had long lost enthusiasm for his enterprise—like the horse, dully soldiering on—when he first caught sight of the lookout, a distant speck of metal on a spire of white rock that was Mount Caroline. Though he could see enough of the trail to chart its entire course—a long line up a timbered ridge and a final series of switchbacks up the white face—the distance was at least five miles, fully two hours considering the last ascent.

"That's not so long to suffer," Abo told the horse, who had shown the same lack of foresight as he in neglecting to stock up at the numerous rills they had crossed in the lower country. Abo recalled a time when Bird commented, "A thirsty horse will let you know if he smells water, but I wonder, I wonder if a thirsty horse ever *thinks* water."

That had been on a dry ride into Sur Canyon and Abo felt justified in barking, "Don't mention water! Don't mention it!"

And Bird had replied, "Ah, this ain't dry. But it's a-getting there."

There, it now became manifest, was near delirium. In these final three hours, Abo sang out, "Whatcha thinkin' about, Little Pete?" And, "Oh say, Little Pete, what might currently be on your mind, other than the drought in the corn basket, monsoons in Bangladesh." And, "Little Pete, I'm ruminating on chemistry: two hydrogen atoms, one oxygen. Whatchoo mullin' over?" It was not a debonair appearance he made, rolling off the horse beneath the pillars of the lookout and croaking to Joan, "Water."

She showed him the tank below the peak at the end of the east side road. He tried to manfully pour a bucket for the horse first, but the sight of the stream from the spigot was too much: he was a maniac in his revel with water. Soon he was spent, lying spread-eagled and moaning, a pain in his belly.

Having tended to the horse, Joan stood over him. "I guess I can forget about a shower this week," she admonished. "Forest Service neglected to mention I'd be dirty as well as lonely."

"You look clean enough," Abo said without glancing from the sky. "As for the latter, well, here I am."

"Here you are," she confirmed.

"I figured you'd get awful busy today. Last evening I saw lightning in the south."

Joan gazed west. True enough, the clouds were building, darkening. A few gray rafts had broken off from the mass on the horizon and were moving overhead toward the sun. The heat and clouds spoke storm, but maybe there would be enough rain to keep the forest from fulfilling the dispatcher's prophecy: "It's tinder and it's a-gonna explode, Joannie; stock up on sleep."

Abo continued, "Thought I might help."

"I see."

"I went to some trouble to try."

She looked at the blustering clouds. "I don't want to see the forest burn, but I'll feel like a slacker until I spot a fire."

"You'll spot a fire today. I'll set one if I have to."

"Maybe you'd better not be overly helpful. Come on up when you quit whimpering."

Thus Abo became conscious of his demeanor. At daybreak, mounted on his charger, he had been a cavalier. Now he was played-out, a carcass. Deer flies and thirst had done him in. He rolled to his feet and looked at the horse. Little Pete was tied short, his back caked with dirt. So. She would stand by to let a horse roll and rally, but would mock a man doing the same. As he headed to the stairs, he stopped to take a further lesson from the horse. Well now, I will adopt that stoicism and see if I'm treated right. I have had my water and my roll, and if this trip is a complete bust I will suffer graciously.

The lookout was supported by steel legs embedded in concrete instead of logs in earth, but otherwise it was the same as what had looked over the national forests since the forests' inceptions: stairs up through the belly into a square of wood and glass, the center a fuss of transit and maps, the outer walls living quarters. While Joan cooked dinner over a Coleman against one wall, Abo reclined on a cot against another. When the stove flame flared around the pan, Joan told him one of the stories that came with the Caroline. Beth Duff, manning the lookout one summer after an empty-nest divorce, spotted the season's first fire. "I got a fire here," she told the dispatcher. "Where, Beth?" asked the dispatcher. "It's right here." "Okay, Beth, give me the coordinates." "The coordinates is in the kitchen and starting on the living room."

Joan turned off the jet and waited for the flame to subside before dishing two plates. She set the plates on the small table. "The remnants of all the freeze-dried packages I couldn't stomach in the singularity."

"Do you get all mystical up here?" Jason trenchered in some food and, when she didn't answer, essayed to clarify: "Like, go out at night and feel the oneness?"

"Nope. Mostly I ponder toilets."

"Are you curt as a shoot-first philosophy, or because you and the oneness think I'm intruding?"

"I'm curt because I hate men." She forked through the hash, looking for morsels. "Not the postman. Not the butcher. Not Mark Twain." She jabbed her fork toward a volume of Twain's essays on the map table. "Yes, even Twain. I just read a long article where Twain ridicules the idea that the uneducated actor William Shakespeare who wrote a banal epitaph could have written the plays. His vituperation is overwhelming. We have pudding for brains! So says America's greatest writer, an uneducated man without notable success in any of several trades—oh, he's a man, he can smear the world with irony, he can't see himself."

Abo tended to his plate, not trusting himself to say a thing.

In a glass house, a person cannot miss weather change. A single cloud in any direction changes the coloration. An unmuffled breeze hums a new tune. Heat flows readily in or out. When the fiercest front of the summer rolled in while the man and woman in the Caroline ate, all these things were dramatic. The temperature dropped, the southeast wind backed, a long inky cloud scudded low in from the northwest and rose to form an anvil. At first the lightning flickered high in the anvil sky to the north, but soon it was a steady shivering web of bolts from inky sky to ground. And Joan had her first fire—not a smoldering isolated tree, but a conflagration borne of many strikes. A lookout's supreme embarrassment is to call in morning fog or an evening campfire, but when Joan first saw a whiff of gray against the inky north she called it in and had the dispatcher hold the phone while she got a read on the alidade. After she hung up she made another read to make certain and by that time the fire was visibly orange on the ridge, thinly gray above, and above that a mammoth white billowing snowcone. The fire was rushing before the wind from many starts and creating its own weather. The fluffy white cone grew to inhabit the northern sky after the front had sailed on and the fire below glowed like a snake of molten iron.

"That is a bad fire," Joan said. She pulled a chair close to the north window.

"I've got whiskey in the saddle bags." Jason put his plate in a galvanized tub and went down the stairs.

The horse nickered and he felt a kinship. He went up with the whiskey and down again with a handful of Quaker Oats. Little Pete swept the oats out of Jason's palm and blew with rolling nostrils, in sadness or indignation, when the man left. Jason intended to return with more oats, but in the lookout he was winded and the whiskey stood rested on a pantry shelf. With the gas lantern respirating behind him, his shadow looked clumsy as he poured a glass.

"An out of shape proprietor of a health club," he said.

"That's probably not so unusual," Joan said. She was watching the fire.

"How about out of sorts proprietor."

"Equally common, I'd guess. How is your health club?"

"Bad luck." Abo settled on the floor against the bed. "A racquetball player took a shot in the eye and his eyeball squirted out and was dangling on his cheekbone, held by the optic nerve. Before the ambulance came, a crowd had snuck up to take a look and turned away with a grimace. Those who didn't see it heard about it. All this graphic testimony put a crimp on the club. Losing an eye is not what one expects from a health club."

"People quit coming?" Joan prompted as Jason stood behind her, staring at the long string of red marking the fire.

"Well, the receipts went down. I've picked some of it up by putting up a display of goggles at the front desk at a four hundred percent mark-up. Plus I've got a camera by the till and instructions to the employees to take a picture if anything gruesome happens. Alas, hindsight. Imagine that picture of an eyeball hanging by a cord and an ad campaign Buy The Goggles Or Are You Fucking Stupid."

Joan tried to imagine. Jason had given her a membership and she had gone once and was having a relaxing time in a hot tub when Jason arrived and took off his trunks and stood on his head against the wall. Only that impetus, and people in the club sifted to their personal bottom ways.

Jason now said, "I think I'd do better giving cowboys a washtub of water at two bits. Instead, on a Saturday night for three dollars they get a sauna, a spa, a eucalyptus room. And since it ain't a Saturday night without a fight, a few figure it best to get it done while sober, and that causes contention with members. It just hasn't been a healthy place to be."

Abo was on his feet now, soliloquizing. "The August ranch payroll checks came back Accounts Closed. I kept the boys working for a while with a nightly keg and a barbecued quarter of beef for all comers, but eventually they had to think about that pickup or diamond ring or college education and quit me. I got Bobby Coles to use his mill vacation and move into the bunkhouse, but whenever he leaves on Saturday night he may or may not be back before Wednesday, and certainly won't be worth a shit till Thursday. So mostly it's just me."

"And how is that?" Joan asked.

"It's terrible. Working your tail off doesn't leave time to think how to get out of the fix. I had time to think today but mostly I was too thirsty to think clearly. I could be the bold Casey Jones or the smart fireman who jumped."

"My last husband would despair at the first scent of business downturn. He wouldn't buck it. So we'd move. We'd check with the van lines and see where people were headed."

"I'm not your husband. He didn't go the distance."

"Who are you, Jason?" She stared at him fiercely. "I've seen you cynical, flippant, and charming. That's not enough."

"Joan, I've been through that inner you, inner child, inner clockworks of the universe. I'm like the Invisible Man—start unwrapping outer appearances and *poof*, dadgum, you got nothing."

Now in the night sky the fire was hot red, and the snake that it had been was twice as long and more nearly the shape of a lizard.

"That fire is roaring," Joan said. "That fire is out of control." She went to the phone and repeated these observations along with a more scientific rendering than the big red lizard which shortly before had been a small red snake. The dispatcher had already heard from the first crew on the fire: it was hot and big and wild. In three weeks it would sweep over three hundred thousand acres. Rattle-dry thickets exploded into ash, thick stands of timber crowned and shot incendiaries across canyons, and in the worst places the earth was scorched to a black moon-dust powder.

Joan had an inkling of the outcome. "For what good it will do, I did by god spot that fire."

They worked on the whiskey and watched the march of the fire. Even though the wind quartered toward the blaze, they smelled smoke. Once Joan said, "I'm glad to have the company." At midnight the dispatcher told Joan the lightning was done and to get some sleep.

"Yes. A nightcap and that's what I'll do." She put up the phone. "At least I wasn't sleeping on the job," she said as she poured a splash on the ice in her cup.

Jason had many times interpreted nuance when there was nothing but straight talk, and so was loath to be commited more than an analyst's, "Yes?"

"Let's sleep together and be shed of that presence that's all over us like a locker room joke. I've alienated a good many men in this town. I had better surrender to the man who is still in pursuit."

He was derailed. He had not felt so business-like at a Denny's restaurant in West Hollywood at 3 a.m. "I think it's a good idea," he said lamely. This was a lady and he had better swing some passion and romance. "Of course, I do love you."

"Let thee count the ways."

"Don't you laugh."

"There are condoms in my purse. I trust you to be honorable about disease. Pregnancy is okay—no, a godsend, even illegitimate."

"I can't think. I'll just shut up."

"Until you get your feet under you, that would be a good idea. I'm not exactly aflame."

"The truth of the matter is, neither am I. And I have been rather steadily since I saw you irate about the bastards that repossessed your car."

"I'll make a final report and we'll see what happens."

The Caroline was one of the last lookouts equipped with a phone rather than a radio. A phone line did not suffer interference or disturbance but did need an intact line. When Joan failed to hear a signal, she knew a tree had blown over the line. It was a party line and could be spliced.

Joan found the pliers and a flashlight. "I'm scared of horses, Jason, or I wouldn't ask."

"You don't have to ask."

He took the tools and had a fortifying pull on the bottle.

The road down the east side was white and coarse granite sand and easy traveling. Aside from avoiding a few limbs that overreached a pickup cab but not a man a-horseback, Abo had little to do but loll in the saddle and occasionally shine a flashlight to verify the swoop of telephone wire in the trees. For a while Little Pete balked against this new trek, but with resolute urging grew resigned, then resolute himself. Up at the lookout the west wind had been screaming gusts, but below the peak it was moaning above and only breezy on the road. Bats passed willy-nilly overhead, so faint and brief in the dark sky as to be quirks of vision. The tremulous *ki-yi* of coyotes seemed to be from a large pack just up the hill, but it may not have been so, for one coyote can sound like several, and several like a regiment, and also theirs is a sound that carries. The clopping of the hooves and smell of woodsmoke grew imperceptible over time as he sloughed off to a timeless, thoughtless lethargy, settled to the rhythm of the fast-striding horse like a baby iin a cradle. An hour into the ride he had a stirring of thirst. He had left the bottle on the ground where he had saddled. Oh, Christ, not that again. Probably the wider, gentler draws on this east side held water, but to look was to lose time and it was impatience that drove him. Time stood between him and water, between him and that woman. Water or woman. Thinking of the one made him thirsty, and thinking of the other made him crazy. He faced a barrage of thoughts about what really was up there in the lookout. He could not think clearly about her or any other woman. He would dredge up fond memories of handsome and glorious stints and then parody himself, *Oh yes he loves the wimmens he surely do.* He would think that she with the broad German face and broad straight shoulders was different, and then see himself caricatured in a cartoon with a thumping heart. He would add and debit her particular accounts, then sully his figures with spilled ink. Finally he slapped his leg and willed a resolution: don't think. To lie with a woman and feel her warmth and discern her thoughts comprised his greatest happiness but probably any schoolyard or barnyard poet understood more than he about love. For him hedging was an anchor.

Two trees angling over the road marked the break. Other fallen trees, broken jagged from stumps, angled in the same direction, casualties of a strange popping downthrust of wind known colloquially as a burster. Abo tied Little Pete to one of the down trees, walked down the road to where the wire dropped loosely into the undergrowth, then slid down the bank through elderberry bushes to grab the wire and begin the slow untangling. As he freed more line it began to snag behind him as well as in front, and he groped back and forth, the flashlight nearly useless with its scudding illumination of countless wires in the twigs and stems. At length he came to the free end, tied it off on a sapling, repeated the process from the upper end, made a serviceable splice, and indulged in a final spate of victorious cursing.

Little Pete had worked loose and was grazing on the roadside a short distance away. Its head came up as Abo approached with a reassuring patter and an imploring outstretched hand. A few feet away Jason stopped, aware of the inharmonious breach that existed between the two.

He stood with outstretched hand, commenting on bats and elderberries. He was patient and distracted and soothing. Then he moved forward a few inches and the horse wheeled and galloped up the white road and disappeared around a bend. The hoofbeats were a forlorn sound. He heard them slow and stop. When he came in sight again, Little Pete trotted away, not far, grazed some, walked and grazed, trotted and walked and grazed, with the man always close behind as though he were herding a horse reluctant to move.

Abo was nearly successful in being reunited when he sat for a long time on a rock and the horse grazed back toward him, tired if not repentant; however, when Abo rose, the horse shied again, and Abo began the hike to the lookout grim and resolute, cursing the horse, and to this real rather than feigned indifference the horse returned and Abo mounted and quirted the horse with his belt on a long gallop on the good road and brought the horse up loose-jawed and frothing at the pillars of the Caroline.

He jerked the saddle and bounded up the stairs. Joan had changed into a flannel nightgown. She fished a dishtowel from a pan on the Coleman stove and brought it to him.

"Is the phone working?" he asked.

"Yes."

He wiped his face and neck and arms with the towel until the warmth ran out.
Joan asked, "How far down was it?"

"Far enough for a zillion thoughts." He hung the towel on a nail and poured
a glass of water. He looked out at the fire and heard the choppy drone of a plane
weighted with fire retardant. "I leave a pretty woman, wallow in the brambles,
watch my horse run away, and still am content, and I wonder if that is love."

"You do wonder," she echoed.

"Yes."

"I'm getting weepy. Christ. For no reason."

"The big sadness."

"I've lived, lately, for myself. That's not whole."

"Maybe so," said Abo.

Maybe no, thought Abo.

In the morning they ate canned salmon and saltine crackers and watched the
lumbering retardant planes appear every quarter-hour to drop fantails of red
spray. The fire appeared to be stalled in the morning, but with the hot dry air of
midday, smoke rose in a thick brown mass and in a short time enveloped the hills
with haze, and the overhead sun was scarlet.

In a tumbledown shed Jason Abo found a rotting manty rope and used it to
tie Little Pete to a sapling which had a treeless thirty-foot radius of thin sere
grass. An hour later, he checked on the horse and found him ensnared in a cat's
cradle of legs and tree and a half-buried two-by-six that had started the mess.

"Thought a smart feller like you would know rope," Abo said as he cut the
rope, gently unwound it and moved the horse to virgin grazing.

A while later he looked out to see the horse plunging, fighting a wrap around
a foreleg. "He doesn't know rope."

"He'll dislocate a shoulder," Joan said.

The two of them went down and freed Little Pete. Jason boosted the woman
onto the horse and told her to grab a handful of mane. He led them down the
rocky brow into the trees, circumambulating deadfall and dense alder thickets. A
tom turkey blew out of a tree over Joan, a monstrous bird slow to get off the limb
and then a feathered rocket down the slope. In a clearing with a view he swung
her off.

"Let the horse eat." He clover-hitched the long lead rope to a limb stub of a
fallen pine. Then he scouted for a comfortable swale. He told her to come.
Below the chosen swale was a patch of tag alders, and a big covey of heavy blue
grouse flew up from the ground alders into the big trees. Jason Abo pulled her to
the earth and said, "You name the terms. I'll prick blood, marry you, give you a
friendship ring, divvy up my estate. You name it, I'm game."

"Terms like those are codicils. Trying to get it all straight so in post-mortem all is neat and blameless." She stared out at the rumpled hazy hills and saw a wisp of brown smoke make a brow, another wisp tousled hair, and enough splotches to make the face of her son Ricky in the vapors. "One very vigorous part of me dwells in the past, Jason."

"The other part will come dwell with me."

Without rising inflection, it was nonetheless a question. And the point was as well-marked as a triangulated piece of earth; the artful dodging, coquettish dalliance, the vapid routine of persevering in Bannock converged at this moment, just as they finally had for her husband and sent him on his flight into the ether. Here was a swain groping to recapture chits of derring-do. She lofted her gaze to the red sun. "I will," she said.

Tom Bird watched the dragonflies hover and dart over the the rumpled sweep of the Big Timber as he rigged his rod. There was no activity. The fish were in the doldrums. Not so the mosquitoes, however. They swarmed his wrists and savored his neck and he had to escape to the water to finish rigging.

The last of the high-country snow was washing down clear and scant. Between the waterline and the bush line was a gray strip of river rock crusted gray with dried silt and moss and the tiny pebble-and-twig igloos of old caddis cases. He floated an ant and got no response, and so gambled on a long walk through the alleyways of brush to a hole upstream where if an evening hatch were to come, would come here. Twilight was gloaming when he reached the hole. Hole was a catch-all term for a piece of water worth fishing, in this case a long smooth run of water knee-deep. He started at the bottom of the glide, working upstream along the bank of osiers, still thinking ants and grasshoppers and other terrestrial strayers until small clouds of midges wafted by, followed by the emergence of a thick cloud of white caddis beating upstream, and then small trout flipping across the breadth of blue water. He had known big trout to come into these shallows to feed late, so he tied on a caddis bigger than those he saw fluttering over the river; unable to distinguish body color under the white wings, he guessed green. With no room behind him for a backcast, he shook enough line through his rod to roll cast. At the end of the first drift, he sidearmed upstream, feeding more line, then checked to throw a slight coil on the water. A small fish hit immediately and Bird struck the rod with his right hand and stripped line with his left and still was slow tightening the coil—with the result of no fish to counter his power, and fly and leader shot back into the willows behind him.

By the time he was rigged with new leader and fly, the glide was busy with fish bulging and jumping. He thought he could see the helicopter-rise of mayflies, but in the bad light they were streaks, suggestions, ghost trails. He roll-cast and on the swing a nice fish went slashing after the fly, missing it three times. On a sidearm false cast, a bigger trout plainly leaped at the fly as it passed in return back to the rod a foot over the water. But on the drift he caught a ten-inch fish.

He hooked the fly on the cork butt and smoked. He thought about the water. He thought about Jason Abo's plan. Both were fantastic. He had a headful of thought. He stepped into the stream, cast to the far bank, stripped a foot across the current, let float naturally a foot, stripped again and the neat V of the fly's wake was smashed. The commotion of the combative trout through the glide seemed to elicit a greater frenzy, for he quickly caught four more trout from one to two pounds with the same technique.

He had enough fish, nothing big but five nice ones in a very short time, and left the river to prowl about Jason Abo's notion of returning the Double Diamond to private hands: namely, Abo, Eleanor Goodnight, Sally Honstead, Al Corbett, whatever Bannock investors could be huckstered, and he, Tom Bird, who, extraordinarily, had a bit of capital to contribue.

Courtesy of those fool racehorses.

Eleanor Goodnight's colt won its first allowance start at Santa Anita, was bought for eighty thousand dollars, and subsequently won a graded stakes. The colt had become a name, which made its sire the newest star in the brilliant Northern Dancer constellation. A smug Hap Meeks gloried in his soothsaying. And Tom Bird owned the stud's entire yearling crop.

It doesn't often happen like this. Owners of thoroughbreds cannot look at a ledger truly. The grandness of horseflesh gallops across the numbers and turns loss into investment. Owners are always on the come. And this is true for the duchesses of the old Kentucky farms, true for the nouveau riche yearling-buyers, true for the franchising trainers, true for the backhills Idaho farmer horse-poor and dream-rich. It is a business averse to quarterly plans. The duchess watches the great sire twist a gut and die; the moneyman sees his two-year-old bow a tendon in its first gate work; the big trainer hears on the telephone that two of his big-stable owners wallowed dead from heart attacks; our Idaho dreamer one winter morning finds the one well-bred yearling—an accomplishment of fifteen years—lying in the snow with one joint too many in a front leg.

But to Bird the miracle happened. He had picked good mares, all runners, a generation removed from the mothers and fathers Kentucky wanted, but all had the lines he thought were forever: Turn-to, Ribot, Princequillo, and farther back Hyperion, Mahmoud, Blue Larkspur. He had flat got lucky on the son of Northern Dancer as a sire. He had seven commodities the world didn't have but wanted. Keeneland called. Saratoga called. An Arab flew in with his retinue. For a fortnight after the first solid offer, Bird trailed streams, thinking hard and fishing poorly, ending this meditation with a sale of six yearlings for one hundred thirty thousand dollars.

Now this idea of Abo's. Bird had thought himself fixed with his horses, adequate pasture, bit of hay ground, and live creek. It was hard to say when thoroughbred racehorses first smote him, but when it came time to leave the Double Diamond he knew how to go. He had moved frugally, with forethought. An old comrade, Jack Townsend, once had two hundred cows bought and paid for, with an income of perhaps sixty thousand in an ordinary year, before he came into possession of his first thoroughbred. Soon Jack had many horses. Now he had nary a horse or a cow and was buckarooing on the O-X. In a small way Jack's fall had goaded Bird into trying the horses: this thing could be done right. And maybe he had done right, but that would not be know, for luck had stepped in and served up Jason Abo in his driveway asking, not for a foreman, but for a capitalist.

In Bannock, Bird swung into the Alforcas.

"How was fishing?" Al asked as he slid a bourbon across the bar.

Bird looked at the drink. "No thanks, Al. I can't afford it."

They looked at each other and laughed and pumped hands over the bar.

"Tom," said Al, "I heard one-thirty."

"And I still have the mares and the yearling I like best."

Al reached over and they shook hands again. Al slid down the bar to pour watery drinks for a rancher and his wife who were working up for a fight, a wild reconciliation, and an up-and-at-'em roundup on a couple hours of sleep. Al drifted back and said, "Tom, you gotta count me out on the Double Diamond. I think the Pretty Boy's figures are right, but he's wrong in his calculations about how much money I have. There is a risk. Hell, after everything's in, your place is the only tangible asset. The mortgage is a yearly thing. The fact that the company seems to have forgotten about the calves gives the deal a boost, but it is still a form of child abuse to let a child inherit a ranch."

"That's your advice?"

"My figuring. I don't give advice."

The ranch couple had drained their watery drinks and stormed down the lip of the bar to assail Al for another round and one for Tom Bird, the primero cowboy who would go up to Horse Heaven and bring down the cows, he just had to (they jointly told him), and unlike last time there was a camp cook with groceries, and there were good horses, and they flat needed Tom Bird. To Bird, the paucity of food the last time he helped out Ernie and Sue was something to remember all right, but more riveting was when Sue slugged Ernie in the Alforcas, Ernie sped off in the pickup, Sue stole one to chase him down, the two of them wrestled in the gravel, the stolen pickup was abandoned, the ranchers returned to the Alforcas to pick up their crew, the night was spent in a teardrop trailer when six tired men were kept awake by Sue periodically swearing "Wait until I get my pants down goddammit" and Ernie banging away and falling asleep, banging away and falling asleep, and then rising with a clamor of "Let's go get 'em, boys" when only he had captured some naps.

"Not tonight," Bird said, and they swarmed him, Ernie and Sue, roaring on to conviviality and a long demented stretch of excess. They each bought him a round. Bird explained, "Your nights are too long on one end and too short at the other."

Ernie brayed, "Give this cowboy another!"

Bird brushed a quit signal to Al and shortly walked outside in a drizzling rain to ponder his future. Analogies: it was like a horse's last stakes race, or like a whore's matrimonial try at a stake, or like an old man's rush at a future receding on an actuarial curve. Buy the Double Diamond, what a thought. His money was picayune. The very real racehorses had effervesced into dollars. Grips were tenuous all around. Well, what was he? He was a fisherman. He had horses. He was a lover of some half-dozen people. He had not yet sold his soul, but he had girded his soul so that it was compact, unnoticeable, of scant value. The Double Diamond was a chimera chase after the most tangible thing that had eluded him. It was the other end of possibilities from Ernie and Sue.

In her later years Eleanor Goodnight would wonder about the buyback. She and Jason Abo could have swung it by themselves. It must have been a fantasy, a Napoleonic mustering of the old guard which even in defeat would be glorious compared to complacency. Bannock was her tribe. She needed those folks. A queen in her country, she did not want people to forget. Contrariness spun her web, an irresistible spinning, but really it was Sally Honstead's throw-in that engendered the lawyerly gathering in Sally's house to indemnify the signators to a mutual hurrah. Afterwards the principals sat around the hot tub while Bob sat in it, trying to drown himself to escape the debacle of a slower death by starvation with the Double Diamond. Abo brandished the handwritten agreement: "I think we own the Double Diamond."

In three weeks they did.

BOOK TWO

1

On Columbus Day Tyree got off the school bus and skinnied under a barb-wire fence to make a roundabout loop homeward. A boy on the bus had spoken of an old bathtub in the ground. Tyree found it easily: a concrete and mossy plank cistern fed by a trickle-tube tapping a weak spring. In this drought year the trickle was about even with evaporation and the cistern was scummy. Nearby, built into the hillside, was a log dugout, the earliest effort of a pioneer to gain clean water. Its bottom was a rock-lined pit. Tyree looked into the dark maw of the open doorway, daring himself to enter. He did not like to open a shed door and have pigeons fly out over his head; and this dark cavern looked to have dark birds, big-winged spooky birds, that would in frantic haste barrel him over. He inched forward, began to see into the hut, lowered his head and stuck it in and was as alert as a mammal can be when a voice called, "Hi."

Tyree dropped to his knees. No bird swooped out. He swiveled on his butt and saw the boy trotting up on the cow trail. It was the boy on the bus, tall and thin and pigeon-breasted, two years older in age and one by grade, a friendly sprite who was as content to do his lessons as he was to climb on the school roof at recess and throw dirt clods at kids and teachers.

"You scared me," said Tyree.

The boy sidled past and bear-crawled inside the sagging spring house. He disappeared except for his shoes. Then his shoes wriggled inside. "Come on in. There's room."

Tyree eased inside and scooted around on the ledge of foundation rock to the opposite corner. He wedged himself solid. "My name's Tyree. Tom calls me Segundo."

"I think I'll call you Shorty."

"How about Ty."

"Okay, Shorty. I'm Ted Coles."

The two boys sat for a while inside the springhouse with delicious security and companionship. When they ventured out they were fast friends. What to do next? Climb Everest! Kill Godzilla! The Coles boy was worldly enough to suggest an outing. Tyree left for home with the words in his chest like a fire. He had never had a friend.

In school Tyree was silent, distant, complacent, and completely ostracized. He had become the third-grade effigy, the common foe, the enemy that rallied and bonded the masses. Kids are not naturally cruel at this age—that comes a year later—but Tyree was so content to be alone that the gregarious bunch roamed around him in packs, uncertain whether they were prey or predator. His classroom teacher Mrs. Eichelberger regarded him similarly and called upon him only when his indolence could serve as a lesson to the group.

But Tyree did not know any of this. He had left the schoolyard, left the classroom. He had transformed. He had learned to read.

For two years the letters had resisted him. In this school year they assembled themselves miraculously. When words came, stories came. To him alone it seemed had come the magic: the class was still chorusing sentences from a workbook while he glanced ahead to see *what happened.* Sally, who had read many Mother Goose rhymes and fairy tales to Tyree, first noticed the transformation. She bragged and fawned. It was magic. Tyree felt himself in the company of trolls and giants and Billy Goat Gruffs. Sally, the author of a published historical article about area moonshiners, unwittingly promoted the notion of writing as a devilish enterprise, and the boy felt simply hexed. The trolls had him.

He read in secret. His desk at school had a lift top and he could raise the lid an inch and read a book opened in the bin. He took a flashlight to bed and read under the covers. He took a book to do chores and nestled in the haystack to read until dark.

Tom Bird thought him the slowest feeder to ever break a bale.

The worldliness of literature, unlike the worldliness of years, makes one more awed than jaded. And maybe innocence is genetic. For Tyree, like his mother, grew with greater conviction that the world would turn more extraordinary each minute. A lifelong shadower of adults, he had known novelty. Literacy now shone a light on everything and he was newly born as a seeker of beyond. In this season, at eight years old, he was impelled to discover.

Tyree sprinted across the home pasture to intercept Joan's carlights and relayed his new friend's Saturday plan. Joan said, We'll see. She was tentative, unwilling to be a step-mother. She too was literate and had read Cinderella, and was worldly besides. She was a schoolmarm, and a moonlighting baby-sitter and bookkeeper. Decisions regarding Tyree belonged to Jason via court order.

But fathers are absent in life as in fairy-tale, and it was Joan who gave the okay and packed a lunch in a fanny pack the next morning and stood in the driveway to wave goodbye.

Tyree walked up an old logging road, now a thin terrace grown over with pine saplings sturdy enough to stop four-wheelers and dense enough to stop motorcycles, now a natural course for deer and cattle and a boy heading for the hills and a rendezvous with Ted Coles. In a fanny pack he had a peanut-butter sandwich and a candy bar, plus a sling shot filched from Tom Bird. It was his first theft. Ted Coles had said he would see ghosts. Tyree was prepared to fight them.

Tyree walked around the flank of the hill into the yellow grass valley of Moose Creek. Tom Bird had told him to follow the road to the fence and follow the fence into the valley to the fence stiles. Bird was sitting on the top rung of the stiles when the boy arrived.

"Segundo, you followed those directions perfect," Bird said. "Here's some more. Don't go farther than the reservoir. If you climb the hill, come back down to the flats and follow the creek downstream to these stiles. Don't go uphill too far and when you turn home always go downhill."

Tyree climbed the planks to sit by Tom. "Okay," he said.

"Tell me what I said."

While Tyree proved he had hold of the essentials, Tom added to his fanny pack dried peaches, jerky, a can of pop, a water flask, a pair of jersey gloves and a stocking cap.

"If you can help it," Bird said, "don't drink the creek water. It's incredible to me that good mountain water isn't good, but some people do get sick." Bird pointed to a rocky spire jutting up from the southern line. "When the sun is over Tit, you be right here. I'll be waiting for you."

Tyree belted his pack. Tom smoked while they waited for the Coles boy. He had called the mountain *Tit.* He should have been genteel and said *Teat.* Manners and dictionaries said so.

Ted Coles jogged up from the county road. He too had to hear the instructions. Then the boys waved so long and dashed up the cow trail along Little Moose Creek.

Frost on the grass and brush wetted their pantlegs, chilling them, but the sun came hale with a warm breeze and soon they were wading in the creek, attempting to scoop up trout fry that scattered like buckshot in the placid bank shallows. Bottom crawdads made languid spurts and were easily caught. The boys held them in the air and watched the languid fanning of the pincers. When released in the creek, the crawdads made langorous mud trails as they backed burrowing.

They began lightly on the lunches, first meting out the dried peaches and baked pumpkin seeds, but their appetites were keen and when they came in sight of the earthen dam they had but a sandwich and the water left. They made a vow to save these for later heroics. The geese that had been laying over at the reservoir were returning from the fields. They were in several bunches, a hundred in all, and their honking, at first singular and searching, became general and fitful as they neared the reservoir. Crossing the dam, they began to tip their wings so as to plummet twenty feet, catch themselves and plummet again, not in unison but singly, so that the flock looked like a bunch of boomerangs flipping down from the sky. Then in a crescendo of honking and with flapping wings they settled on the water. The clamor ceased, and the silence was then so deep it took time for the leaves to rustle anew and the creek to burble and the woodpecker's staccato work to begin.

The water was low, a dam-pond in a horseshoe of dry jigsaw cracks. Walking on this cracked silt, they found quarter-sized toads, partly buried and winter lethargic.

"Warm 'em up in your hands," Ted Coles said.

This they tried but the toads would not rouse beyond slowly stretching a leg when the boys set the toads down and nudged them to hop.

"Shorty, this ain't much of a race." Ted hurled his toad toward the water. The legs twirled and the toad was aerodynamic.

The boys laughed. They found toads to throw. The geese paddled away from this new activity. A few waddled up on the far shore. *Luck-lute* rose from the flock. *Luck-lute...Luck-lute-lute.* This nervousness was short-lived. The geese adapted to the shouting boys throwing toads and rocks. Most rested on the water, maintaining a radius of danger from the boys. The grass foragers on the far bank sometimes raised wings and made a few steps as the boys came to the upper end.

Tyree said, "Tom said do not go beyond the reservoir."

Ted Coles said, "Let's look for better toads," and started them up the creek.

Within a mile the brushy watercourse through grassland became a tangled tumbling stream overloomed by hillsides of spruce and alder thickets. They crawled and scrambled through the bottom brush and laughed when they were trapped and had to back up to find a new route. The creek pinched tighter and they clambered up the hill to game trails that scythed through the undergrowth. With hands covering their faces, they charged through branches, dropped on knees to rest, and charged again. They covered a fair distance before ending up prone, submerged in alder, elderberry, sweepers, and deadfall. They broke out the last of the lunch.

They took one bite when below them came crashing. Then silence. Then a bugle and a coughing grunt of a bull elk. The crashing came again, slicing up the hill toward them. In their blind woven-brush world they wondered. The crashing stopped. Then the downhill brush was shaking and suddenly, close enough to lasso, was a bull elk, heavy-antlered and dark brown on the neck. It froze for a beat and then was gone. Its antlers glided uphill over the brush and the boys could see tawny glimpses of the harem moving uphill ahead of the bull.

"Dadgum," Ted Coles said. "He was huge."

Ted grabbed a spruce limb and tried to chin himself up to get another look at the fleeing herd. He got up on the first limb, and the second, but missed the next and careened around the trunk, grasping, and fell through the boughs onto the downhill slope. He landed on his feet and hands amid a scatter of small white bones. "Come look at this," he said. Tyree scooted down and they began pocketing the polished trinkets of bone. Tyree found a big splintered bone and turned it in his hands. He looked up and saw bones angling across spruce limbs some fifteen feet up the trunk. He pointed. The Coles boy swung up, hooked a leg over a limb, shinnied over a lashed pole and fell onto a human skeleton. Many pieces were missing but it was hideously human, with long hair tangled around the skull and teeth like T-Rex.

"You boys need to do me a favor and not say nothin' about those bones." Tom Bird let the truck idle and gave the boys a long look. "Remember what I said."

On the way to take the Coles boy home they stopped at the pasture where Jason Abo was making his third count of the day's gather. The Double Diamond had two more head than had been turned out in May. Close enough, Bird figured. They hazed the herd through a gate into the big twelve-hundred acre pen. Two thousand cattle were now in the pens. More were still in the hills. Bird was sorting every day, fixing for the cattle buyer due in a week. He and Jason were discussing the next day's gather when up the county road came a bunch of pigs, nearly a hundred, with Worthless shooing them along.

Worthless jogged up through the pigs, holding onto his straw hat with one hand and an ash cane with the other. "Can I foller up those cows?" he yelled.

Bird motioned for the boys to block the road. The pigs funneled through the gate and promptly went to feeding on the fresh manure. Worthless took off his hat and wiped sweat off his forehead. "Thankee, thankee." He had jogged over a mile with the pigs, kicking and caning to keep them on the road. For the effort they might feed for two hours before he had to make the return trip. Like all the Coles tribe, he was motivated by anything free. He dug out a cigarette.

"Hiya, son," Worthless said. "Have fun?"

"Hi, Dad," Ted said. The boys were petting the horses tied to the trailer. "Lots of fun. Saw some elk."

Abo was engrossed watching the pigs scurrying and scarfing. "Jews and Moslems have seen this," he reflected. "I think I'm done with pork."

"There's only one smell better than frying bacon," Worthless said.

"Which is?" Abo asked.

"This." Worthless stood among the snorting manure-eating pigs. "The smell of money."

A family bush of Coles squatted around Bannock. The Knutsen mill had been the source of the first paying job of a Coles, and relatives had poured after. Even now, three generations later, the clan trickled west from Arkansas, drawn by the mystique of paychecks. One smart and shy Coles boy had managed to work a charm on a daughter of the well-landed, well-ensconced Yraguens, but Basque vivacity found the in-law a foil and named him Worthless. At first it was a sobriquet, then simply a name. Alice, meet Worthless. Worthless, show me your drill bits. I love you, Worthless. At this urging he became lazier and more of a rake. The Yraguen woman left him. He remained Worthless.

"Oh, shit," Worthless said. "There they go."

A vanguard of pigs nosed under the bottom strand of barbed wire and then there was a stream of pigs across the county road up the hill into the pines. Worthless harried the main herd back under the wire, but more than a dozen had scattered up the hill like buckshot. He hollered for his son to hold the bunch in the pasture and ran after the convicts in the trees.

In a short time he came back. "Tom, they's scattered. Can you go get them on your horse?"

Bird mounted. The sky was gauze, whispering snow. The pigs, rooting and grunting, were easy to locate. Bird found two together that would constitute his herd. He drove another to them. When that seemed accomplished, all three lowered their heads and went scurrying pell-mell on stubby legs through brush too dense for a horse. Bird used the last of the day's light to push five pigs to the road. Another pig was draped dead over the saddle. The horse had tromped it and Bird had finished it with a limb.

"I've got you one for Sunday dinner," Bird said. "Got a pit dug?"

"Nope," said Worthless, "but it ain't hard to scare up a butchering crew."

"What to do about the rest of them?"

"Cousin Bobby can get them. All the missing ones are his." Worthless grinned and began hurrahing the manure-fed bunch home. The pigs went down the road in haste and Worthless had to hurry to keep alongside. He called back, "That one on your saddle is Bobby's, if you want to give it to him."

Bird drove the Coles boy and the pig carcass home and spoke a last admonition.

"Not a word about the bones. Got it? Only we three will know."

2

The last bunch of Double Diamond cattle had to be brought out from the gorge of the Sur Fork. It was a warm, grassy place, where cows could drift up the hillsides with the sun or stay cool in the brushy hollows. It made for a tough gather. The flats of the old river flood-plain was a tangle of thorns and willows and vetch. Cattle made alleyways through the brush to pockets of grass and would flee through these like elk as soon as they spotted a rider. Horses could not go through these low tunnels of thorns and whip brush. Three hands could expect a full day in repetitive sweeps through the flats, and even then a man, at dusk, might have to cut a deal with his conscience and not look any longer.

Bird and Abo and Bobby Coles sat on their lathered horses after the last sweep and watched the long strings of mallards ripple across the orange sky.

"Let's get these beeves home," Bird said. He would return in a few days to pick up strays.

A splinter of moon was rising when this herd summited the gorge and were hazed into a pen of deeded ground. Joan had scattered hay and was waiting in the flatbed to shuttle the men the last three miles to the home place. They threw saddles onto the flatbed and turned the horses out with the cattle. Bobby Coles had a pint of whiskey. He had to work graveyard at the mill and had a plan to drink fast for an hour, sleep hard for another, and spend the third with an energy drink he had bought by mail order. At the home place, they departed in separate rigs, and Bird followed Bobby into town and played guardian, puttering around in the trailer where Bobby was quartered until Bobby had to be waked, handed a cup of energy drink, and shoved out the door.

Tom Bird went to the Alforcas to have his three drinks. Two women from Bobby's trailer went with him. They were nearer Bird's age than Bobby's and had ceased looking for a ticket out and were sighting only on something better than Monday night football on the T.V. Bird seated them at a table, bought them a round, bid good evening, and went to stand at the dark end of the bar. Al came over and said, "I wish I could make those women you brought in lesbians. They're decent enough but they have such hard luck with men." He was letting his hair and beard grow, as he did every winter, and was now scratching his neck and chin. "I've read that AIDS is devastating the choreographers of Broadway," he said, rubbing his underchin. "Gertrude Stein was right: women love more decently than men." He poured drafts for two men off swing shift and came back to add, "Homosexuality so upsets natural order that the buggers have to be creative just to live. I say this, Tom, because the cousin that I had always thought of as simply weird was very queer and as of yesterday very dead with AIDS."

"My condolences. That's a bad way to go, I hear."

Al caught orders on the wind and set drinks on the bar. His help had gone north and he would not demean himself by tending tables. Familiar folks picked up their drinks, while a table of stubborn customers waited and waited and were told to pay up whether they took possession of their drinks or not. The four men were torn between wanting the drinks and the justification to fight. They had not yet decided when the county sheriff stepped in and preened. He was pear-shaped, and just a few eggs from a heart attack, but he practiced often with his .357 and was good with it. Being sheriff atoned for flunking out of law school. He came to stand by Bird and asked the bar owner for a glass of water.

"I heard about the kids finding a body," he said.

"Not a body," Bird said. "Bones."

"Will you show me where?"

"Let it be," Bird said. He was speaking to the sheriff but looking at Al.

"Now how can I do that?" the sheriff asked.

"If people went there, it was to have peace."

"Tom, you told the boys not to tell."

"I didn't give it much chance of working."

"Well, shit. You know something."

Bird tapped his glass like a gavel and glared at the sheriff. "That is Indian burial and you ought to leave old bones alone."

"I'm sheriff of this county and I can't do that. I'll see you tomorrow. Good night."

After the sheriff left, Al leaned fiercely over the counter and said, "Jesus, Tom, you didn't honor that romantic shit, did you?"

The next morning Bird gave the sheriff directions to the bones by drawing a map in the gravel. He said again no man should trifle with an Indian burial, and the sheriff reasonably calculated that every Indian to die in the last thirty years had been interred in the Bannock cemetery.

That morning the cattle buyer came in his Cadillac, all two-hundred-ninety pounds of him, to look at the steer yearlings held in scattered pens. He had a good eye for yearlings "on the gain," mostly divined from the appearance of the hide on the flanks; if it was thick and curly, they were marbling, and the buyer was flat committed to marbling, in himself and his feeders. He made the Double Diamond owners cull a few marked beeves, though it was mainly for his self-respect and leverage that these culls were to be sent through the local sale yard. By the pound it was insignificant. It was late afternoon when the buyer looked over a milling herd and said, "Worst goddamn bunch of steers north of Mexico." He snagged a cigar from the pocket of a corduroy jacket with suede breast patches; it hung around him like a teepee. He grew suddenly resolved. "I'll pay top dollar."

"Which is what?" Eleanor Goodnight asked.

"Well, it ain't even really a dollar. More like seventy-three cents." The buyer puffed his cigar, an aristrocrat of cow country, enjoying himself. Back at the plant in Tacoma he was another fat suburbanite with a tender ear from daylong phone wrestling. "That's generous," he continued, "when I know Tom Bird will deprive them of water, feed dry hay, mill them some, then send them to the creek just before they load on the trucks. And even as we drive off he'll be clinging to the trailer with a baby bottle trying to coax another ounce into one before weighing."

The owners milled. They demanded another dime, then a nickel, then a penny, which they got. The buyer waved his hands around his head to fend off their words and shuffled off to his Caddy. Bird followed him.

"Nice car," Bird said. He had known the buyer when he was skinny and drove a red Rambler.

The buyer scooted behind the wheel. He closed the door and spoke out the window. "Yeah, and if everyone was like you this car would be a Volkswagon van I'd bought off whacked-out hippies and I'd be spending nights on the mattress they'd left in it." He squirmed into the seat and tilted the steering wheel onto his gut. "You folks enjoy this. Next year you'll have to sell some cows to make payments, and the next year sell some more. Without cows that good grass is just fire fuel. Plus Pretty Boy here will read all those ag magazine articles singing hymns to the latest hundred-thousand dollar machine and the latest spray and the latest fertilizer and maybe miss the connection with the ads that support the magazines. I give you three years max."

The buyer drove off and Eleanor Goodnight pantomimed a kick after him. "I'm sorry and ashamed I opened my mouth. To get a penny, I cost us a dime. That the seller should speak. It's a travesty."

Tom Bird said, "If he thought it was a steal, he would have drawn up a bill of sale right then. He's still dickering."

Jason Abo was scratching multiplications on the loading chute. "The fat guy's just about right," he said. "Seventy-four shipped from here is a plus for us. But I'd like to get him into my health club."

The partners discussed holding onto the light calves. They too could cull. While the debate went on, Abo tried to nail down the concept of a health club that charged by the pound. He would give the fat folks granola and sunshine. Cowboys would haze them around corrals. He would be the first meat man to put his thumb *under* the scale. All he needed was capital. When the debate traffic dwindled, he said, "You folks keep an eye on this, okay? Our long range plan ought to be to leverage out in a dozen ways, cook ourselves into a growth stock, and go public and get our poke."

Sally Honstead said, "Mr. Abo, I want to be richer tomorrow than I am today. And et cetera. But it doesn't have to come all at once."

Abo whisked Joan to his car. They drove through a drizzle that became snow before they reached town. He said, "I've got a blanket in the back seat if you would be willing for some teenage front-seat sex." She scooted next to him and they parked behind the grocery store. They kissed and groped like teenagers and got jammed against the dash while reclining. Abo raised up and studied the geometry of the car's interior. "I've forgotten how," he said, perplexed.

Joan giggled like a very young girl. They arranged themselves like scientists. They were analytical. They solved the problem and that was satisfying. Then they couldn't disentangle and Jason got his foot caught in the steering wheel. Finally they were sitting under the blanket, listening to the great band Cream on the radio.

Joan said, "When I first thought of you this way, up at the lookout, I thought of an old boyfriend who extolled his faithfulness by telling me that while I was out of town he fucked mud. This was Santa Fe."

Jason thought about this for a long time. "Did he draw a human form and make mounds in the right places?"

"I never asked. I right away went shopping for an upgrade and hurt his feelings, wrongfully, considering his relative faithfulness. Worse, my upgrades were all cads. I should have cast my lot with the Santa Fe mud."

Jason Abo wondered if he had ever been this happy. They dressed and rubbed the condensation from the windshield and drove to the Alforcas. Jason explained how the Double Diamond equity could be made to work. Why was he saying this? he marveled while they sat in the car by the neon-lit window. He was designing a rosy future. It was scary to design a future and share it. He quit talking mid-sentence.

"Think of Tyree," Joan said quietly. "Think of the boy."

"I do." His exuberance was rote on this point. "All the time!" There was another long silence. "I think we should all go somewhere south cat-fishing and get our mail general delivery." He catapulted out of the car and spoke to the moon. "I think we ought to live under a dock in Memphis with the best stinkbait money can buy. I think we ought to get to know Memphis mud." He stalked in through the door, picked a wet napkin off the bar and hurled it against the ladies' door where it stuck like a tiny hornet's nest.

Al plucked off the wad and trashed it. "Nice throw," he said. He nodded to Joan and leaned close to Abo. "It's getting hard to bounce folks since you got them on Nautilus. You've got a slim margin, Jason."

"All the time!" Abo crowed.

The buyer arrived at Bird's place in a cab, the only one in Bannock. Tom was frying elk backstrap in pepper and onions. He put on some more meat for the buyer and got a commitment for another penny.

The buyer sopped up the drippings with a biscuit and said, "Tom, I went to the doctor and told him my dick was going independent. Gaining free will at critical times. He told me I might try losing weight. Then I was at a Fort Collins bookstore and a young man was buying a software package called 'How to Host a Romantic Evening.' Tom, I sit at a computer a whole bunch. Think there's any connection?"

"Nah, you're just old, Leonard." Bird slid him an iced whiskey and sat at the table. "The doctor might be on to something, too."

"Well, anyway." This worldly cattle buyer slowly spun his glass and studied the amber liquid runneling greasily around the ice. "I figure he spends the evening running the program and then goes and jacks off." He hoisted his glass and drained it, the ice clinking on his teeth. "If'n he knows how to do that."

Bird groped blindly on the shelf above him for the bottle. There was a flash of light in the windows from a car turning in, then the throbbing of a rusted-out muffler.

Leonard poured a dollop over the ice. "I still ain't convinced this is whiskey. I've drunk every kind there is and I ain't sure this here is even a third cousin."

The visitor knocked once and entered. It was Worthless wearing a ski mask and a slicker. He looked around, nodded in the four directions. Ice clung on the mask around his mouth. "Tom, I didn't kill me a deer this year."

Tom Bird grabbed a .30-.30 off the deer horns above the door. "Want to come along, Leonard?"

"Nope, I'm going to stay here and poison myself."

Bird hung a knife on his belt and handed four cartridges to Worthless.

"Workin' for a cowboy's wage," said Worthless, "a man needs to hang some meat. You're the only man I ever knew to make something out of buckarooin'."

"It's all them poaching fines I saved."

Worthless got in the back of the pickup and they drove down to the creek and crossed the rocky bed and jounced along until they found a doe in the lights. Worthless slipped around and crouched below the lights and cocked his head so the sights were illuminated. The deer humped at the report, went two jumps, and fell.

To keep from being complicit, Tom Bird sat in the truck while Worthless dressed the dear. It was a facile distinction. He knew that. But now he was not the poacher. Hunger was too strong, sometimes, to honor game laws. Bird remembered his fine when Swen Johanssen, the warden then, stopped at a line shack and shared a fine noon meal with eight cowboys, and afterwards cited all eight for possessing the out-of-season sage chickens that had fed him. He could have cited them after the first bite. But no, he cleaned his plate.

When they returned to Bird's place, Worthless danced around the carcass in the bed of the truck. "Boy howdy, I truly was meat hungry." He shouldered the deer and carried it to his car. He slouched back. "Tom, that pig is done inside our ribs. Next one that dies, okay?"

"I might need a hog someday. I'll tell you when I do."

A cab idled in Bird's driveway. The buyer came down the porch steps with the exaggerated care of an inebriate. "Meat," he said. "I can smell it." He thumbed to the cabbie. "Damn fool. He's the only cab in town and he keeps telling his number to his wife the dispatcher. He tells her number one and she answers number one and the only possible explanation is them computers cuttin' everybody's nuts off. Let's go see Al."

"You buying?" asked Bird.

"Sure," said the buyer.

"I do hope you're right about having bad software. You'll be less likely to run off."

Leonard banged on the roof of the cab as he opened the door and shouted, "Onward, number one." He backed in and lifted his legs with his hands, lamenting the demise of the Checker cab. "Anyway, Tom, I tell them that maybe I can't cut the mustard but I can still lick the jar."

Worthless was pulling onto the county road with his poached deer as a sheriff car waited to pull in to the lane. Leonard saw the light bar and said, "I don't know you, Tom. I just stopped to ask directions."

The cab rolled away. Tom sat on the steps.

The sheriff had another man with him. This man was the County Prosecutor. They were both dressed in hats and sheepskin coats. The two men scuffed, unknowingly, through coagulated jellies of deer blood as they stepped forward to shake hands.

"Who is it?" asked the sheriff.

"Tom, I have enough to charge you," the prosecutor added. He was young and had a red handlebar moustache and was from Brooklyn.

Bird scooped a mix of mink oil and beeswax from a tin on the step and began coating his boots. "For many of these Indians," he said, "burial is a big deal. Let it be."

The prosecutor said, "I have a computer full of missing persons. And I have this box of bones. I've got to match if I can."

"You moved the bones?" Bird asked.

"They're in a box," the sheriff said.

Bird threw his hands to the sky. "See, Katie? They boxed you anyway."

The prosecutor and sheriff looked at one another.

"The bones," said Bird, "are Katie's. They belong to Jason Abo. You talk to him. I put them there, as she wished. The coffin in the cemetery is empty."

"Why the hell did you do this?" asked the sheriff.

"She asked me to," answered Bird. "I suppose I broke some statute. If you're going to arrest me, do it now. I want to rustle up a bondsman before he goes to bed."

Neither county man wanted much of this. Bird wiped the wax residue from his fingers onto his pant legs and walked between the men to his pickup. He dawdled at the door and sniffed the air like a hound. Late fall was a good time in the northern Rockies. In the very high country, above seven thousand feet, snow was deep enough that a man wanted a big horse to break trail. But even that high the sun was not long absent and was plenty strong. A man might go about in a t-shirt as often as in a coat. In the valleys and high prairie the days were warmer yet and mostly windless, an easy time for humankind.

Bird said, "My old man worked so terrible hard to be so terrible broke and his only grievance was that soon it would cost money to die. Probably he would have checked out sooner if he hadn't been beholden. He was a good-humored kind man to his family and neighbors but a mean cuss to the stars. He could read the fate that would lead him to the end of time trying to get even with the bills." The county men were standing together by the fender of their car, backlit by the porch light. Bird liked having them hear but he was talking to the scraps of stone and air and life that make up a world. "Katie was joshing when she said she wanted to be food and fertilizer. I think she wanted to leave a story to tell. And now here you are and there's a story and as usual she's several campaigns ahead of us when it comes to fun."

In the silence of the men rose a coyote's yip and trill. The men listened to the cry and went to their vehicles. Bird drove to town because he said he would, but town didn't beckon. Katie and his father and the coyote were not to be found there. He would have his three-which-means-four and bolt.

At the Alforcas door he met the wag he had slugged with a clenched shot glass. The man skipped away with upraised arms and said, "Whoa hoss." Leonard had improvised a dance floor by scooting tables and chairs around the pool table and was jitterbugging with a hefty woman to Merle Haggard on Al's new CD system. Al liked good sound and liked electric Chicago blues and acoustic Delta blues. He kept a few George Jones and Waylon Jennings and other non-squealing country types around for when that peculiar contagious itch to dance swept the bar. Two other couples now moved to the floor to twirl and sashay. Leonard saw Bird and stepped forward, jabbing a finger. "Tom, you ain't never had a dime. You can get jerked down so fast you won't remember up." Leonard wheeled back into the mix. Bird summoned an Early Times on ice from Bea and went outside to his truck. Shoot, the buyer didn't need to say that. Of course expecting cows to pay off debt was risky. Why did Leonard say that? In the Twenties when meat-packers concentrated into twenty big companies anti-trust action was brought against them. Now having three packers was dynamic business. Leonard's plant in Tacoma would within a year be swallowed by one of the three and the union busted and *e-coli* sent out with a graveyard run of hamburger. Bird knew that raising cows and calves was a pursuit of the profits attached to the trail herds of a century ago. The motive lingered in people like a bad gene.

But what else to do with a cow ranch but raise cows?

It was midnight when Bird parked at the Sur Fork where the riverbank was sand as fine and white as dune sand. The stones of the riverbed above the water were crusted with dry silt and moss that were whiter than the sand in the moonlight. Ice webbed the stones on the fringe of the water and the current ran black, dappled with starlight. He fished an oversized midge and caught one whitefish which he threw in the pickup bed for Worthless' pigs. He built a fire in the sand and made a bedroll. It was a soft cushion but before long he was squirming in fine sand that had infiltrated his bed while he rolled. He stripped and dunked in the river. Then he shook out his bedroll and carried it back from the river and made his bed under cottonwood trees.

Fog was thick in the morning and hoarfrost limned the tree limbs and brush. A tint of yellow was beginning to touch the fog when Bird gave it up, fishless. Driving out of the canyon, he burst from the fog into a crystal sunlit day and was a lord of all he saw, prairie and canyon and the blue and white escarpments on the horizon where individual trees seemed distinct. His possession was sublime. It faded while he tracked the highway signs to home.

3

For a time Joan maintained the fiction of schoolmarms and was a moonlighter at the Double Diamond to pad a chintzy salary. She kept a stock of withering replies at hand and felt a bit dark for her delight in their deliverance. Only evil people could jolly in causing such discomfort. So she spread the truth: she was Abo's lover. That exoneration freed her to be meaner.

In fact she was overdosed with cynicism. She and Jason were practical. She could chart their future acts of devotion which are also liens: remembered birthdays, phone calls when out of town, the midnight trip for tampons. And then one of them would fall sick and require humiliating care. Oh, they were stuck that far at least. They had stumbled into one another and were still stumbling.

In winter Joan was on an ancient schedule of sun: she left the house at dawn and returned at dusk and sat the night away with a lapful of papers. Each morning she painted herself for the attack and sallied off to school. At war with the world, she campaigned mostly at school. She climbed on kids and embarrassed slackers on the staff. Jason Abo commented that the upswing in bitchiness correlated precisely with the downswing in the health club business. He showed her a graph with a blue bitchy line and a red profit line. The lines ran together like cheek-to-cheek dancers. He was a realist and not much help to another realist.

The problem was Joan did not fit the skin of an assistant principal. The hierarchy was a mirage. She had gone at the job with vigor, and as such had condemned every idiocy to greet her and scuttled every innovation, however meager. She was the lead commander of the status quo.

These thoughts congealed like candle wax in the cold morning after the Thanksgiving vacation. She reached the school door and shook off her anger and combativeness with a head-to-heel tremor like a dog shedding water. Two steps inside the door she heard the fire alarm go off. There was smoke in the hall. Joan went through the building, chasing people out, and met the firemen obscured by smoke drafting from the boys' bathroom across from the library. Most of the kids were just arriving and were herded into the gym and kept there two restless hours while the main building cleared of smoke with every door and window open. Then the rooms were cold and the cooks were behind in cooking and Joan helped in the kitchen to feed these cherubs and finally in the afternoon tracked down the culprits and faced the two boys in her office with its frost-bit plants from Arizona and with her clothes and hair reeking of paper-smoke and paint-smoke. One boy was tall and white-faced and scared; he made a show of bravado. The other had seen enough police cars and courtrooms to know the value of reticence. "That fire will cost you four hundred dollars apiece," Joan said. She crowded them against the closed door. "I'm going to tan a piece of your hide myself and just haven't figured what piece and where yet to hang it on my wall." She sent them home, regrouped by snipping off the wilting Arizona leaves, and then got an audience with poor beleagured Gary, the principal, in his office. She said, "I can take two classes—sophomore P.E. and sophomore biology—to reduce teacher load. Referrals can languish in the office for a period. I'm going to dispense with every damn nuisance of paperwork and just do things. Once a year lack of documentation might prove inconvenient. For that one time I should be a file clerk?" She brushed some smoke from her hair and turned the doorknob. "I'll change schedules before I go home." Gary tried to drum up a show of passion but it wouldn't come and he watched her go.

Joan was enlivened by the classroom. In the biology class she leapt into reproduction, which gave the farm kids a leg up when it came to ovulation cycles and gestation periods. Her goal was to foster curiosity, and the life and death of a mayfly was more poignant than a salmon's because mayflies copulated. She used the old practice of dance cards to have students work out genetic probabilities of their issue with different classmates. This caused mostly revulsion at the idea of mating (of course a few of the combinations were done deals). But the exercise intrigued and forged a path to the learning of genetic diseases and AIDS and T-cells and immune systems and antibiotics and why cockroaches would survive fallout. She could ensnare their distracted minds with sex and death.

In her sophomore coed P.E. class, her primary function was to dent the egos of the several stud boys in class. To the extent she accomplished this, everyone got some exercise, learned some skills, and were able to feel part of a team.

One day a new boy showed up. In his nose was a metal ring the size of a silver dollar. The class was playing volleyball; Joan told him he would have to take the ring out lest someone catch a finger in it.

"I can't," the boy said, "it's soldered."

"I don't see how you can be in this class," Joan said.

They went to the counselor to explore scheduling. Nothing fit. Joan said, "All right, we'll tape the ring alongside your cheek."

The boy's eyes grew wide. "That would look ridiculous."

Wendell Adams, the chair of the Bannock Disaster Auction committee, met with Joan Collins at the local coffee house to solidify plans for the auction at the school. The annual auction raised funds for burnt-out and flooded-out families. People paid high prices for donated sacks of onions, quarter-beefs, farm miscellany, haircuts, and merchandise from town businesses. Cake-walks and basketball-shoots and craft-booths and greased-pig contests made the event fun and even bigger than the Fourth of July for civic participation.

Wendell was tall, gangly, bald, slow-moving, with huge hands. He owned the hardware store in the old Main Street, squeezed between a floral shop and a barber. Thirty years ago his father had told him that it was better to be poor in a small town than in a big one, and without much self-confidence Wendell came home from the defense of West Germany to hang around Bannock competing with high school kids for low-rung jobs until advancing middle-age made that unseemly; he got a steady job as a hardware clerk and then, miraculously, came into possession of the store, a wife, and a double-wide mobile home. And since then, for a dozen years, he'd done all right, awful close to the vest, but all right, keeping an inventory of most of what a rancher could use, along with some yard and house items. One cold day his entire sale was an eight-cent machine screw, but generally someone was in the store looking for the means to get a job done, and before Christmas he could move some toasters and bicycles. He had done all right and then some. He contributed to the fireworks. People asked to post in his store circulars for auctions and rodeos. He always had fresh-brewed coffee free for the taking, and people regularly partook. Once he'd addressed the school board in favor of a bond issue, but that proved overly venturous amid arcane terms like mils and retirement schedules. In his store he was a master and would home in on a customer's needed item with the directness of a missile. He was mechanic, carpenter, plumber, metallurgist. The Main Street folks drinking his fresh coffee had enlisted him for the Disaster Auction and he had become, improbably, a wheel.

And then to have a Wal-Mart come in on the north end of town and drop-kick his ass.

He was morose and beaten when he made the final preparations with Joan. His last civic duty was to subscribe his entire inventory to bidding without reserve requirement. That would ensure a large crowd. The hardware store was brought on flatbeds to the school parking lot at noon. The booths and frivolities opened about then and Wendell got a notion to set up a card table and offer a hundred dollars to anyone who would pony up a dollar and beat him in arm-wrestling. A few men tried him for fun and were flopped down as quick as thought. Jason Abo, in his bored meandering while Joan worked, came upon this table, viewed this man, and donated one hundred dollars for the chance of keeping same. The gesture was more theatrical than charitable, and drew an audience. The arm-wrestler was long and bony and not very muscular. Jason was bulging in taut skin and grinning with civic magnamity as he clasped the bony hand...and the grin was still there when his forearm was torqued and slammed to the table. "They used to call me Fingers," Wendell said as Abo counted out the money to a cheering audience. "In the army I was the European champ and one giant Air Force man said my arm was the size of his finger. After

I beat him he said two fingers at the most. So then my name was Fingers." Wendell was suddenly very sad at the thought of leaving town. He scrawled a receipt on a donated memo pad. "Thank you from the Bannock Disaster Committee," he said.

Tom Bird and Sally Honstead were in the crowd. Tom had donated to the auction a dozen flies, a hybrid pattern of green floss, peacock herl, and hare's ear fur. It was a very good nymph and Bird meant to buy them back if they went cheap. He did not like to tie, and that dozen was a season's supply of his favorite nymph. Sally had donated a half-beef.

"You're most generous," Sally said to Jason after the crowd dispersed. She viewed the Auction as a ceremonious occasion and was dressed for show: white-coyote jacket, black satin dress, kid-leather black boots. "Old-timers remember the armed-forces bulletins sent to local papers. The compensation for picayune lives is intimate knowledge of other picayune lives. No one is a mystery."

"Sally, please." Abo massaged his elbow.

"Mr. Abo," Sally said and shook hands. Then she departed to admire the quilt the Ladies' Auxillary had made depicting pine trees, double-bit axes, cross-saws, and peavey poles."

Bird and Abo snaked through the throng in the school halls and grabbed floor space in the gym to where the auction had moved. Abo slipped a pint of mezcal from his jacket. He motioned Tom to a corner and flung up the bottle for a quick swig—a useless furtiveness; every lady in the gym recognized the gesture. "The coffin," he said, passing the bottle to Tom, "is under a tarp in your pickup."

Tom Bird swigged and waited. The auctioneer made a quick recitation of protocol and a long spiel about the Christian charity that was sneaking like heartworm into everybody's hearts and the only worm medicine today was great big bids. Tom Bird swigged again and waited.

Jason narrated in a low voice: "I told the mortician I wanted a plain box, pine. He trotted me through all these glorious caskets and I almost had to pin his thumbs back before he'd talk about cheapo. Even then it was ornate. I called the state licensing agency in his presence and learned there were no standards on caskets, that I could cobble up a box from junkyard plywood if that's what I thought of my beloved. Then the mortician drug out the pauper's coffins. I bought two. I liked the craftsmanship so well I would put one in storage for myself. I waited while he transferred the bones and brought them to the chapel. When the mortician came into the chapel at the end of my private meditation, both caskets were on gurneys side by side. One held Katie's bones; the other had taped to the top five C-notes. He swished around a while and took the one with the bills."

Bird gave back the bottle. "Thank you," he said.

"Oh, fuck, it cost me five hundred dollars," Abo said. "I've paid that much for the company of bones only a thin medical definition more alive than those."

"I've got a ride to make," Bird said and left.

Abo lingered and made a bidding run at the first offering—a Wal-Mart shovel—and then strolled the wing where the crafts and baked goods were. Tyree was standing by the pop machine, hawking "bones of the lady in the tree." He had an assortment in a rucksack. Abo's first reaction was parental: this was an abomination, selling his mother's bones. His second reaction was also parental: damn good marketing. The boy had a pocketful of quarters when Sally collared him and squelched his business. Jason found Joan and propounded on entrepreneurship: metacarpals were selling like pearls. "Don't go grave robbing," she advised and darted off to tell a boy to remove his hat.

Cop on the beat, she was, and Abo followed a moving throng into the cafeteria. Cafeteria tables laid on their sides made a pen and the crowd stood around these tables as boys under ten were called inside to catch the greased pig. Thirty boys and one girl were assembled when a man toted in a cardboard box, told the kids to be touching a table before the go, and slowly tipped the box. The pink shoat, about thirty pounds, looked about as the horde of kids converged, then shot squealing through the phalanx and ran several laps before a red-headed boy captured both hind legs, held on as though to an animate wheelbarrow and kicked at interlopers and himself squalled for a ruling. Wendell Adams threw the boy a burlap sack and declared the contest official. The red-headed boy used the burlap to grip and nestled the shoat against his chest and named him Buddy. Joan and Jason brought out the mop buckets but the detergent didn't cut the grease; they left the job to do later.

The auction in the gym had a hitch when Conley Brunell told the crowd that the stud fee he had donated was for his paint who was an aggressive breeder, and Conley had a short video to prove it. First on the TV screen was a mare cross-tied. Then Conley entered leading the stud. The stud was pulling Conley about, then broke free and with flashing hooves mounted the mare. The breeding began with violence and ended same. "That paint will leap on a dust mop," Conley said proudly as he flicked off the tape.

One woman yelled, "Is that horse a logger? He sure acts like a logger."

A hubbub of women's voices welled up.

"Did he take his shoes off? If he didn't, he's a logger."

"He said he loved her, didn't he?"

Joan shouted out her own sisterhood rebuke: "Did she get dinner?"

Even those women severe in judgement of Conley's *faux pas* were in good-humored rebellion. Women who had hied to cloak their girl-children from the video now expostulated on the lesson: "That there is Everyman."

Joan was still shouting sisterhood witticisms when two girls slipped up and shyly said two boys were snapping off car antennas in the parking lot. Joan gathered Abo and walked the perimeter of the parking lot in the poor light of the two mercury lamps. Jason saw the boys skirt through the schoolyard pines at the edge of the moonless night. He gave perfunctory chase but they had too much lead and too much dark territory. He and Joan got in her car—with its broken antenna—and patrolled the streets in search of vandals. Jason described the boys.

Joan recognized them: the unrepentant arsonists. "I'm gonna kill those bastards."

"Now you're talking," Abo said.

"The surly shit told the radio station I threatened to cut his balls off and hang them on my wall. I said no such thing."

"You should have." Abo swigged with vigor from his bottle as they circled through the parking lot to the school. "There they are!" he said suddenly.

Joan saw the boys at the edge of the headlights and wheeled to fully expose them. Slack-shouldered, they strolled, turned to look at the car lights, and strolled with deliberate indolence. Joan tracked them in first gear.

"Hell," Abo said, "they still have their hands in their pockets." He lifted a leg across the console and pressed her foot to the gas feed.

The car lurched. The boys looked dumbly on for a moment and then went akimbo out of the lights. Abo let up but Joan's foot was now jammed toe under the brake and heel on the accelerator. In a blink the car shot over the sidewalk and crashed through the hollow steel doors into the foyer of the school. The car, except for being crumpled, sat there amid the tables of crafts and cakes like an offering in a drawing.

Finally, Joan said, "The blood in my lap is from my nose."

"Are you okay? I'm going to make those lucky bastards real unlucky."

"Please don't."

People were opening the doors.

Joan murmured, "Don't go. I don't know how to explain this."

Someone outside yelled, "It's on fire!"

Abo bailed out to look beneath the car. Flame ripped along the ground and leaped in a sheet to the leaking tank. He darted around the car, pulled Joan out, and with the other frontliners swept people through the cafeteria doors. Wendell Adams jogged up with two silver fire extinguishers. He handed one to Abo, but they were one beat too slow, for the flame went conflagration. Now it was a scramble away, and this spirit shot through the exodus like a light beam, the surge upset the crowd balance, people began falling on the patina of grease in the cafeteria. Bodies fell over bodies. Panic went general. Individuals willfully fought this welling beneath their breastbones, but it settled in their legs in the old fat-belly prey-herd urge to goddammit run! to get freed of everyone else's rathead panic. One instinct not discarded was familial: mothers and fathers were hustling broods, breaking back through the crowd to look for missing ones.

The fire became known throughout the school, but some had to look, and the crowd spilling from the gym hit the crowd fleeing the cafeteria with a result that

118

would gladden any stampede chaser: the colliding groups mingled and came to an utter stop. Cows don't knock one another down. These people did. Black smoke was rolling against the ceiling with an ugly plastic smell and the fire *whumped whumped*, audible over the babble of voices.

For a time the outcome appeared gruesome, but then the throng got moving into the gym and panic was drawn off into the spaciousness of the gym. Men gallantly lined up at the outside exit to usher out women and children and preserve the romance of duty in extremity. There were volunteer firefighters in the assemblage and these made haste to the firehouse. The boy with the pig lost his grip a few paces from exiting. The porker skeedaddled back to the cafeteria. "Shoot," the boy said matter-of-factly, "now I gotta catch him again." Other boys saw the chase was on again and flew off in pursuit. Sally and another woman were rescuing cakes from the foyer and putting them on the cafeteria floor when the pig barreled through, hounded by a dozen boys. Cakes were trampled and Sally thrust out her arms to barricade the foyer. Adults streamed in to corral the boys, destroying the cakes, and Sally made one last sally to save the Ladies' Auxiliary quilt and then gave up the scene to the firemen. The woman who had so assiduously aided Sally in the preservation of the cakes arrived outside begrimed and resigned. "This is a disaster," she said.

The only casualty of the school fire was the pig. He had holed up in the cardboard box in which he had arrived, and was found there, asphyxiated.

Jason Abo and Joan Collins were married at the Chapel of Love in Las Vegas, Nevada. The newlyweds caught a show of an aging comedian spewing profanities without a semblance of wit. Abo tossed onstage the cherry from his drink, was immediately accosted by three gracious house thugs with name tags. "The house requests you to leave," one said, a stock phrase not to be construed as polite in Las Vegas. Abo was delicate in his resistance, meriting no more than the perfunctory manhandling in the foyer. Joan trailed dutifully but reminded him that a marriage of convenience ought to be more or less convenient. Jason was chastised. He led her to their room and they reveled in love. When he was sure she was asleep, he went back to the showroom. One houseman was in the foyer, bending to hear something from an elderly couple. Jason stepped between the couple and busted the startled houseman in the nose. The man lurched upright and staggered back and Jason shot four jabs to his face and then clocked the man with a right to the chin. The old folks said not a word. It had been so unexpectedly easy. Jason strode through the casino and made a hundred-dollar roulette bet on a wheel near the door. He saw the commotion in the pit and would have made the street if the bet had not been a winning one. Collecting his chips led directly to jail.

The newlyweds left town after paying damages, which to Abo's dismay did not even include x-rays—just dry-cleaning for a shirt, tie, and jacket.

4

Tom Bird drove down from the timber into the valley of cow pasture and over the hump of sagebrush hills to the Little Timber where it ran over lava rock. Moss hung from the rock in long undulating tails which marked the main current like a trough. Tom stood in this trough in his hip boots, tying on a tellico, when he was enveloped by a white-winged caddis hatch. It was a snowstorm in reverse, swelling to the sky. They were on his hands and in his ears. He walked downriver, sometimes coming to a break in the hatch, only to be enveloped again. He couldn't raise a fish. They were sated or overwhelmed by the blizzard.

He stuck the hook in the cork butt of the rod and left the river and made a fast hike until he no longer saw a snowrise.

Here the river had a milky green color, ran flatter, collected run-off from the hay fields, plunged into sheer gully walls and swept around bends of willows. Foam edged the current and trout were making dainty rises in the foam. The trout weren't fussy so long as the artificial floated, and Bird changed flies often, seeking empirical truth. A bucktail caddis eventually seemed best at drawing the boss of the hole, and Bird headed back upstream to fish this too-orange impostor against a fallen cottonwood that hadn't yielded right on the downtrip. He came around a bend and saw the gnarled roots of the tree and started across the river to get above the roots when he heard a squeal. On a sand spit below the tree were two women. One held a bent rod. A four-pound trout was flopping on the sand. The woman without the pole rushed in and netted the trout in the sand.

Bird crossed to them. The women had bought their togs and gear that morning. When Tom told them they had caught the largest trout he had seen taken from the Little Timber, they gushed about the wizard at the fly shop and gushed how much they loved this fly fishing. The netter wanted to release the fish and the rod-holder wanted to show it to her husband as he came off the eighteenth hole. "Keep the fish," Bird said. "It can't live now." He had an inkling the fish wouldn't be cleaned before it was shown to the golfer, so he offered to do it. After the fish was stripped, one of the women noted it didn't look as big. The other woman followed this cue and they looked at Bird as a saboteur. The shop wizard, in comparison, loomed romantic.

Tom slept that night in the cab and the next day made a long drive measured by the small streams where he stopped to dab a fly. He was ready for big fish when he slid into the trapping country of eastern Idaho. At a town called Beaver he pulled alongside bubble-head gas pumps next to a pink shanty and told the gray scarecrow with yellow fingernails long as chicken toes, "Gimme a pint of brake fluid, two quarts of oil, a gallon of anti-freeze, air in the tires, and a dollar's worth of gas."

"Nice truck," the scarecrow said of the 1972 Ford with rumpled, rusted skin. "The last good pickup."

Before Bird made the next town the last good pickup threw a rod which skewered the block and busted the timing chain and bent all the lifters and generally made a fishing-line snarl of steel.

He had the truck towed to Pocatello, ordered a new engine, then grabbed his duffel bag and caught a Greyhound bus headed north to West Yellowstone. Three hours later the bus climbed out of the potato fields through the lodgepole slopes onto the caldera, and Bird asked to be let off at Osborne bridge. He toted his gear from the bridge to the Forest Service road and was digging into the bag for some jerky when a van came by and took him over the ridge to the west fingers of Island Park Reservoir. The young couple said the fishing was good. "Here is fine," Bird said where he wanted out.

He walked through the roadside fringe of pine and came onto a broad meadow on the longest peninsula just as darkness became complete. He walked along the water's edge, listening to the pipers and ducks demarcate the cove. The surrounding peaks were defined by stars blotted out. He fumbled and fumed rigging up his rod in the dark, then lay on the bank waiting for the moon.

An oblong moon came up and gave the world three dimensions. The lake, no longer an ink pool, had weeds growing to the surface, and weedless channels. For thirty years Bird had celebrated fall shipping by shipping out himself, and those voyages had taught him much, humbled him much, and the residue of humiliation and triumph had given him fishhawk sense and a little craziness, for he jabbered excited predictions about the channels as he waded out. "I'm going to catch a four-pounder on the plop at that weed line," he said, double-hauling. The leech landed, began to sink. "On the first strip." When he had retrieved halfway across the channel, he said, "Big hit now," and two seconds later it came just as he envisioned it and he was onto a leaping ripping rainbow that eventually tired of the fight fantastic and doggedly weaved basket hitches around the tule spires and broke off.

Bird horsed several lesser fish from the weeds and landed them along with another big rainbow that also went to the weeds but did not weave so well. He called it good fishing and rolled out his tarp and put on his long-handles. Clouds swirled blustering around Sawtelle Peak. They weren't gray sheets of fall but black summer scythes. He tucked the tarp around his bedroll and dug out the chicken sandwich wrapped in wax paper. Prior trips had taught him that weather *originated* in Yellowstone, but there was not much he could do except eat his sandwich while it was dry.

The horizon winked with light and there was low grumbling thunder. Before Lewis and Clark saw the Rocky Mountains they heard them groaning. Now a breeze flipped up. Then wind was bending the treetops. Lightning bolted and thunder cracked. Bird ate the last bite of sandwich as the remainder of the sky disappeared behind galloping thunderheads, and hail and lightning and rain danced on the caldera. He got soaked and could not sleep but passed the time agreeably in awe of the tempest, scooping from his cache of hailstones into the Jim Beam flask. The fury spent itself before dawn and when the sun hit him he slept well.

The day grew hot, a continuation of an entrenched system that had been syphoning heat from Arizona for several weeks of Indian summer. At midday trout cruised the shallows, feeding on nymphs that had been tossed from the deep and ants that had been blown from land. Bird hooked eight in a short time, three to five pounds. Two pelicans spent that time floating nearby, still as decoys, and when the rod quivered and the reel sang, he spoke for the birds: "Doggone, how *does* he do it?" A midge hatch followed the wind flotsam, and Bird suddenly couldn't do a thing. He ran through patterns and finally sat on the bank as still and studious as the pelicans.

Two pickups drove onto the peninsula, and a bunch of men and women and kids fell out with float-tubes, and hurriedly donned waders and fins and began waddling to the water. Bird intercepted the migration and asked if anyone might be heading for the highway soon.

A man near forty, with a long brown beard trimmed thin so it hung down his shirtfront like a cravat, said, "As soon as I commandeer some keys, I'm out of here," and waddled backward into the water. A float-tuber entering a lake is a sight as ungainly as you might ever see. The bearded man who acted shanghied into this fleet was most ungainly: he waddled until he hit soft deep mud; he staggered backwards, teetered, then launched into a fancy dancing reel that led to a big splash as he plopped onto the tube seat and his lost flippers tipped to the muddy surface a rod length away. "Fucking bourgeosie recreation!" the man shouted, then paddled around with his hands to get the flippers.

A blonde full-made woman came up and stood by Bird, watching the tuber's struggle. She said, "Homer is one of those sons of riches who got into microchips." She had braided hair, strong carriage, sun wrinkles. "City fathers clap and cheer when he announces that because of state and urban tax incentives he is sending out the call for more minimum-wage peons. But I knew him when he was poor and a lovelorn chef, and he was just as fussy then."

The man Homer was contorting several ways inside and outside the tube to get on the flippers. The woman walked down the bank, and though wearing good leather boots she waded in and squeezed the man into his flippers. She gave the tube a bon voyage push and came up the bank smiling. "I'll make that run," she said. "My name's Rose Harbinger."

"Tom Bird." They shook hands and headed for the truck. "Doesn't he like to fish?"

"He don't like to do nothin' except think. When we were young, his way was fun; now it's mostly aggravating." She lifted a cooler from the pickup bed and toted it to the shade of a spruce, provisions for the tubers. Bird tossed his duffel in the truck. She drove fast over the rutted two-track. When they got on the good gravel, she said, "I think he's cranky and he thinks I'm cranky. I guess that's age." Bird didn't think she was forty. She was vibrant and very pretty.

"That man your husband?"

"Old friend. We were a tribe."

The switchbacks up and over the spine lulled Tom to sleep. He woke when the truck slid to a stop. The woman was pointing at a bull moose twenty yards off the road. The bull stood black and huge amid the lodgepole, his horns spanning five feet. The bull looked at the truck for a time and then shifted to face it square.

Rose said, "He's studying whether to charge us."

Tom said, "He is. And so's his buddy." Another black bull, with a heavier spread of horn, trotted up behind the first. "I don't think they'd do it, but why don't you tap the horn."

The moose stopped at the horn, and walked away.

"Were they going to charge?" Rose asked as they finished carving switchbacks and gained the flats.

"They aren't scared of anything," Bird said. "I know that. Folks have told me of them charging log trains rather than yield the track, but maybe they just lower their heads, being fearless and dull. Those two up on the hill were cantankerous, facing up like that."

They crossed the river and went at a tear over the hump to the roadside community of Last Chance. She stopped at a skimpy road market to buy ice and beer and white gas. Bird thanked her for the ride and crossed the road to join the waders in the river.

The river here was a big rain-gutter, waist-deep, clear and fertile with weeds and bugs and, according to lore, trout. Tom Bird drifted a Goddard caddis on the way out to good water. After a few good drifts, he started looking for bent rods in the community while he made drying false casts. What one looked for in such populated water was if everyone was catching fish, which meant the pattern was known and the answer was the pattern, or if one person was catching fish, which meant that he was doing something very different. Bird changed flies and water. He was not one to flail a hole and he worked more quickly than usual, for he was hustling to leave. He knew some of these people were good fishermen who had changed depths and flies. He was making a final drift with a blood muddler when he saw the dorsal and tail fins of a big trout rise as smooth as a bubble to intercept the fly. He struck and the trout swirled, then went slashing upstream on the trail of a blue dragonfly. The trout bolted in a frenzy like a steelhead shooting rapids, and seemingly would have caught the dragonfly if not for the resistance of the line slitting through the water. The fish shot into the air, on its tail, now fighting the hold of the line. Marveling at a hooked fish made manic by a passing dragonfly, Bird played it longer than he needed to and was cradling it against the current to revive it when Rose hollered from the bank, "I want that fish to eat."

"It's yours if you run me up to Box Canyon," Tom said. He dug up a river rock to rap the trout's head and splashed to shore.

The river through Box Canyon was an immediate predecessor of the gentle flow of Last Chance. In the Box it bucked a bit more, but it hadn't carved much of a canyon, and wasn't really rough water, and mostly showed whitewater spray when the sports and guides in drift boats lathered it up casting. The basalt wall was sheer, but no higher than a three-story building. One stretched the definition of canyon to measure its length three river miles. It was almost undeserving of a name, except for the lore. This day a big gray mayfly almost as big as a green drake was hatching and Bird spent his time in ecstatic delirium trying to sell his match, which was close enough to elicit some takes and many splashing short refusals; he came out of the canyon not knowing how long he had fished, but only wanting to get a rock out of his wading shoe, grab a bite of jerky, and get back into the river.

Rose was waiting by his duffel bag. She had finished some laundry at an RV park and thought he might want a ride. A cool breeze was dragging in big flat-bottomed clouds. She said, "End of Indian summer, I guess." She wore a leather coat and gray felt hat blotched with light saddle-oil and heavy machine-oil and ragged salt lines around the crown.

"You ranch some?" he asked.

"We run pairs the other end of the state."

He walked to the canyon rim and looked down at the pea-green river, pocked with kinetic rings of feeding trout. If he stayed to fish, he had a three-mile walk to the phone. He grabbed his duffel and they headed across the timber flat to the pickup. Gusts of wind flitted about the compass, and the sky settled low and gray. They made a walking race against a sunlit blue wall quartering at them from the northwest. The last hundred yards they ran but the hailstorm won the race and hammered them.

"What brands on your ranch?" Bird asked after they dove into the pickup, hail clattering on glass and pinging on metal.

"The main one is JA BAR."

"Over Owyhee way." She looked surprised and he said, "There's a lot of talk in a bunkhouse."

The storm blew over and left a floor of hailstones like ball-bearings on the forest road to the highway. Twice Tom Bird had to chop with an axe through windfall to make a path for the truck to skate back onto the road. Rose confessed to the sin of leaving the handyman jack at home. She wasn't a completely idiotic traveler, she wanted him to know, she had a live credit card.

The blacktop had melted and the truck was zipping through Last Chance when Tom Bird hollered for the woman to pull over. In a turnout Eleanor Goodnight was sitting on a lawn chair, just far enough off the highway to escape the fantails from truck tires. She had a *People* magazine in her lap, and was gazing at the fishermen in the river when Tom stepped before her and introduced her to Rose Harbinger.

"Tom, we need to buy fall calves to get up to capacity." She had tracked him down to say this thing. "As it is, we can't cover the notes. We need to use the whole ranch. I know you can put the weight on them. It doesn't pencil otherwise." Then she turned to Rose and said, "Pleased to meet you."

Rose whooped. "Goddamn cowfolks." She pumped Eleanor's hand. "Even the Lord might not be stout enough to save you all." She waved them together like a boxing referee. "You finish your cow talk while I fetch us beer. Then I'll sermonize. Rassling a cowman for his soul is tough duty. His mortgage is his soul. The one he gives the Lord is provisional." She walked away, chuckling. "I'd be canonized if I saved one cowman."

"How the hell did you find me?" Bird asked, pawing at a spate of wind-blown mayflies to grab one and see its color and size. This was like early fall, so buggy.

"I intended to find you, and I would have, even without this bit of happenstance. I want you to go with me to Dubois."

"Dixon?"

"Well, Leon's dead. His son-in-law is accursed now."

"Shoot, accursed with that place? Even Stewart could have grown fat on that range."

"Tom, stop that. I liked Stewart just fine."

"I just meant it was good cow country."

"Is this a new thing, disparaging my dead husband?"

He took off his hat and put it under his arm. "I sure never did it while he was alive, Eleanor."

"No, you wouldn't." She accepted a bottle of beer from Rose and spun off the cap. Foam ran over the fingers of one hand while the other jabbed at Tom's chest. "I think fish is a bad diet for you."

Rose said, "Brain food for cowmen goes direct freight to their balls."

Eleanor said, "Cowmen have rubber bands put around their testicles when they're weaned."

"Mama does that?" Rose asked.

"They do it themselves. Little boys just off the tit grab their little chaps and the rubber bands and decide to grow beef."

126

Being a non-belligerent in the presence of a sisterhood alliance was not new to Tom Bird. His intent of falling into the world of trout was now bricked by sisterhood dams and he would have to consent to being savaged in order to be allowed to fish.

He endured it and thought it was over when Eleanor said, "The man does have ninety-eight point six degrees of honor, Rose. He will honor himself broke and alone before he dishonors you. He will honor himself before he dishonors anyone anyhow because such a thing is vile and he thinks someone is keeping tally and he means to have a pure scorecard."

"Eleanor," Tom said, "I don't know you."

She watched an osprey plummet to the river. It flipped at the last second to thrust out talons before it splashed. Unsuccessful, it flapped heavily, drying its feathers with a shudder between wingbeats, and looped back up to an observation track eighty feet above the stream. "Tom, I'm tired and cranky. But you don't know me."

The lawn chair fell before a gust. Bird picked it up and leaned it against the trunk of Eleanor's Buick, frowning while he thought. She had molted, like a mayfly. From the subimago of Stewart's wife, she had become the imago, the perfect adult. The imago, at fifty-five years old. She would copulate once and die. He told her this conceit with a jaunty vulgar air. No, he didn't know her. He was looking for clues.

Rose had walked off discreetly and now returned. "Come on to camp," she said to Eleanor.

"I've got a room in the lodge."

"Remember, I've got a sermon." She fetched three beers from the cooler and methodically popped the tops. "I've been a Jesus freak nine years. Even Jesus wasn't a Jesus freak nine years. We raise on our ranch good Angus artery-cloggers and mucho hundredweight of Christians. Last summer we had a retreat for women and it was the most un-Christian man-bashing imaginable. No wonder men hate us. We hate them. You ride along with me, Eleanor, and we'll bash this fishing cowboy to the top of the hill and then I'll talk Jesus at you and we'll become good and by camp you'll want to do that mayfly thing Tom mentioned."

"Tom won't like having a master." Eleanor tossed her keys to Tom while looking at Rose. "We worship an intolerant power-drunk codifier, the big policeman. The God of the Old Testament is vengeful and wrathful, an inane tyrant. But He's powerful, all right, if measured in cannons and canons. He has conquered deities at every meeting."

"He had to be tough," Rose said. "There were some hellacious battles. And when he won, he sent his son."

"I've known brave men," Eleanor said. "The ultimate sacrifice is no stranger to history. A Lakota chooses to die in order to remind his fellows of courage.

Japanese pilots by the hundreds volunteer to be divine wind." She carried her chair and magazine to Rose's truck. "Such a paltry thing it is to die in order to redeem all of mankind for all of eternity. Only a churl would not make that sacrifice." She turned to face Tom. "Is this all right, Tom? Tomorrow we'll go to Dubois and see if Leon's son outlaw has done anything with the fall calves?"

He nodded. He didn't know her.

On the road to the west fingers of Island Park, Rose said, "The bottom line is power. God kicks ass and Jesus heals. That is power."

Eleanor said, "I've seen power; I've bought a glass of orange juice for twelve dollars and fifty cents. Tom has seen power only in a penny-ante refusal to acknowledge a captain of his soul."

"Satan and stubborn are one yoke," Rose said.

"I doubt that is true."

"You're damned, Eleanor. It ain't permanent. I heard you two talk. And I'm just trying to get you and Tom a bit of earthly bliss to cushion the shock of Judgement Day."

"Tom deserves a bit of bliss," Eleanor said. "Lord knows."

5

On New Year's Eve Jason Abo put on a navy-blue suit, made of good Scottish wool, bought in London when he had need to be pampered by London tailors. He slipped on black kid-leather shoes bought in Italy. The maroon tie he had stolen from a fop KOed early in a brawl in a San Diego navy bar. He splashed on Old Spice and dabbed his cufflinks with vinegar. He looked in the mirror and contemplated his appearance. The umbrella he hurried to find was from seditious Wales and sported a stilleto in the stem.

As he drove into town to pick Joan up at school, his courtly preparations failed to sustain his verve. He didn't like the night of amateur drinkers. Dinner and dancing and bed, that was the consequence agreed upon. He could conjure no greater design. And boredom so early was no way to treat a wife, nor himself. Nevertheless he squired Joan through the New Year's Eve haunts of Bannock and tried to work up a nasty scene as was his wont but was curtailed by his wanton love for the broad-shouldered German woman, and accepted as his unavoidable lot a smidgeon of happiness. His mission since birth to escape boredom was now nearly accomplished with a bellyful of boredom and prime rib and Irish coffee: is this contentment, then, to sit back in the shadows of a steakhouse and watch your beloved join in the countdown howl of a new year? How exquisitely dull to delight in another's delight!

That night she refused him. Who can say why. A whim, an ailment, a preemptive strike—what matters the aim to the one who receives the blow? Abo drank a cup of coffee on the porch steps and pondered. Work was his consolation. That old embraceable standby. A goddamn faithful friend. He knew true blessing: misery makes a man work. If a maudlin panegyric be sung, let it be to accomplishment.

A thin moon rose as he saddled the roan gelding named Chief. The snow grabbed this little bit of light and made it big. He could see bushes and rocks and cow trails far out into the fields. He whistled up Eleanor's blue heeler Jiggs and trotted out toward a herd of heifers bedded down amid scattered hay stems. The herd watched horse and rider come and then all rose at once and teetered on the cow-thought of run or no. Jiggs lit into the philosophers and made his thought prevail. The heifers walked and jogged smoothly into the barn corrals. Abo further split out a half-dozen into an alley that ran into a squeeze chute. With help of Jiggs and a crimp pole he ran these beeves one at a time into the chute and vaccinated them for brucellosis and scours. The big dipper spun around the north star while Abo ran heifers in and out of the chute and filled syringes. Every blasted one bawled like Satan when the vise closed on its neck, and for

Jason the sound of foolhardy brute panic that lapped steadily at his wife's bedroom window was the very sound and sentiment stifled in his own throat.

The stars were fading when the last of the lot were treated. The fatigued man leaned against the chute and daydreamed of real sleep and real dreams; the dog curled up on a pile of baling twine; the horse stood stoic and slack-eyed with tipped hind hoof.

"Good morning," Joan said and all three stirred. She wore a blue housecoat and black rubber boots, picking her way through the snow, carrying two mugs of orange juice mixed with tequila. "Welcome to the new year," she said, passing a mug to Jason, begrimed and blooded in his fanciest clothes, "although my husband has yet to the put the old one to rest."

"This is a trial," Abo answered. He looked at his ruined clothes and drained the mug. "I'm going to bed."

"And I with you."

Abo didn't get this. He ought to brandish logic. He ought to throw up the hours in the corral for them to bicker over. But rebuke couldn't find a spark. He was fatigued and truly in love and glad to move rather than maneuver.

A crew assembled at Number One at ten: Tom Bird and Tyree and Sally Honstead and Bobby Coles and a groggy Jason Abo. They were to brand the fall calves from Dubois. Joan Abo put coffee and snacks on the table and reminded all that she would neither fork a horse nor be a foot cowherd nor abuse cute little calves. She opened up an Ivan Doig book and curled into an easy chair and said she would be available to call an ambulance.

While the riders moseyed out to bring in cattle, Tom Bird lined out things at the corrals. With a plastic snowsled he made a tray of vaccine and worm medicine and dehorning shears. He lit the charcoal drums for the irons. The plan had been good, but the riders were slipshod, and he had a long wait. He passed the time sacking out a sorrel filly that had eaten her way out of a home with one of Joan's teacher chums. The winter sun was traveling fast by noon when the weanlings came into view and entered the home pasture.

Sally and Tyree, on horses, moved the brutes into the alley. Jiggs hustled them up to where Abo worked the crimp poles. Bird hazed them forward and Bobby Coles worked the squeeze chute. When a calf was locked, Bird applied the iron and the calves bawled with hanging tongues while Bobby vaccinated and Jason dribbled the worm medicine down the backbone. Bird then cut the horns to the hairline close to the skull. Blood founted over the chute in a thin stream while Bobby cauterized the wound and released the squeeze chute and Abo jobbed the hocks of the treated calf to get it to walk through and Joan pulled and inserted poles down the squeeze alley to move up calves.

Conscripting Joan had given the job efficiency. Her husband had gone up to the house with a spiel about being one hand short of fluid quantum assembly-line physics.

The job was nearly done when a dozen calves broke through an alley gate and went under a high fence into the pasture. Tom Bird climbed aboard the young sorrel still tied and saddled. He tested her again in the hackamore. Satisfied she was compliant, he urged her forward after the fugitives. The filly began to trot and Bird, to straighten the saddle, threw his weight on the left stirrup and gave a simultaneous jerk on the horn. Provoked by the slipping cinch, the filly lunged into a run and then flat came disassembled. Her head was somewhere below Bird, her rump was somewhere above, and the part he was sitting on was nowhere. Somehow all the parts reunited and Bird jammed his feet hard in the stirrups and reached for a shorter rein to double her. The rein broke from his grasp when she again broke apart. She sunfished, pile-drived, swapped ends. She was a grand bucker, a writhing fury of fear, and as Bird made another grab for a shorter left rein he leaned too far and slipped his right stirrup. The next jump was to his left, settling him hard in the left stirrup. When the next jump went right, he was as a loaded spring, and he catapulted off the horse, his feet to the stars.

With a numb shoulder and faceful of snow, he rolled to his belly and watched the horse tear off in running rodeo bucks.

"That I could have ridden," he muttered, rising to his knees. The filly skidded to a stop a hundred yards away and stood still as a statue.

Sally and the boy rode up. Their mounts stamped around with rolling nostrils, infected by unease.

Tyree said to Sally, "Is Tom dead?"

"I don't believe so," she answered.

"Tom, are you dead?" asked Tyree.

"Only a little bit." He tramped off to the filly, caught her and straightened the rigging. He shortened the stirrups in case she should try again what worked once, but she never did; she complied with every human touch and eventually became Joan's pet and then Joan's partner, the only horse Joan ever did ride with gusto, so ultimately anthropomorphic that a human could feel praised to be likened to the horse's subtlety.

The calves had reached the limit of their cocksure flight and were already turning back toward the corrals when Bird mounted again. Tyree had got behind them and was chasing them in at a gallop, waving his hat.

"That boy is you, brother," Sally said.

"Well, he pleases me."

"It's the Pinoccio story. He's become a real boy."

They put the horses in a pen, pulled saddles and bridles. The sorrel filly lay down and rolled. "Sign of a good horse," Tom Bird said, toting the saddles while his sister gathered up the blankets and bridles and followed him to the tack room. The yard lamp burned on. Sally dumped her load of gear in the doorway and said, "Ramey's 'bout give up everything. She's coming back."

Tom blindly sorted the tack. Abo and a calf bellered a duet.

Bird said, "She's a liar and a whiner and a goddamn menace."

"Yes, but she is my daughter."

Bird threw a few flakes of hay to the horses. He rammed a post through the ice in the water trough and pulled out the cakes. Rubbing the chill from his hands, he walked up to his sister and looked her in the eye.

"I'll give her my love, but I won't turn my back on her. I suggest you do the same."

"Thank you for the love. That's really all we can do, isn't it?" She hooked his arm and put her cheek on his shoulder. "I did something godawful wrong, somehow."

"Shoot, sis, look at how we were raised. Deprivation and meanness were plenty stout, you'll recall."

"Fear and despair more than meanness, I'd say."

"Fear and despair, yes," Bird said. "The worse sort of meanness."

They walked back to the chute, both bearing memories of jackrabbit hunts and Papa bringing the latest bad news from town.

The last calf was run through and the crew hurrahed. They repaired to the house to feast on wok-fried hash and burgundy. Soon everyone was bloated and just able to burble "Happy New Year." When the company later talked about the Disaster Auction, with much winey witticisms and guffaws (*Bid faster Bid faster You ain't keepin' up with disaster*), Abo at first dismissed the accident by noting that it raised citizen consciousness about the steady presence of misfortune, and that the only victim was the town's insurance company. Then he vowed to engage in further civic duty. He would upgrade the buckaroo breakfast come rodeo time by putting mescaline in the pancakes. No one doubted Abo's enthusiasm for such projects and in general steered him toward a consideration of the children. Bobby Coles added that to have the rodeo judges riffing on the clouds was unfair to the boys trying to get good scores on their rides.

The jocular evening went on too long for a boy, and Tyree found Tom Bird's lap and made a nest. Tom waited until the boy began his fledgling snore and then carried him to his truck and went home. So far, being a company man meant pretty good company. Aphorism ruled: *many hands make light work.* At his house he toted the limp boy to a bed and bent to kiss the sleeping forehead. The boy made pig grunts while burrowing into the mattress. Tom sat on the edge of the bed until the boy stilled and fell into the slow gone breathing of slumber. Then Tom sat some more. He went out of the room to pour whiskey in a cup and returned to sit some more. Light work was an ill goal. He had grown too comfortable. Tenderness, he decided, asked to be as carefully identified and avoided as bad cholestorol. Comfort might slip in and steal what had been won by cranky work. That's what Abo was alluding to when he climbed on the chute and howled, Let nobody get none! Put all men's hearts in their throats and they'll grub like coolies and this ranch will *fly!*

It's also what Sally meant the day they'd agreed to grab the Double Diamond. Her husband had turned up her palm and traced a few lines. He then said, "We're fucked." The short fortune-line had intersected with the very long lifeline and dead-ended. She could look forward to many years as a washer-woman. Sally said, "If the lifeline proves long, pray it prove penniless before being vapid." This was oratory, Tom knew, this was a dig at a spouse—but it showed something true about her will to move, and the fire made new by a child come back to her.

Ramey Honstead had by degrees become a worthy person. She had a B.S., M.F.A., M.B.A., Phd. She had known for a long time she was a dozen IQ points lacking of being first-rate, but cunning had given her the degrees, the degrees had made her worthy, and cunning still availed in post-degree worthiness.

She took this personage to Washington, D.C., and presented it to the senators and congressmen of her home state. All thought it good to have her on staff. Congressman Tolbert Evans created a position for her with the most freedom. Outside the chain of influence, she made a new chain and linked up with Tolbert at the top. When he capsized in the next election, she sidled over to Senator Rod Hansberger in a nebulous slot, was sniped by staff in her quest for advancement, and jumped to the senator of the other party. Then back to Congress, with the chairman of the Ways and Means. This Southerner still had an eye for legislative detail, but he also had an eye for women, and had developed a modest venality to finance his wooing, and went about it in long hours, as once he did to master taxation and revenue. His staff was large and busy and were accepted as agents of the Chairman.

Ramey foresaw the Savings and Loan fiasco. Unregulated, these white male bank managers would abandon secure home mortgages and get hard-ons for big projects like oil drilling, wharf construction, high-rises, Polish bonds. Taxpayers would fork over to cover the wrecks. Afterwards she would claim she was fired for trumpeting a warning, but in truth she was banished from the beltway for lack of loyalty to man or principle.

Blackmail was her last chance, but the target cowardly died of a heart attack. She looked around and home seemed suddenly dear; to return prodigal was romantic, heroic, a humble mission of atonement.

Oh yes, she had the consciousness of atonement, but desire to atone did not have attendant humility. She mostly thought in inequalities: greater than, less than. She could pay the debt of her upbringing with attention to the ranch.

Putting a fire under the bucolics might make everyone well and get some good marks with St. Peter for service to county and country. As a collateral effect, she might get her due. She pretended to have these reasons in her heart when they were only in her head.

So it had always been. When Ramey was three, she learned the power of telling a parent, "I hate you." When she was seven, the power of disdain grew to mean freedom. Punishment only engendered a firmer declaration. When she was eleven, the sentiment was true. Power and hate were twins. As a teenager, Ramey fell for the first black leather jacket, scorned the small town mores, and earned unlimited funds for education by demonstratively courting the alternative. The heir of Hondo Motors spurned the gift as being too burdensome—she bought a ticket out with a pregnancy and an abortion. Sally Honstead knew something about recessive genes. She knew the parable of the lost lamb. Bob was unacquainted with genetics or philosophy, and only despaired. His girl was lost in the wind. He oiled hurt and guilt with a handwritten will that stipulated his daughter Ramey must personally put flowers on his grave within twenty-fours of each solstice or equinox, or else forfeit the previous quarter's dividends from a trust. It was a chasing sort of parenting, trying to append to a fleeing child a moral tail.

Ramey dropped out of the sky onto the Double Diamond airstrip, kissed her mother and father and began the gathering of data.

The fall roundup had brought in a passenger, a mare and foal. Tom Bird had recognized the mare, which had been missing three years from the Double Diamond. The mare had foaled in late summer and Bird was surprised when she began horsing in January. A friend had a Doc Bars stud he wanted tried and Bird volunteered to bring over the mare.

He had to rope the colt to put on a halter. He made a stab at halter-breaking by twisting the tail as he walked alongside tensing and easing the rope. Often that lesson takes hold in ten minutes, but hardly ever when you only have ten minutes. Bird had said on the phone he was on his way, and now he had a snorty colt too big to manhandle.

When he got between the mare and the colt, the little horse would rear against the halter rope and throw himself. He moved behind the colt and mare; the colt ran past the mare and slipped around her and then fought. Bird darted around the mare, switching hands on the lead rope, trying to head the whirlwind in the general direction of the trailer.

His predicament was he could not lead the colt close enough to the trailer to lift him in. The colt fought mightily; he threw himself over and over, squealing and blowing. The mare would not enter the trailer without her foal. Bird's heart pounded. He panted and sweat. In lulls between new tries he thought, What would I do if I were younger? Nothing. I would still have the same problem.

He tied the mare to the trailer and worked around so that the colt reared and fought towards the trailer. Three times the colt hit the trailer and Bird rushed him, but each time the horse surged past, and came up again snorting at a taut lead-rope with stiff, spraddled legs.

After a rest, Bird tried again, and as the colt backed fighting against the rope toward the trailer, Bird shook the rope to create panic and the colt reared and went writhing over backwards a few feet from the trailer. Bird pounced on the rising colt and with a lift and a shove sent the horse akimbo into the trailer. The horse scrambled up and surged to escape, but Bird met him like an offensive lineman. He checked the colt three times, hard. Now the mare was stamping. One hand fended off the colt and the other jerked free the mare's tie. He swung her around and jumped her in the trailer, which made a happy colt.

The colt was missing pieces of hide in several places. He didn't look too bad.

Sally will not herd her daughter so successfully, Tom Bird thought. And everybody but Ramey will get skinned hide.

Sally had followed her brother to Bannock. When his hopes for marriage were strong, he sent her a letter to come at once. He didn't want her to marry a man who would curse the bank, then stalk a jackrabbit or a whistle-pig for dinner. That prairie country was too poor. Sheep were money but coyotes worked on them, and in a bad winter there wasn't enough hay. One winter a teenage Tom had to sign a note for shells to shoot the snowshoes and jacks that fed them. Sally did escape, and it took most of Tom's wages to maintain her in the hotel and all of his free time to make sure no Bannock men had the wrong idea. She clerked at Woolworth's and then became a secretary for a small legal firm.

About the time Tom's prospect foundered, Sally coyly slid into a match with Bob Honstead, client of the legal firm. Bob by then had wrangled exclusive dealerships from Ford, Chevy, and Chrysler. When this contradiction was but a G.I.'s post-war chutzpah in the boonies, it went unnoticed. When Bob began to move cars, Detroit began a play for boundaries. The upshot was that Bob painted yellow lines of demarcation in the gravel lot to separate the makes of the manufacturers. Wind and rain obliterated this fiction within a month. The legal teams were quibbling when Sally and Bob honeymooned at the Indy 500. By the following May there were three separate car lots and three separate ownership groups and a big house undergoing blueprint revision.

An inveterate grease monkey, Bob found solace in pistons and ring-seats while enduring his wife's flame to win. Fortune would not have him be less favored. By the end of Eisenhower, Bob had cash-flow that embarrassed. He forever closed the hood of the magnificent machine and dwarfed himself to accountants and tax codes. He fished and hunted, and very nearly liked these things. When a vehicle broke down in a desolate place, he very nearly gloried in the exploration into the machine; but he grumbled as he reconnoitered, like sensible folk, and thus despoiled the reunion. At this time he had a mundane marriage to money and had all but forgotten the romance of being betrothed to cars.

Sandwiched in a sequence of miscarriages, the child Ramey arrived in the year 1960. The dealerships except for Ford were wrangled away in the next decade. Mustang was a grand hurrah, Torino an abomination, Pinto a sordid joke, and Bob went fiercely after Toyotas. Then he felt pressed to keep the wolf from the door. Survival was philosophy enough.

Ramey had become a teenager when Bob assayed that the earth had buried all his hopes but one. But he was mostly a spectator by then. Unconditional love sure enough got tested. The boy in the leather jacket sat on the pole fence, swinging his legs, while Bob explained to his daughter the theory of manners; when the boy said, "Why don't you lighten up?" Bob busted him off the fence. The next day the boy was on the porch with a victorious mouse beneath an eye, and Ramey was lost. A month later Ramey had a bruise, from the boy. When Ramey left, Bob was immensely unburdened and immediately started courting fancies about his daughter. Revisioned, she wasn't cold-hearted—just tough. Of course, revisionism changed Ramey not a whit, but it fired up Bob to strike a new acquaintance with prosperity. With his last hope made chimerical by distance, he could fill in the details any way he damn well pleased, and the picture sifted out to be a stalwart reckoning of truth and honor; her crusade was an extension of his; she weaved policy and law from the threads of his conversation; they were a team.

The thing unraveled as easily as it was made. When Ramey came home, Bob boiled with glee. Shortly she gave him cause to remember the night the leather jacket slouched on the porch with a mouse under an eye, giddy with the whole legacy of the outrageous punch, while Ramey feigned shame as she slumped out of the house with his good Payne rod and Hardy reel under her coat. Within a week of her return a decade later, Bob knew she was still carrying off things; he just didn't know what. "For crying out loud," he implored of his wife, "I'd just like to know her angle, that's all, just have a clue why she's here and what she's got planned."

"She is our daughter," Sally said. They were drinking coffee late at night, comparing notes, trying to discern the size and color of this thing called derivatives.

"And I love her," Bob sighed. "And because of that I am totally at her mercy." He scooped up his notes and gently placed them in Sally's lap. "And because she is smarter than me, it's futile to try to keep up with her. Good night."

"Bob, she's not the devil."

"Nope, and we're no angels. We're middlin', the lot of us. I'm tired. Good night."

Sally went outside and stood in the good wind. Thin bits of snow swirled down from a starlit sky. She stood staunch and impervious to the swirling flakes. Spring would come with the whistling meadowlark. Remember the tune. Chin up and whistle.

She whistled.

6

The next snow laid firm and slick over the heavy February pack. Tom Bird harnessed his thoroughbred mare to a bench-seat sleigh that had come to Hondo Motors as down payment on more horsepower.

The mare stamped in the snow of the driveway when the collar was fitted, then stood calm and stoic while the traces and driving reins were strung. Tom grabbed the bit and led horse and sleigh to the road.

On the road the mare balked. She reared and pranced and got tangled. Bird removed the harness, punched new holes with his pocketknife, and made a good fit. This mare had raced on a chariot and would understand the sleigh.

Led by the bit, the mare tucked her neck and dog-trotted, then finally seemed studious. Bird was about to climb up when she commenced again to skittering sideways and lunging and backing. Bird vaulted onto the seat and slapped the reins on her rump, meaning to line her out before she tangled again. She skittered and stamped. He snake-slapped the reins and hollered. The mare plunged into the collar and started the sleigh but then ricocheted back against it and reared and pawed the air. Bird threw his slack and was a futile bystander as the mare teetered on her hind legs and fell heavily to the right.

Air whooshed from her and the subsequent groan was like a cat's purr. Bird swore and stepped off, thinking it a good lesson that the mare should lose her wind. Then he saw blood welling from her ears.

He freed her from the harness and looped his belt around her lower jaw and pulled her head and neck off the snow. She stretched out her front legs and seemed ready to lunge up when she quivered from hoof to forelock and flopped in the snow and with a final spasm died.

Well, Bird thought, how about that. That wasn't much reason to die. He looked a long time before he could believe.

He jammed a stout limb in the snow to lever up the forequarters of the horse to slip off the collar. Then he piled up some brush and topped it with his handkerchief to warn cars. He threw the harness on the seat, grabbed the tugs and pulled the sleigh back to the lane. Being a draft animal is the ultimate indignity, he thought, opening his jacket to cool his sweat while he went inside to call the county about the carcass. He kept thinking that a week ago he almost sold her because the last two breeding seasons she had slipped.

The next mare he brought out of the pasture, the furthest from foaling, had taken well enough to packing but was a bundle of spark and springs when mounted, and expendable. Bird cross-tied her head between the lane posts and harnessed her during a diminishing dance. He let her stand while he ate a sandwich. Then he reattached the harness bells he had removed. They might help to calm or distract her. He hooked up the sleigh, brought her into the bit, sat in the seat, and stepped off to untie her when Ramey drove up, three hours late for their sleigh date.

Clothes swirled in the car and when Ramey stepped out she looked like a colorful inflated mummy. "Uncle Tom!" said her muffled voice. "What happened to that horse on the road?"

"She died in the traces of old age."

Ramey clucked at the horse before she climbed up. "I figured a lecture was attached to this sleigh ride. I can handle it. Uncle Tom. Roughy-tough on the outside, sweet and tender on the inside."

He clucked and flicked the reins. The mare plunged forth, humped a bit as the sleigh gained on her, then for a time fought the reins as she kept leaving the trot for a lope, and they were careening down the road as Bird sawed at one rein or the other. He had been looking forward to putting a horse in a sleigh, which he had never done, and he knew he had been careless in his haste, but it was a careful thing now to slap the reins and hurrah to consume the horsefire. And so it was: the horse made galloping spurts and then quit thinking and went a dog-trot, and the sleigh schussed over the snow and the bells jingled and the horse blew strong and even. The top layer of snow was so light it rose up like dust from the hooves and runners, eddied around to sparkle their faces with a pleasing frostiness.

Ramey relaxed her grip on the seat and asked, "Where'd you get this killer?"

"His daddy was a sawhorse—his momma a nightmare."

As they passed a big wind-contoured drift of snow, Ramey pointed to a small white thing with black points crouched upon the snow ledge.

"Weasel," Bird said. "In the winter it's white and it's spelled E-R-M-I-N-E. I've never known how to pronounce it. I've never heard anyone say it before."

The sun shot an astonishing shaft onto an oval of creek bottom, and the brush and trees were bright and colorful like Oz in the old movie. Within a minute thin low clouds shuttered the rays and then swallowed up the glow.

"Wow, that was something." Ramey brushed back her hood and scarf and let the ringing bits of ice melt on her skin. She had a long, thin face, and a voice that purred. "When I was a little girl, I loved running into your arms. I never saw you without running. Do you still love me, Uncle Tom?"

"You know I do. It's those things I hear about you I don't like."

She thought a long time. "Most of them are true, I'd warrant." She was not conniving now. "Tom, money has never had a freer ride than today. I remember learning that to attract capital the return must be three percent above inflation. Tom, twenty percent is a piker's return. Tom, you can service that debt with your sweat and good grass and good operating, or you can use the loan to be a capitalist. There is eight million here, if done right, that could be doubled in three years."

"The grass will keep us flush," Bird said.

"Maybe this season, maybe the next, hell, maybe five—until the certain day that beef bottoms and fall-shipping doesn't meet the interest, and Mr. Packard or Mr. Turner or Mr. Simplot sees a doggone good ranch with a good lease and your pockets are inside-out and your bankers aren't friendly anymore. Since it's a down cycle, the working ranches can't deal, and so you sell out or flip out or peter out, depending on your style."

Bird hummed whoa and tapped back on the reins. Halting, the horse tried to look back through the blinkers and then shook and blew. Tom Bird cradled Ramey's chin so he could look her in the eyes. She had bottle-green eyes and a face almost gaunt that was long and pretty like the old miniature oval portraits. "It is not your ranch. What do you care?"

"Our senator is a faggot and I love him—I loved him, you understand, more than life...in some terrible way that you might love a tree. And when the rumors began to drift west, he married a decent-looking clerk with five kids and got re-elected." She wiped tears with the back of her hand. "I had nowhere to go, Uncle Tom." She had pale skin that was blotchy now like a ripening peach. "And how do you love a faggot senator? With buckets of PAC money. That's how you love a faggot senator. I came back here to create a PAC of anything so I can have access to this tree I love more than life."

Tom Bird was holding the reins and saw that the mare's ribs were no longer bellowing. "Is it possible I understand you?" He wakened the horse with the reins. "I'm going to take you to see a young couple with a young boy who are partners in this mortgage you'd like to bet."

"If they're happy, it will only make me envious. But I like the sleigh."

They came around a curve onto a bunch of yearling steers against the drift fence, who with the suddenness of trout fry put up their tails and fled.

Bird said, "With your experience, you could be captain of pert near any PAC you want. And Sis could fix it for sure."

"Tom, PACs are too constrained by law. I don't want to support a candidate; I want to get out the vote. That money has different rules. Getting out the vote is Good Samaritan. Kind of like a non-profit hospital. Nothing makes more money than a non-profit hospital. A non-candidate fund can dispense money by the bushels with no constraint. I want one hundred thousand in my mitts and I'm going to take a shot at everything in front of my nose to get it before the May primary."

Tom slapped up a faster trot. "Do you see I why I don't trust you?"

"Of course I do. Do you see why I love a mealy-mouthed closet boy with five instant kids? Everything's so explicable."

They veered onto the lane to house two, which had a steep pitch down to an old beam-and-plank bridge over Bruin Creek. The mare surged ahead of the spurting sleigh and clattered over the bridge.

140

"I've got a harness horse," Tom Bird said as they came to a stop in the yard.

"Tom," Ramey said, "please don't introduce me the way Mother would, a thermometer of successes. Just say I'm your niece. Okay?"

"Do you see where your pride and shame lie?"

"Oh, for godsake. Enjoy the day. No afternoon's sermon is going to make me change."

Bird swung down, tied the reins to the seat; he used baling twine to make a bowline around the mare's neck and lashed it to a drunken picket fence. Joan came out the front door and began snatching bedsheets from an old lariat stretched between lilac clumps. "Santa back already?" she called to them, gathering the sheets against her belly in a roll. She hoisted the roll on her shoulder, sniffed it for the good smell of air-dried linen, and put out a hand to Ramey. "I am Joan Abo and you are the picture of health." Joan took her load into the house and came back tugging her husband. He shut down a cellular phone and said, "I don't understand why I can't get advertising dough for bleaching the Nike swoosh on cows." He looked again at the mouthpiece, amazed. Tyree squirted through the group and grabbed Bird's coat cuff.

That was a day of feast. A casual call had gone out and food poured in. People who had planned other things quit those things and dropped by. Bobby Coles brought the underworld and Sally brought the upperworld and word-of-mouth brought the netherworld.

As the crowd grew, people began to push against anonymity. "It's Valentine's Day!" shrieked a woman who then began to plant kisses on the men waiting in the food line. Tom Bird was in that line. He motioned Jason Abo outside. Leaning against a corral, they forked up slabs of ham from paper plates and decided to put the first-time calvers in the Two Trees pasture. Twilight gloamed as they headed back to the house. Bobby Coles was in the backyard slinging a bullwhip at a yellow pine, spraying needles. Three women, feeling amorous, were working toward him, dodging the lash.

"I have always been the pursuer," Abo reflected, watching the theater in the yard, "never the pursued."

Bird went off to unharness the sleigh horse. People were milling on the front yard. He thought he heard "interface" but when he saw the young man pump his fist and do an NFL sack dance he knew it was *In her face!* and knew also that the young man, still sorting out a pecking order in a young marriage, would track his wife to the bullwhip in the backyard before long.

Bobby Coles was sweating. He had started with the whip to combat a drowsy drunkenness. It became performance. Astute enough to recognize that accuracy was less important to the women than power, he worked into lather and exhaustion. He leaned against his pickup. His good German shorthair bitch was curled in a corner of the bed. He prolonged his spot as maestro by calling out the dog and running her through commands. His rapt audience grew discerning and he told the dog to "run out" and find lost women and children. Then he sauntered in for some chow.

Inside the house a consortium of bankers and lawyers professed not to divulge deep secrets about the Double Diamond but divulged enough as bait and became jointly possessed of a dreary inside prognosis. Eleanor's entrance was tragic, according to their lights. She was in Levis, windbreaker, knitted scarf. She poured herself a glass of champagne and roved through the wheels, reminding them that to owe a bank fifty thousand is servitude, to owe a million is to be master. She exuded dignity. Their sympathy became fright. Business had necessitated this social call, and now business tweaked them to be wary.

Tom Bird came in and sidled next to Eleanor and said, "I think the best bet is to drink ahead of this crowd. I'll watch you if you'll watch me."

Eleanor hooked his arm and led him to the flock of bottles. She poured him whiskey over ice. "You'll watch me regardless," she said.

A mill-worker with a thick bandaged hand, notorious locally for his nine DUI citations, popped in from the yard and shouted out: "Bobby, can I use your gun on a coyote?" He was running out of fingers but was a third-generation sawyer and a wonder with wood for an otherwise idiot.

Bobby Coles said, "Magazine's loaded." He stood at the finish line of the potluck table, loading up scalloped potatoes and sizing up the three crazy women from the yard.

Joan Abo came up beside him and said, "Those are theater people. That outside was theater. They'll try on a role, then shortly leave here to make intrigue, and they will not even remember who flailed that whip."

"What do you mean, theater people?"

"If you aren't of them, you're scenery. Or theme, like you tonight. Motif, maybe. I think you should avoid my theater friends, but do go see their performance of Wilde."

"Those hot women? they've been play-acting?"

"Don't kill the messenger, Bobby."

Tom Bird stopped by to clink a glass. He pointed to Eleanor by the stone fire place. He didn't say anything. He just pointed.

Drinking this early made him sleepy. He headed for a straw bed in the barn. As he walked through the men on the lawn, the report of a rifle rent the gabble. The thunder-stick fired again. Bobby Coles, inside the house, wondered why his dog wasn't raising a ruckus. Then he darted from the house onto the lawn.

It was phenomenal that his dog held the point while skylighted and while fired upon by men taking the silhouette to be a coyote serenading the moon. "Don't shoot!" Bobby hollered. "You fucking idjits!"

In the barn Tom Bird was wakened by a voice. He was wedged as neat as a mitre cut between fallen straw bales. The voice said, "Tom Bird, I seek you out." It was spoken in a broken foreign voice. She stepped into the light, a black-scarfed stranger. She moved toward him.

Bird rolled to his feet and shook her hand. "I think you ought to vamoose," he said.

He went to water the sleigh horse. The mare nickered to the bucket, like to a friend. The woman in the black scarf slipped up and climbed into the sleigh.

Tom Bird looked up at the Big Dipper dialed around past midnight. He recognized the woman. She was one of the theater persons, the tall milk-white mute one. She was stuck to the seat, posturing.

Bird said, "Can your boyfriend drive a horse?"

"Here he comes," said the woman. "Ask him."

The boyfriend was big and angry and looking uncivilized. He slapped the sleigh and asked the woman where the hell she'd been and scowled at Bird.

"If she's been missing a while," Bird said, edging away from the likely lead, "chase down some other varmint. I saw her about three minutes ago."

"All it takes."

Bird saw that his deference had inspired the fellow to push.

"Taking her home," the man said.

He motioned the woman down, and she obeyed. The trouble, for Bird, was she exited on his side of the sleigh, and he was standing between the happy couple. The boyfriend squared up and rubbed his hands on his belly. He was coming.

Bird backed another step and said, "She was trespassing on my sleigh." He felt that another step would precipitate it. The pale woman was hanging behind his back, peeking over his shoulder, not helping this detente.

Jason Abo hustled up. "It's Mr. Kick-Your-Ass," said Abo. He grabbed the boyfriend and made a light head butt. "How are you, Al?" Jason had seen trouble from across the yard. He now shook Al's hand and turned him so Tom and the woman could slip away. He asked the man if the Celtics had a chance.

Jason Abo saw a white flash of wood, heard the thunk of wood on skull, and momentarily held Al collapsed in his arms before the man spun and wilted away. Tom Bird stepped up and cracked his head again. Al flung to his elbows and knees. Tom raised the stick over the man's head, then swung it onto his buttocks. The stick broke and the free end flew off and hit the woman in the knee. Bird dropped his end on the man's back. Blood was dripping steadily on the snow below the man's head.

"Don't you come at me," Bird said.

A crowd gathered to watch the snow turn red. Bird drove off in the sleigh. Jason Abo wrapped gauze around Al's head and said, "I'd take that advice." He secured the band with tape and tossed the roll of gauze to Bobby Coles, who was determined to find a bullet nick on his dog. Abo washed the blood from his hands in a trough and whooped. This party was earning annotation.

The woman who had come to the haystack was a Polish refugee. Her caseworker had placed her with Lindy's Hair Chop. Lindy witnessed the first snip and hustled the woman into the alley. "What the fuck, Marie? You've never been a barber."

The woman quailed. She dissembled. She had inherited an obeisance to officialdom. Jabbering was an escape route from the gas chamber. She'd never been nothing. So she could be anything.

And so a boy on a rail crew, a gandy-dancer, saw her cowering on the street and bought her. In three days she was a successful whore. She felt sly but dirty. Mary Magdelene surely had not entertained a cowboy who mounted from behind and said, "Let's try her," then tried to hang on for ten seconds. The cowboy paid multiple entry fees in a night, and bucking kept her strong, but customer whims scared her, and she deduced she was not as strong as Mary Magdalene and would have to find something new.

She had thought to recover some respectability by hooking up with Al-Kick-Your-Ass. That proved demeaning. After the Abo party, she took to bunking with Bobby Coles in his trailer. Her third night there she told him she was a barber and cut his hair; the next day his hair bristled like straw, giving millworkers occasion to comment, which meantime brought up what was known about Marie.

"I never seem to have a dime," he told her that evening, "so I don't begrudge you working. But I think I'm man enough to keep you occupied."

She cried and wailed and dissembled. Bobby comforted her and himself and later went to work replacing brushes in a used D-10 generator he'd swiped from the mill. Marie said she was an electrician before she was a whore and a barber. Bobby reached out a greasy hand, and Marie flinched. He studied her. "There's a left-handed screwdriver in my jockey box, if you care to fetch it."

She went to fetch it.

Bobby muttered the refrain of diplomats and pundits, "Never trust a communist," and put in the scavenged brushes and then wondered where in the tarnation he might sell this heavy piece of metal he'd picked up as discarded junk and was now worth a thousand dollars.

"I will get a clean job," Marie told him that night. Her face was blotchy from crying. "I will work at your mill."

"You used to be a logger, did you?" Bobby was gnawing on a slice of cold pizza. "Paul Bunyan's sidekick?"

She reminded him the Pope was Polish, and that she thought the way he did.

"I really doubt it," Bobby said.

With the coming of the spring, the woods crews looked to their tools and their trucks. A single reef of logs remained at the mill, and the crews expected an early push to feed the mill, though some wondered at the company's passivity in the Forest Service timber sales. No timber people felt rosy about the next few years; though everyone had scapegoats, the simple truth was that trees grew slowly in the northern latitudes, and a century of logging had gleaned the easy pickings. But there was work for some yet. The union's wage dispute was in its fifteenth month, and the workers were resigned to givebacks on health insurance and pensions, but were consoled by the company's move to a two percent hourly bump. That, at least, gave them tough talk with which to abide their whipping.

In truth, for Bannock, the whipping was yet to come. The company was building a mill on the west coast of Mexico and was planning to outfit it with the machinery from the Bannock mill. Flow charts in company computers showed how the local timber was to be trucked to other mills. The deal was done, if not yet public.

Into this gutshot mill stepped the Polish refugee Marie Chayevsky, prospecting for a job. She demonstrated to the plant manager her skill at imitating a rooster's dawn crowing. It was a loud shrill rendition, and she was hired and given her uniform.

Dressed as a chicken, Marie stood on the office balcony after the morning-shift whistle and jotted down descriptions of latecomers. She made her first hit on the kiln line; she grabbed the tardy man's elbow and crowed in his face. The men on the line laughed. Twelve men were serenaded that first day. The next day, only four. A memo of congratulations was posted, and of course the next day fifty-two people were late, and Marie crowed into the noon break.

The next day she was hoarse and could only walk around like a big bird and wave at the late men.

"If it was just that," said Owen Fink, lead man on the green chain, who pushed his guys plenty hard and always had, "it might not slow work down so much."

Marie regained her voice. The men no longer laughed.

On payday Bobby Coles told her, "There's a morning ritual to work. You're fucking that up." She was beaming as she studied her paycheck. "Getting people out of bed is a new twist for you." He could see this wasn't going well. "You have to quit."

"It's the best job I do good," said Marie. "All the rest I was bad."

"Marie, you're a big chicken doing stupid animal calls and pissing people off."

"I am a singer," said Marie.

Irreconcilable differences, a pure case. She said she would move out, and she moved from Bobby's bed to the couch. This went on to the next payday. "All the way out or back to the bed," Bobby said. She made a bed out on the porch. Bobby figured she'd lost her ambition, and by next payday she was just a roommate and he was fixing porch screen.

That was the paycheck accompanied by a note explaining that health insurance had gone up $120—hence the reduced net pay. Also, in the absence of a labor agreement, the company had subscribed to a new carrier, an HMO with a Bannock affiliation. The note went on to say the HMO had agreed to insure some pre-existing conditions, for extra cost, providing the insured climb to the office at the summit of Mt. McKinley to sign up.

The next morning Owen Fink walked into the mill, a pepperoni stick in his mouth. He was late. He told his men for god's sake not to get hurt, since only healthy people were insured. Then he saw the rooster come his way.

"If that fucking bird crows in my face," he said, "I'll gut it with a peavey pole and hang it to roast in the kiln."

Bobby Coles heard this and came down the catwalk at a gallop. He grabbed his crowing roommate and flung her back against a stack of pallets and pinned her there. Owen Fink said, "I'm not going to take any of this," and shut down the chain. The crew followed him out, making obscene gestures to the chicken. The mood in the mill was sour, news raced, and Bobby Coles was the last man to join in the wildcat strike, his chivalry rewarded when Marie said, "The Pope thinks this way," and doffed her chicken suit and went out to the cars to be with the men. Those who would have surely killed the chicken now hailed the woman.

Some strikers were in the Alforcas that afternoon. They were boisterous and talked tough. Al called state AFL-CIO boss Con Kearns and said they'd better go general or at least string a decent picket.

Con Kearns agreed and said, "Between you and me, I doubt we'll succeed at either, and I guarantee you'll see some big fucking payback. They're routing us, hoss. They were more clever than us. Somehow exporting capital and importing labor got grafted onto flag and marriage and work. We're whipped. I'll do my best for your town, but I know I can't lay the woods folks on the line. I wouldn't want to, if I could." Con Kearns took a breath. "Al, I've written my letter of resignation. I've got to let someone else try. It's always been a race between our logic and their money for the voters, and for a while we kept even. I'm done. I'll do what I can for your town. I might be able to keep the trucks out."

Al stretched the phone cord to pour a glass of coke. "Jesus, Con, I didn't think it possible to be more pessimistic than I."

"Oh, I'm cheering up already. What's another big loss when you have your virtue?"

"A reason to resign."

"Yes. It is. Five years ago the capital newspaper called every day for a reaction to some story. I haven't been called in six months, and none of my calls to them have got me so much as a quote. I don't have a journalist that can pipeline Gannet. And I can't say with a straight face that we've got a strike fund. And there are two politicians in the state who might give me a listen. And that whey-faced wimp from Virginia came from Jerry Falwell's band to head up the Right-to-Work-for-Less initiative, and it passed. And now he's a Republican voice. That stupid pompous shit whupped me."

"You won't look good resigning. Con, you were the best electrician our lab ever had."

"Requiem already. Thanks for calling. The local still hasn't."

Al hung up and thought about Con's pessimism. Whence it came, it had come honestly. For twenty-five thousand a year, he toiled longer days than a farmer for his people. That runty back-East shill who'd been sicced on Right-to-Work, that's who was killing Con; it blew his trust in the American idea when that lump of goat cheese escaped universal scorn.

Jason Abo happened in to the Alforcas and heard about the wildcat. He got on Al's phone and reached his broker, ordered stock in the company. He cradled the phone on his neck and asked Al, "You want some? Wall Street loves it when workers get their ass kicked."

Al gave the bum's rush to Abo, who went graciously while explaining to Al that he was an Old Testament man rather than a New.

Later Al got a phone call from Con Kearns. "That mill's history," said Con. "It's closing, the machinery going to Mexico. It's incredible. They'll vamoose and the world will think we spoiled brats got too greedy and chased them away and, ha ha, end up with nothing. Oh, it's a civic lesson. Ha ha."

The Knutsen mill in Bannock was one of hundreds of craphouse sawmills in the mountain West before the big money exhausted the easy ore and turned to trees. Corporations had short lives, but the heir company was always bigger. The small mills were torn down, or left to rust and rot and to eventual fire. Nearly every mountain town now has a Mill Street, but no mill.

Knutsen was lucky: his river location was good enough so that he was bought out rather than squeezed out. He lived a contented old age while the mill provided the town with good wages and steady earnings for shareholders.

Then one day the profits were a low rate of return on that big chunk of capital. The mill was a malingerer. It was as weak as the U.S. Savings Bonds that Knutsen had bought with the first pension contributions.

Workers were laid off, and the return fattened. But not enough. Each new labor contract had brought union givebacks (in overtime rules, in pension payouts, in petty procedural insults). And now the mill was to achieve capital success by ceasing to be, and as a side note the Bannock local was to be busted.

Who made this decision?

Owners, surely. Yet the majority of shares were owned by people who didn't know their funds were invested in the lumber giant. A chunk was held by United Auto Workers.

Okay then, the Board of Directors. These were twelve white men paid thirty thousand dollars to gather for a quarterly luncheon and try to have a harmonious and harmless viewpoint, because that ass at your salad elbow might someday be sitting on your own board.

Management, doing their job, God bless 'em, maximizing return and getting themselves a poke and riding hard as patriots behind a popular president, over trade unions and into a dawn of freedom.

Madison Avenue, making us all agree to it.

This is what Jason Abo tried to convey to Bobby Coles one boozy wretched amphetamine-jangled morning, parked along a cyclone fence with ten sacks of sugar in the trunk, the immediate question being whether to cut through the fence and dose the fuel tanks of the mill machinery.

"That's what the people want!" Abo snapped. "They want to be confirmed. They want you to go to jail. They want me to go to jail. They want sugar in tanks and speed in anarchists and fat duck in themselves."

"I'm happy to oblige."

Abo got out and opened the trunk. "Time for me to mosey on, Bobby."

They stacked the sugar against the fence. Abo leaned against the car while Bobby worked the boltcutters. "Maybe I can still get ahead of the curve," Abo mused. "I can revive the Pinkertons and contract for Indochinese scabs." After Bobby wiggled inside, Jason passed the sugar through the slit. "This might be a bad idea, but it don't matter cause it's just an idea: why don't you take that sugar to your grandmother for canning jelly."

"She's dead."

"Then that is not an option. Is felony the only option to possession of ten sacks of sugar? It must be."

Abo drove around town for a while to check for alarm and then went home to once again astound his wife with tales of where he'd been. She made a face of anger, but Jason didn't like to duel. And Joan hadn't found scolding very effective. Either he or she was a novice at love.

They were pulling calves. Tom Bird rode a midnight to noon circuit bracketing the calving hour. Bobby Coles and some mill hands split the evening ride. Jason Abo at first helped when he felt like it, then saw how it was and thereafter swung into saddle at first blush of dawn.

One morning Abo saw a new foal lying in the snow in the pasture of horses not being used in circuit riding. The herd was grazing a furlong off from the foal. The newborn stood, looking healthy, as Abo rode by. He saw a cow lying flat and swollen in the calving pasture, and loped over.

This one looked bad. Tom Bird had given him cigars, so that he might light up after deciding to help and not undertake a thing until the cigar was gone. Abo took only a few puffs, then knelt by the cow and leaned onto her sweaty hams while he reached inside her and found the calf's head. He maneuvered the head up but still there was a thing pushed tight against the uterus. He pushed and guided and found another head.

With both hands inserted, he pushed back the second head and brought out the nose and forefeet of the first baby; the head emerged further, to the eyes, and writhed while Abo cleaned its nostrils. He looped a cotton rope around feet and head, and waited for an effort from the cow. When it came, he tugged gently— then he dug in his heels and heaved. That one slipped out alive. The dead twin had to be pulled out by his horse.

Abo was wiping dry the calf, waiting on the cow's fate, when Bird rode up. "She ain't decided yet, has she?" Bird stood down and looked beneath the cow's tail and then into her eyes. "She can live, if she wants to." He straddled the calf and lifted it in the sling of his hands and lurched with the calf between his legs to the head of the cow.

"Damn," said Abo, "that cow is just not very pleased with life. Postpartum blues on a thousand pound scale." He tied his ropes and sack onto the saddle and told Tom Bird about the lone foal and the general need for parental ethics in these pastures. He was flattening a latigo knot when he heard Bird galloping away.

Bird made several sweeps through the remuda of geldings until he found the impostor. He lapped a rope on her and led her toward the foal, now lying in the mud and snow like a snake. Abo helped lift the foal and guide him to the udder. The mare kicked. She kicked again and again, initially with annoyance and then with a deliberate searching reach. The men scotch-hobbled her and eared her to distraction and put the baby on a nipple. Still the mare fought.

"Let's take them up to the house," Tom Bird said. "We'll have to do this every three hours until they bond." Cradling the foal, he flung it over the saddle and sprang up behind, then snugged the mare to his saddlehorn as Abo released the hobble. "You been talking bad mamas," Bird said, "and I'll fess up that I ain't never seen a mare toss away a baby like this."

They put mare and foal together in a small corral, and still the mare kicked, whinnying to the distant herd. They scotch-hobbled the mare onto three legs again and put the colt onto the teat.

"Do that every four hours," Bird said as he mounted to finish the circuit. "They'll click soon, I'm thinking."

Jason Abo said, "Tom, all we have is trouble, it seems."

Bird pointed off to the snowy knoll where the brindle cow was walking alongside the live twin toward the water trough.

That was the day Ramey Honstead gave two speeches. The first was to striking mill workers gathered in a Lutheran church basement for an informational meeting. She was introduced as a political pro, a privy hometown prodigal, and she told the workers, "You dumb fucks. I know how you voted. you hate the IRS and worship the president who cost you the sales tax deduction, interest deduction, subline employee expense, casualty deduction, and who blessed you with increase in our FICA flat tax, decrease in capital tax, who sanctioned bond and banking thefts, and saddled all your children with debt. He's sure a good American, and you're such dumb fucks."

The woodworkers weren't really reacting yet, and so Ramey jabbed elsewhere. "I saw Right-to-Life bumper stickers in the lot. Whose wife has had a miscarriage? Say, in the car, blood on the floorboards, your wife is passed out and her skin blue, and you're tapping her chin and jabbering as you race for the hospital...now, when exactly are you concerned about that aborted fetus? Except in your fantasy months later, when did that mess matter at all?" Ramey was back on the Hill, pontificating. "And did you have a funeral service, a casket, a body?" She had said all this to the faggot, who had agreed that God likely did not put souls on to cells with an eyedropper, but who nonetheless fought the good Christian fight to save souls in another's womb. "You dumb fucks."

Some workers spewed bilious words, some felt bile in their gut. Ramey slapped her hands on the table, "The Company is doing the right thing. You're in the way."

She left the basement, trailed by a union rep who wanted to debate. He called for a take on environmentalists closing mills. "In Coos Bay," she said from her car, "I saw ships of logs going across the ocean, and why again did you say the mills are closing? Christ, I'm one of the architects of splitting the left."

The second speech she delivered at the meeting of the Double Diamond owners. Twenty thousand dollars she had, she told them, and she would give it to the Double Diamond if the ranch would then capitalize her new company for twenty grand, and for lending its name would receive a quarter of the profits. "I know people who, if were led to believe I had two shiny dimes, would credit me. As a subsidiary of Double Diamond—and as a name it doesn't hurt a bit, better than the Lazy 4 or Crooked Y—I'd have the bluster to make two plus two equal five. Derivatives are futures you can play both ways. Beef and yen and feed and dollars are linked, and all I need is a phone and a calculator to get a profit when there is fluctuation in a currency against a commodity."

Jason Abo said, "I believe the next sentence will contain the phrase minimal risk." He was slinging together snacks of canned baby clams, raisin bread, nachos.

"No risk, actually. Strike one and I'm out."

Jason Abo went to the well house to get salsa for the nachos, thinking he was moribund. Ramey knew more than him. She would get to play with the liquidity, not him. He selected Joan's hot jar, marked with a red X on the lid, and came inside to hear Ramey say, "I'll pay for Tom's choice of lawyers—he hates every word I'm saying—so you won't be out a dime if you get the chance to say the bitch fucked up, which might be worth a bunch."

Bob Honstead ladled a dollop of salsa on a corn chip and scooted around the kitchen like a wind-up toy before able to bellow, "Goddamn it, Ramey, don't call yourself a bitch."

"Dad, join the crowd. I really don't mind. It's like having a good pair of shoes. I can always put on the bitch."

"Sally," Bob pleaded.

"She became that way when you punched that hoodlum boyfriend in the nose," Sally said, abdicating.

"Oh, Mother, I'd have run off the next time you bought the wrong kind of cocoa." Ramey had always been plagued by intimate lapses just when everyone wanted to pay phony homage to reason. She cleared her throat: "There's no regulation. It's OTC."

Silence tended. Tom Bird said, "Let's think about this."

"Fast, Uncle Tom. Forty-eight hours."

"Overnight is good enough," Bird said. "Meet at noon at my place?"

Joan Abo entered the house with a box of Sippy's chicken and Sippy's hardest cider. Sippy barbecued from the back of his truck in the post office parking lot on days he felt like it, and to run across him was a nice bit of luck. The cider was chancier, but Sippy wouldn't sell his ribs or chicken without a purchase of cider. Joan's husband helped lay out the table and told her, "Wary greedhead nods, is what you see." He told her the rest while the guests dived for the chicken.

Joan waited until their plates were full and said, "Imagine a government that proposes to tax income from capital at a lower rate than income from wages. Just imagine." She filled glasses from the cider jug. "In Turkey or the Congo a thousand years ago such a thing would be a callous dare to revolt."

Ramey waved a drumstick. "Oh, I've got absolute confidence in our police and national guard. They have job oaths and subscribe to the fallacy of the ladder of success—always room for more at the top! It's a pyramid, baby, and the riffraff begins at the level you just left."

Eleanor Goodnight said, "Stop it." She stood up and brushed off Sippy's leached barley crumbs. "Just stop it. Please excuse me. But I don't want to hear the philosophies and the snide bragging. The ranch needs money. That's enough. Tomorrow at Tom's place, for lunch."

Bird saw Eleanor to her car. On an alkali knoll in the bull pasture a male sage chicken strutted and stamped and puffed up glorious to an audience of drab hens. They watched the ritual.

"Eleanor, I want to court you. And because I don't know how, I want to do it the way I once did know. Who can I ask?"

"Tom, would you run get me a glass of cider. I want to think."

While Eleanor thought, Tom Bird wished: he wished he could retract three sentences. But if wishes were horses, bears would ride. He returned with the cider.

Eleanor drank the cider in her car and passed out the empty glass. "Hap Means. That's who to ask."

"Well, that's who I'll ask then."

Three sentences, and Bird had to follow through. That scamp Hap Means guffawed on the phone. "Isn't she a trophy? Breeding like those Northern Dancer whelps you finagled me out of. You might bust me here too, hoss, but permission to go a-courtin' is granted. I don't figure to lose twice."

"I paid the dollar you asked."

"Oh, it takes a while to know whether you won or lost. I could have proved that stud a number of ways. I thought I had something mighty fine for our homegrown stock—and I undervalued him, because of my own pessimistic heart. I offer Eleanor the world—because why not? I want to make her mine, you want to make her mind. Do your best, hoss."

Bird hired a hard-luck jock named Baumgarten. He had the jockey ride the cows one evening while he went to Eleanor's hotel room. He asked if she would like to play cards. She said she played hearts, pinochle, bridge, poker, and canasta, and he said he would like very much to play any of those. She said she also liked solitaire.

Bob Honstead was distraught about the mill closing. Workers bought cars. It was distressing to deal with the town wage folk and compute for them the impossibility of making payments. He wanted everyone to have cars. He liked cars. Everyone liked cars.

"Then there's these belly-flopping cattle prices," he told Sally the night their daughter climbed onto an electronic aerie, scrutinizing prey. "Tony Croft showed me indisputably how the cattle market is a seven-year cycle. We're troughing."

"Tony Graft was never successful at anything besides getting elected."

"Quit calling him that. It's getting around town and making Tony reluctant to do favors."

"He's a Senator and we're dirty reminders. Favors will come hard."

They ate a quick salad dinner and Bob went to submerge in the hot tub. His pull with Graft—er, Croft—was diminishing, and his own ambition was straining toward purity. His thoughts were of cars. He wanted to recapture that purity. It was the sweetest thing in his life.

North Koreans had brokered the love affair. Bob Honstead was a corporal driver in the motor pool during the war. One time he drove north with a colonel and a lieutenant and a bad map. Retreating Chinese stumbled upon them. Corporal Bob Honstead drove off the mountain road and bucked down a ravine and crossed a stream while the Chinese cantilevered an automatic rifle against a tree and sprayed fire. The Jeep rang like church bells and the aide was asking the corpse at his side if he was all right *sir* while Bob fell in love with his vehicle. He was a goat, an odd goat, sprinting and crawling, and leaping and crawling, as the colonel's blood sloshed on the floorboards. Bob told the lieutenant, "I'd feel better if you fired that .45 so we can say this was a running fight rather than just a running." He said this as rimrock forced the Jeep back into the stream and under the Chinese rifles. The Jeep floated, chewed, bit, then hauled up the cut bank into an aspen grove, out of sight from the retreating column.

Bob jumped out to check damage. The bullet holes, except for the one in the colonel's throat, were cosmetic. The lieutenant, from Brooklyn and West Point, was very brave and went to reconnoiter, and didn't return. Bob sat vigil over his Jeep with a pocketknife. Then, for eighteen hours, he toured Korea, eluding straggling Chinese while tormenting the transfer case and tie rods and tires of his goat-buggy. He threw his knife at one rifle squad apparently out of ammo. The knife came back and stuck through his right shoulder above his clavicle; eventually he reached an American forward aid station and learned armistice had been declared.

He mustered out with motor pool acumen and a blood brother's debt. He opened a garage in Bannock and was seduced into displaying a few Buicks out front. He was a most recalcitrant herder of a cash cow. The G.M. rep had come to Bannock in the engine of a log train a month later. Thereafter the carload came by the month, and monthly Bob Honstead asked, "What happens when everyone has a car?" But cars began to be parked next to the red mill-shanties and Bob finally saw there was no end to this.

Sally put him over the top; he went from having a good seat at the Rotary luncheon to having bank acquiescence and congressional pull. She turned his attention from pistons to franchise agreements. Her main point was this: "People will go a hundred miles to buy a car. They won't go that far to get one worked on. Shop hours are steady income. So quit treating every car that leaves Hondo Motors as guaranteed for life." And Bob evolved from a grease monkey to a millionaire.

And with this in mind he finished his proclamation to his wife: "I've often thought of running an Indy car. I like race cars a whole lot better than cows or racehorses. I grew up here and know what it means to be a big ranch owner. So I've done that. It isn't worth an ice cream sundae to me. If we make money, someone can buy us. If we lose, we bail: I won't feed the ranch, not a single year. You got me into grubstaking Tom and his horses, which was reasonable because Tom knows horseflesh, and somehow we got catapulted into a big ranch and thousands of beeves and a monster goddamn mortgage; and that too is reasonable, because your brother ran the place when it bankrolled Stewart's bad investments; and so I speak as a reasonable man when I say that if your brother can't make dollars out of cows, it can't be done; and I'll squander our wealth in something I love. By god."

Bob said this from his lair, the hot tub. Soon Sally carted out six gin-and-tonics, disrobed, and slipped into the tub. "Remember this incredible thing: Tom is the owner of the Double Diamond."

"That was a piece of luck, all right."

"And a piece of luck that I left the prairie, at my brother's bidding, and met you."

"Romantic."

"Yes, it is romantic."

Hearing the guests come through the front door, they slid apart. Ramey and a covey came onto the deck, gesticulating with bottles, blurting greetings.

"I'm glad you've found friends," Sally said to her daughter as the covey stepped out of their clothes. "Found exactly where?"

"Mother, your radar is right on," said Ramey. She pointed to a small man slow to join the soakers. Then she pointed to an artificial leg lying on a bench near him. She said to the one-legged man, "Dennis, take out your teeth." He did, a flourish in the night air. "Take out your eye." He shook his head, but picked up a twig and tapped on his glass eye. "Honey," Ramey said to the small man, "when you get to the part I want, toss it on the cot." Ramey at that moment began plotting how to be rid of the crowd she'd seined from town. "It was funny the first time I said it."

"Ah, doggone it, Ramey," said Bob Honstead as he climbed from the tub.

"I love you, Dad."

He headed inside. "Doggone it, Ramey."

Sally stroked her daughter's hair. The covey was splashing and drinking and prattling. "That a man who's not a man should gut you so," Sally said.

"Mother, I was unsatisfied from birth."

"That you were."

Dennis Baumgarten was forty years old—a jockey for twenty-four years—and had lost his leg in a starting gate, his teeth in a pile-up, and an eye to cancer. He embarrassed himself trying to ride with the mechanical leg, and spent the next year gaining pounds in beer joints. Bottom, it was, when he made another try back, in a Montana weekend meet, and was better than any of the jocks, except perhaps for an old competitor Lloyd Stevens, and won some races. But he knew. He could barely ride. He had rapport, but not a good seat. In a race his mounts were uncontrolled. Even a slow morning gallop might jump to trouble.

The Sunday morning in Montana before Lloyd Stevens was arrested for a hit-and-run homicide, Lloyd went around speaking to the jocks before the first race—astounding, for Lloyd hardly spoke except to yell on the track, *Here I come, mamma mia,* when he had chosen a hole and meant to have it. He showed one bug boy the grip he used for the gentle raking bat on stride. He told Baumgarten, "You cannot ride anymore. You know that. Here is the address of a man Tom Bird. He has jobs. He said that to me. And he has good horses."

"Trainer, or farm manager? Groom? Stall-mucker?"

"You can be anything with a horse except for a rider," said Stevens. "In a race I see you fighting to hang on and I wonder what to do. You will get the guys hurt."

Red and blue police lights bounced through the windows of the jockey room. Lloyd Stevens stripped off the silks and put on his street clothes. "I hoped for one more ride," he said. He stopped at the door and told the jockeys, "Get your horse relaxed and push the gas pedal slowly."

The hit-and-run had not been happenstance. Lloyd Stevens' brother had been bludgeoned to death, years before, on the Wind River reservation. Lloyd drove through the Wind River and saw a swaggering brave and stomped the gas pedal. "I was drunk and would have hit him anyway," Lloyd said. "Instead I counted coup."

Dennis Baumgarten thought of his thousand races against the Indian jockey and drove to see Tom Bird. Lloyd's voucher was enough for a job, but it was no insurance against being fired: "If you miss work," said Bird, "because of drink or car trouble or pneumonia or rust in your leg, you'll get your last pay."

Baumgarten was fearless on a horse and a fast learner about cows. Plus, Tom Bird pumped him for his last molecule of memory about racehorses. Baumgarten was one to keep. When drink started luring him, Tom Bird stole the coil wire from his car; when the ploy was exposed and countered, Bird made him check in his leg at dusk; that led to a four a.m. leg-delivery, and a discovery that Dennis Baumgarten, when held to his old jockey hours, was a hand to covet;

three a.m. to four p.m. he was a working fool, if plied with wine and a monster supper in the evening.

Baumgarten and the boy Tyree clicked right off. Baumgarten's only child had vanished because he couldn't maintain the adjudicated support; he had been a hot jock during the divorce proceedings and had his alimony and child support based on that freak lucrative year. Subsequent petitions to reduce support had mostly showcased him as a malingerer. His boy, wherever he was, was Tyree's age. Baumgarten showed Tyree how to balance and post and jump off ("Like teaching a man to pee on himself," was Tom Bird's verdict of this latter lesson). Tyree had gained size enough to control the reins, and he rode light as a breeze.

On a Saturday in April, Baumgarten and Tyree and Tom Bird were riding together when they found fence lines drifted over with snow, and mingled cattle. Baumgarten rode off to fetch Eleanor's dog Jiggs; Tyree galloped to get Worthless' mutt. Tom Bird put up the fence and waited for the dogs by shooting baskets at the Abo house.

Joan Abo drove home. In dress clothes she rebounded for him and said, "My man is a gem and as egocentric as the sun."

"He's genuine in his affections."

"I know that. And I know if he hurts me even a little bit, the shrew inside me will climb on him like ugly on an ape."

Bird had always seen their alliance as fragile. He said, "Don't keep score."

"You should have married."

"I may yet. I'm courting."

"I heard that on Indian telegraph. Sign that license, is my advice. Jason and I married like androids, but he's the man I want and deserve."

They shot baskets until the riders returned with the dogs. Joan saddled the sorrel filly that had thrown Tom and helped bunch up a pasture. They sicced the dogs on the cattle to make the the calves mother up. Heifers and barren cows they threw on the road. Baumgarten's job was to stand on the road and shy the cows into a corral. One stout cow stood obstinate. Baumgarten swatted its forehead and gave it a push on the neck and the cow stupidly swung its head. He gave it a disparaging slap across the eyes with his hat.

The swinging head was no longer stupid cow, but all bull. The bull made a short rush, and Baumgarten dodged. Then came a longer rush, Baumgarten stiff-arming against the massive skull. The next rush was faster, more deliberate, and so was the next; whether by accident or design, Baumgarten was being maneuvered against a barbed wire fence on the snowy road shoulder. The bull was as methodical as Joe Frazier or Roberto Duran slicing the ring. One step from the five strands of barbed wire, Baumgarten made his break. The bull rushed and got to his hip and he was down in the snow. He curled and covered. The bull didn't finish him, and he jumped to his feet and made the corral across the road while the bull rushed again. From that safe perch he kicked the bull's nose, and sang out merrily as the bull plunged into the railroad-tie corner post and staggered off with a lusty curling lip.

Tyree rode up to the jockey on the corral. He told of his witness. He kept telling as they finished the cut. Baumgarten, who had escaped the charge on his phony leg, was Tyree's friend.

7

Jason Abo was in a line of cars slowing at a traffic light when the passenger door of the red Toyota ahead of him flung open and a man fell out head-first, his feet flopping toward the curb. He rolled on the asphalt and came up glaring at the car. A woman was driving and a young boy stood on the back seat, staring back through the rear window. The man began to walk to the sidewalk, holding his eyes on the red car. He wore a tank top and his left shoulder was welling with blood. Suddenly he grabbed his arm at the elbow and ran serpentinely down a gravel alley. His dramatic exit had been spoiled by impetuous, excessive force in shouldering open the door.

Straddling the center line, Abo pulled alongside the Toyota at the light. He leaned over to see the woman: a freckled blonde, also in a tank top, much younger than the dramatic passenger, early twenties, somewhat sullied. Her window was open.

"Did you notice that a man fell out of your car?" he said.

The woman glanced at the vacant seat. The boy in the back still stared out the rear window.

"Why, I guess he must have. I plumb didn't notice." She shoved her face into a rigid commuter's stare.

"He might be hurt." Abo was unsure of his motive here. Voyeur. "He didn't look so hot."

The woman held a steady gaze on the traffic light and said, "Oh, I'm sure I'll hear all about it. In the meantime, go fuck yourself."

Oh, those hard trashy women with freckled chests. "Do you want lunch?" Abo said.

"Do I want lunch."

"That's right."

The light turned green. She looked at Jason Abo. "Hellfire," she said. "I'll follow you."

They ate at a franchise steak house on the edge of town. It had ubiquitous class: oak partitions with ferns and flowers, dim ceiling lamps...an eatery where the cook hardly mattered, where the Ohio headquarters determined the supper fare of thousands across the country with its bulk frozen purchases. The boy, who had polite manners, piled ketchup over everything and ate right through the lima beans to a slick plate. His mother's name was Connie, and she too had manners and was quiet and graceful in this muted place. Jason liked to hear her talk. Connie was plenty tough but not crude nor a conniver—an innocent! Jason and the tough freckled woman Connie stared at each other over coffee while the boy humped a video game next door in the mallette.

"Where can this go?" speculated Jason Abo. He lit a little cigar. Then he put the cigar in the ashtray, scooted close to Connie, and drew her close. "I sure enjoyed this lunch," he said, kissing her forehead. "So long."

Pulling away, she dropped her hand and made a discovery. "You don't want to go," she said.

Joan Abo, hearing some things and guessing the rest, flashed anger and accusation at her husband one night in the driveway of the headquarters house, beneath the gray sky of the spring equinox. Jason was a meek devoted husband, by his reckoning. He hadn't bedded that woman, he explained, she had this boy with her. Later he confessed to being a bit off plumb, sexually, and then volunteered to consult a psychologist, he had one in mind, a health club subscriber with a mop haircut and intense way and erect breasts.

"I'll bet Laura, the psychologist, can tell me whether I was noble or perverse," he said.

She left him sitting on the porch and brought back martinis; she was going to take this interrogation as far as she had to.

"Now, Jason," she said, "what did you like about this chippy?"

"A man was pissed off and tried to break her heart, but made a mess of himself exiting a moving car. A boy watched, stupefied. She told me to fuck off."

"That's it?"

"Our drama king really didn't know what to do when his bravado imploded," Jason added. "Good breeding would have come up with something better than running off wounded."

She picked up the glasses. "Misbehavior along those lines and I'm gone."

"That was in my mind quite a bit."

"You. The thoughtful cavalier. While you're defending womanhood, I'm doubting quaint notions like love and fidelity and honor."

He sidled between her arms and gently pushed down the glasses in her hands. "For crying out loud, I'm not noble enough to give you up. I'm craven enough to stalk you."

"Bad choice of words." She clasped his neck, struck again by the simplicity of this good but unreliable man. "Men have scared me."

"If I were to see your ex, I'd buy him a Cadillac. I'd be forlorn if it weren't for his bad way as a husband."

"Forlorn, Jason? You couldn't tell the difference between forlorn and a toothache."

"Sure I can. A toothache lasts longer." He waltzed her to the couch.

They nuzzled. Presently Joan sat erect and said, "I am trained to man-judgement. I won't accept second-rate love."

"You said all this before we married."

"We married because you wanted Vegas and some mumbled vows to change your luck. That's my thinking. What a fun convenient thing we got. Nobody frets about the other's approval, because we don't care!"

"I don't approve of your heavy thinking," Jason said, truly forlorn now, looking into his lap. He left the couch and drank off the remnants of the drinks. "Your philosophy must recognize that I'm not philosophical at all. I've got some physiological thing stuck in my throat because my notion to roll in your arms hasn't got pedigree."

"A chippy boots her trashy man from the car. It doesn't make sense, Jason. But don't give up."

"Give up? Me, never." He moved back to her embrace with stiffening ardor. She was soft, like a woman. "I'm just an unphilosophical accountant, and I have a credit for a roll in the hay."

The expression hooked him, and he sought verisimilitude by leading the soft somber lady to the barn for a shivering, prickly congress on a pallet of alfalfa—which made him laugh at the disparity between soft words and harsh sensation, an observation that lent him some small claim to being a philosopher at last, which led straightaway to more martinis and a conventional roll in house quilts. Was it philosopher or hedonist or love-struck moon-calf that bade him resolve to steer clear of chippies? He puzzled over that for five seconds and nestled against the soft breast of the somber woman just beginning to snore.

A phone tolls ominously at four a.m. Jason Abo was not much surprised to hear Bobby Coles asking to be bailed out of the city jail.

Buying twelve sacks of sugar in the grocery store was sure to stir gossip. In the mind of a young policeman, the first bewildered guess of moonshining gave way to the hypothesis of sabotage, and for the cost of a few gallons of drained fuel, he ingratiated himself to the mill.

"Bobby, I won't go it," Abo said. "You won't pay it back. Worthless can sell some pigs. The honor of making a hopeless loan should go to family."

"Jason," Bobby implored, "I'm plumb sober here. This ain't no drunk lockup, no see-you-in-the-morning deal."

"You'll get fed. It's cheap board. I'll check on you in a few days."

Abo hung up. Incarcerated, Bobby Coles was easy to babysit. He leafed through a *Forbes*, repulsed by the snide and laudatory airs given to greed, though he concurred it was a truer editorial slant than the masquerade of general good. He fell asleep with the magazine and awoke to knocking on the front door. He heard rain. He slipped on pants and let in Tom Bird and Dennis Baumgarten. Day was breaking gray and wet. "Cousin," said the ex-jock, "have you got some coffee?"

Tom Bird said, "The Supervisor of the Forest is coming here this morning. It won't be good news."

They were eating sausage and eggs when the supervisor came, wearing the brown uniform of a Forest Service minion, though he was supervisor. His name was Hyman Thorpe. He had a lumpy face with heavy folds of boxing-scarred eyelids that made his eyes downslanted slits. He accepted a plate of fried eggs and minded his plate until slicked. Then he spoke: "A big part of your allotment has been rated in fair condition. That rating makes us act. We're cutting you twenty percent. Of course, you want to know about other lessees: fifteen to thirty percent over this whole district. Plus York Creek and Starveout are degraded." He put a folded paper on the table. "This map lists nine springs on Big Hat Mountain that must be fenced off." He brought another folded paper from his shirt pocket and set it by the first. "Those are our specifications."

Tom Bird said, "I didn't know there were nine springs on Hat. You count funny." He looked into the hooded slit-eyes of the Forest Service. "This is the first time my landlord said I was doing fair."

"Those two creeks did it."

Bird unfolded the specifications paper and scanned it. "And what percentage will the government pay for these improvements to its land?"

"Discretionary. Likely not much." The Supervisor drank down his coffee. There was nothing more to talk about. He stood up to go. "The Double Diamond has been a good steward. The ratings might be bad science, but those streams are degraded. Give my best to Mrs. Goodnight."

Tom Bird wanted to thank him for coming but couldn't work up the spit. He looked at the map while his government, coalesced in a man, departed. It was a true map. Big Hat springs were seepage now, short bogs rather than long clear rivulets under brush. The country was steep, and the cattle didn't roam to feed, but stayed in the spring draws and cropped new growth and tramped out the brush. Bird put the papers in his hip pocket. My range is fair, by God, by science. I should have fenced those springs, without Hyman saying so.

"Stick a sandwich in your shirt," he said to Baumgarten and Abo. "We're going to ride to Big Hat and figure how to fence those springs."

Jason Abo shook his head. "Count me out." The very idea amused him.

Thirty minutes later, with a sandwich tucked against his belly inside his shirt, Jason Abo rode toward Big Hat, though he couldn't see it in the charcoal fog that was partly mist welling up from soaked snow, partly sodden-clouds settling down. The snow had a heavy crust which cut the pasterns of Abo's good horse Chief and of the nameless geldings ridden by Baumgarten and Bird. On the flank of Big Hat they rode under trees that dropped cold, startling bombs of water on men and horses.

Baumgarten, hunched against the cold water bombs, said, "Cousin, this is climate for frogs."

161

Abo replied, "Too wet for amphibians, I think."

Baumgarten, while adusting his hat, jostled overhanging spruce boughs and brought a creek down his neck. "I wish I was an environmentalist and could see the beauty of it."

They stopped in a ravine to clean the ice from hooves and to apply another coat of Vaseline to keep the slush from balling.

"The York springs are above us," Bird said, flagging a tree with orange tape. "Four of them, about two hundred yards apart. They're already piped for tanks. One-pole squares are good enough for them."

Jason Abo said, "Tom, I'm going to sic Ramey on that forest honcho, through her favorite senator."

"Okay," Bird said. "In the meantime we fence the springs."

"Will that bump us up from fair?"

"No. The scientists wouldn't give Eden a good rating. But Hyman shouldn't have had to tell me this thing."

They rode on through frosted brush, sopping their pantlegs. The fog thinned and had a yellow tinge, and for a time the square summit of Big Hat hove above, and then a black mass came swirling up a draw and enveloped them again.

"Maybe we won't break through this," yelled Baumgarten to Tom Bird, who was ahead crisscrossing a slope, looking for a cattle trail to give them a line up the scree slope into the Starveout drainage. "It's hard to find springs when you can't see the ground."

"That's a fact," agreed Bird, trying to place his lawn-sized world on a world-sized mountain.

They seemed to start up on a trail, but then they were on the shale rock hid beneath the snow. The horses grew tremulous, doubting each step, sliding splay-legged. Chief balked and fidgeted against the reins, wanting to retreat, a contagion the unnamed geldings caught to the marrow. Bird plow-reined his mount to a vertical cast and jabbed in his heels, and ascended in a stumbling, scrambling plunge up the slide of skittering shale, hurrahing with hat and heels so the pony would have no leisure for prudent thought. The other two horses followed, falling on their knees, slipping back on their hocks, driven by panic of being left behind, and all came out of the shale with red distended nostrils and foaming neck hide. And then, in a forty vertical-foot climb, the fog grew white, then yellow, then was gone from the blue sky; and the awesome midday sun flooded the mountain and the cloud-estuaries of the lower world. Every rock and branch and leaf was scoured bright, ringing with color. In the minute the men allowed themselves to stop and marvel, pants and horsehide were wafting steam.

They rode to an overlook of Starveout and ate their sandwiches while the horses grazed. Bird pointed out where the springs lay. "I'll get Bobby to get some quiet mill boys and they can do some timber thinning to make the fence poles."

"Bobby's in jail," Abo said. "Anyway, I'm sure you don't want Bobby for clandestine duty."

The jockey's horse, on a downhill grazing drift, raised his head and started traveling home. Baumgarten hotfooted to get below the horse and intercept him.

"Jason, you fence this," Bird said. "I should stay with the cows. Forty years of calving seasons must account for something. It's not a big job if we use government trees."

Abo looked for something on which to sketch the country pointed out by Bird, and found that something in a sheath of charge card slips in his wallet, a bloom of onionskin debt. He shaped them into a smooth wad and buttoned them in his shirt pocket, bulky as a pocket New Testament. He was dismayed by the prolifigacy, the lack of accounting. He decided he couldn't afford to be a buckaroo. "That jock can run the crew," he said.

"I don't think so."

"What the hell *can* he do? Give him the power of writing paychecks and he can sit up here and make wreaths while employees build fence."

"No." Tom Bird could feel Jason waiting for him to explain. The jockey was climbing the hill, awkwardly, sidestepping like a man on skis as he led the horse to a rock where he could mount. "It won't work," he said.

Quiet voices travel far in mountain air, and the jockey, leading his mount, approached and said, "Mr. Bird, way up here I can't run off. I can drink myself into the blankets without anybody minding."

Abo looked at Bird, who was observing decorum by observing the lower cloud-sea. The confession bothered Abo not a whit, and he asked practically, "Tom, can the boozer get through the day?"

Bird turned his gaze to the jockey. "Listen. Ride to the lots and take my pickup to the union local. Get six men who'll work with a chainsaw and sledge. Pick up sixty pounds of ten-inch spikes and plenty groceries. Tell the men to bring a bedroll and outfit for three days. I'll have a pack string ready with camp and tools." Bird waited for the man's nod of comprehension, then added, "Leave your saddle bags."

Baumgarten unbuckled the left bag and slid out the bottle and tossed it to Jason Abo. He said, "I was a goddamned good rider, and was treated with respect by everyone, every day. I had my backside out to the world then, but so long as I was booting home winners no one kicked it. Tell me: do you look up twenty times a day and see buzzards?"

Baumgarten rode off into the fog. Abo unscrewed the bottlecap and drank. "With me," he mumbled, "not more than ten times a day, I'd guess."

The jockey's going-home horse stopped frequently to bugle loud rib-shaking whinnies to the two horses left behind, a measure of time and distance in the fog-bound world, while the men took big drinks to burn their gullets.

163

"Tom, why don't we hire a real foreman? We get these itinerants and cripples and coke fiends. It's good business sense to have someone between the owners and the peons."

"There's only one cow boss, even when he's biting his lip and taking orders." Bird stood up and caught his horse. "I've always been the man who took care of Eleanor's cows."

"So it's true—" Abo swung the bottle up—"what I've heard."

Bird paused with a foot in the stirrup, then swung on and cracked the long reins on the horse's rump. The horse crow-hopped, plunging uphill. Abo intercepted Chief and tied the bottle to the strings. "Very true," he said to himself. His partner was flashing through the brush like a deer. Chief picked his way up the brim in the tracks of the fishing cowboy, who was far above in the shadow of the Big Hat crown, tasting bile and spewing venom on an unnamed gelding.

Much later, Abo approached. He had never seen anxiety in the man, and anxiety was conducted right into the horse, which was side-stepping, tossing the bit.

Bird said, "Do you think my pride is so little I could waller around a woman like a buzzard?" He shook tobacco onto a rolling paper and made a bad roll and abruptly tossed the cigarette. "My god, the shame of it." Before Abo could speak, Bird yelled, "Follow!" and pushed the gelding into a traveling lope over rough terrain along the crest of Hat and finally into a brutal gallop and a sliding descent down the west face.

Abo came to this face much later and saw no sign of Bird in the long brushy draw. He followed the tracks in the snow, Chief picking his way where the other had made long sliding ski tracks. Then far down the draw he saw Bird waving his hat and riding in a fast tight circle of discovery in the brush and big spruces that carpeted the north slope. When Chief started through this thicket, Jason brought his slicker around his face and lowered himself on the horse's neck and thus torpedoed through the rattling brush. Presently Chief stopped and Abo emerged from the slicker. Bird was afoot, leading the gelding who was weaving and hadn't the strength to keep its head off the ground.

"Do you see that burlap in the spruce above you?" asked Bird. "Those are your sister's bones. I didn't love her. She was my good friend." While saying this, he stopped walking, and the horse slumped down on knees and hocks, its brisket as a keel. "I wasn't clinging to Eleanor; I had to stand up to that part of it: I was cow boss of the Double Diamond. You ride for the brand."

"Tom, did you kill that horse?" The gelding's neck was now outstretched.

"He's quit. But he'll rise, I think, to follow you out."

Then Abo looked up and saw the burlap bundle lashed in hemp, dangling from a limb twenty feet from the ground. He urged Chief forward, to see better.

Abo stared at the bundle aloft and said, "You've filled her in about her boy, I bet."

"It comes up."

"Tom, why don't you trash the notion of redealing the past and ante up for the future. It wouldn't be the same as the past, but it might come off passing fair."

"What are you thinking? Didn't I tell you Katie was my friend? You're her brother. You've got what she should have. And her son is a part of it. You can't run after women here in Bannock. You have to cowboy up. That's what these bones want to say."

"Tom, you are preaching to the choir." He scratched Chief's poll. "I could have sworn the two of us"—he glanced up in the tree—"okay, the three of us—were preaching to *you*." He scratched the foamy neck. "Thank you for showing me my sister's grave."

"You ride on now. Let's see if my pony is tired of life."

When Abo rode down the draw, the tired, left-behind gelding rose to its feet, shook, and whinnied. For a long time, the separated horses whinnied their lonely stories across a chasm of tree and brush.

8

The boy Henry was sent up from San Diego to the ranch by Jason Abo's father. The boy was black and inner-city and an orphan except for having living parents.

He was gangly, all elbows and knees, a thirteen-year-old gangbanger name of Henry Cruz. Jason welcomed him to the ranch and drew up a charter for the GM Foundation—which stood for Good Manners, but was mostly meant to be an allusion to the Ford Foundation for whatever credibility it might show the IRS or potential contributors. Jason understood his father was offering opportunity along with atonement. All he had to do was tame Henry.

First, he confiscated Henry's drugs. With rueful integrity he flushed these down the toilet. Then he interviewed the boy, found him smart and sunny, and led him to Tyree's room and granted permission for music to be played before bedtime. Within a week Henry infected Tyree and a makeshift school gang with the hip-hop ethos of outlawry.

Henry came before assistant principal Joan Abo as a tagging culprit, nabbed by the shop teacher who said the west entrance was much improved but he didn't have a spray-paint can left on the shelf. Joan ushered the boy to the painting, a wall tableau of black fist, melting clock, rockets, and rainbow swirls.

"Is this a gang sign?" she asked.

"Shee-it," said Henry. "Should I call you Mom? My mom's churched big-time, and you is schooled big-time."

"Henry, from now on you is sticking with me," Joan said. "And yes, call me Big Momma."

That night her husband remarked on how cute it was to see Tyree paint on the number two barn; and how imaginative it was for Tyree to say he had stolen the cans; and how mathematically astute was his imagination to reckon he had thirty-three dollars yet to swipe; and how brotherly Henry was to share a secret palm-and-fist gesticulation with Tyree; and how "one-eighty-seven on an undercover cop" had replaced "If I had a hammer" in the boy's droning song to himself. Abo had been strutting before Joan as he spoke. He froze.

"God," he said.

Joan looked out the kitchen window. "Where are the boys?"

"I showed Henry how to work the .22, the Remington," Jason said dolefully. "I sent him and Tyree off to shoot magpies."

"Here's a gun, have fun."

"'No one mess with me and Lil Homie now,' is what he said."

They went outside and hollered at the setting sun. Presently the boys came walking into the lot. Abo cleared his throat and stepped forward to take the rifle.

Henry said, "Tyree done a one-eighty-seven on a jailbird." Tyree hung back in the yard while Henry flopped on the porch. "Poor goddamn bird," Henry said, tattooing the porch planks with his open hands. "Despicable. No way I'm gonna jack a car for him now."

Tyree slunk into the house.

The following Saturday, Big Momma went to a feminists' meeting at the High Prairie Quaker Oats and Pepsi Health Club. Her husband had taken Tyree with him to the state capital to attend to his yearly IRS audit. He claimed the boy would profit by learning business acumen; covertly, the boy's presence in the IRS office was a tactical diversion. Henry was placed with Tom Bird.

Bird prodded his charge into barn-hoop basketball and was disappointed again at a black's game. At twilight they drank ice tea on the porch.

"You play good, Birdman."

"You've probably spent all your time on your studies, you little bugger."

"Nah. Just chillin' and watchin' my back."

They took the pitcher of tea inside at dark. Henry bolted up to grab the .270 rifle off the deer rack above the door. Bird bolted just as fast to wrench away the gun.

"Don't ever touch someone's gun," Bird admonished, reseating the rifle on the antlers. "Guns make mistakes irrevocable."

"What you need is a Glock," the boy said as he pantomimed a two-handed fan of automatic fire. "Get one before they's illegal," he further advised.

"Illegal they should be," Bird said. "If I'm to be shot, I want the shooter to be aiming at me."

Bird brought out the cribbage board. The boy learned the game rapidly and was fiercer competition in cards than with a basketball. Bird enjoyed the boy's hooting and jive. Then it was nine o'clock; the motherfuckers were starting to square dance at the Tenmile Creek Grange Hall. Bird had exorcised *motherfucker* from Henry's vocabulary with many stern rebukes; the word would not consent to die, and had taken root in Bird.

That motherfucker Hap Means had taken Eleanor to the square dance. He had flown in to do this. Bird hadn't done anything half so romantic. But still he couldn't figure he was tallying behind Hap. He had to be several notches ahead of Hap Means in any accounting.

Still, he grabbed his hat and said, "Henry, we're going to town."

The graveled county road had deep pits and standing water, and Henry whooped at the big gushers that flooded the windshield.

"Henry," said Bird, "be proud of being black. Don't let people feel sorry for you. Walk tall. You ought to develop some habits of honesty pretty soon, so you can walk tall."

"There ain't another blood in this town, is there?" the boy said.

"A few broken down railroaders. No young people."

The wind whistled and the tires hummed and the boy tattooed a rap beat on the truck seat. Bird pulled into the Grange lot and shut off the engine.

Bird said, "People will like you to death."

"Whoo," the boy said.

"Whoo," Bird echoed, and they entered the Grange Hall.

The entryway was congested, the main room a beehive, the heat greasy. The square dancers in the main room promenaded by. The caller said *Honor your partner* and the couples bowed and made new unions.

> *Swing her high, swing her low,*
> *Don't step on that pretty little toe.*

The dancers weaved. Henry's foot was tapping. *Form a star* the caller said, and the dancers folded in.

> *Once go left, once go right,*
> *Let that girl sashay tonight.*

And the sashaying women burst the star.

"That be cool!" Henry purred. He clapped, spun on one foot, added hop to the hip, flopped and bobbed his head. "Get down, white boy!" he howled.

Skirts flew and the pot-bellied men minced along to the call of *Grand left!* As the dancers filed by, they ratcheted their heads to take in Henry's august glare.

And the sashaying women burst the star.

Then Bird saw Eleanor in a turquoise summer dress, floating across the floor like a candle flame. As she linked up with Hap Means in his new boots and 4x beaver hat, she looked eighteen years old, with a smile and buoyant feet and swirling new dress.

Tom felt sick in his belly. In a short time—maybe minutes—she would be lost again. What he felt in his belly was what he felt forty years ago in the Goodnight lots. *Dammit, Walker, tell me what to do? You wouldn't begrudge me my time, you being worm and tombstone and epitaph.* For a moment he was seeing Walker's fallen face after he pretended at the corral gate to head Walker's horse that was saddled for Eleanor, but really made a belated rush, after the horse was committed to the open gate, to ensure the horse would hightail through the gate and away. "You won't stop at nothing, will you?" Walker had muttered as he rode by Tom on his way after that good Chance horse.

Bird grabbed Henry by the arm and hustled the boy to the truck. Away they sped to the health club.

"Wait in the truck," Bird said and went inside.

He tracked the sound of a woman speechifying. His route led him through the basketball court where karate students were intensely drilling against air and imagination. In an adjoining squash court he came upon the rows of women seated on the floor like Indians. He scanned the array for Joan, vaguely hearing the speaker tell of living in the breast-cancer habitat of Utah, downwind of atomic testing. Finally he asked an acquaintance in the second tier, "Where's Joan?" The male voice got attention. The hushed room and multifold stares made Bird feel pinned like a butterfly against the door behind him. A lone voice cried something and then other voices joined in, rising in tempo and volume like geese fixing to land or fly, and then it was a synchronized chant like at a football stadium: *Block that kick!* But that wasn't the cry. *Kick that block! Kick that block!*

And then like a slap Bird understood the cheer from the echoing stadium: *Kick his ass! Kick his ass!* The walls were shaking. A young woman bolted up and lifted her sweater over her breasts and waggled and added a contralto refrain *Tough-titty-said-the-kitty* to the booming *Kick his ass!* With a last scope for Joan, he opened the door behind him and edged through to confront the chop-chop folks advancing, juiced up by the cheering and ready to pass the test. Tom did not want to explain the commotion behind him—in fact, didn't know how to—and was saved from the scene by the appearance of Henry on the court with a shrill shout, "Whatchoo mother-fuh...sistah-fuckahs doin' to my man Tom?" The cheers in the squash court behind the door had collapsed into muffled laughter, and the karate folks wondered at their purpose, some with keen disappointment at this fizzling miracle of a villain delivered to them, and Tom Bird strode through them and told the boy he simply couldn't explain and off they went to the Alforcas.

Bird bade the boy come inside and burst through the door and beckoned to Al behind the bar. "Al, I hate to impose, but I need you to keep Henry here until I can get hold of Joan." The boy, rising to the bar scene, had found his walk. "Henry, quit strutting and shake a leg." Bird made a hurried introduction and said, "It's a long story, Al—"

"No sir, Tom, a very short story. They were in here earlier talking about the dance." The barman opened his collateral drawer and held up three string ties; he chose one with an elkbone clasp and handed it to Bird. "You got a little free at the mouth at that party of Katie's brother. Everyone knows. You might just as well try and claim her."

Bird gave Henry a dollar and some words of admonition and drove to the grange in a pique of shame, a feeling too damn common and automatic when Eleanor was on his mind. He saw the picture as viewed from outside: a fool romantic boy whose wealth was a saddle loses out, and hangs around for thirty years as a hired man (a sweet gesture of Eleanor's, topped by Stewart's forbearance), and in his muddle-headed age misconstrues the lady's long kindness, and presses and persists...and damn it must have been creepy for her, with him hanging about all these years.

And the shame flushed his face even as he slapped away this picture for being untrue. I stayed for Walker, not Eleanor. And then for a job. And then one day Katie was a waitress at the Alforcas.

The Grange lights hove ahead. He thought, I will make a game try, is all. The sun will rise tomorrow. He parked in the back lot and stepped out into the brisk air, feeling better, stronger. He was at a dance.

Bird entered the hall just as the skinny caller whooped and said he had to see a man about a dog. People spilled toward the front and back doors. Eleanor was leaning against the far wall, idly swinging one foot to make the knee-high hem of her new dress dance.

Bird approached and asked, "May I have the next dance?"

"I'd be honored," said Eleanor. "Where's that boy you brought earlier?"

"Strutting in the Alforcas. Punch?" He offered his arm and they went off to the kitchen to the punchbowl. "He can't play a lick of basketball," Bird said. "But I did get myself limbered up to dance."

Hap stayed around town three days looking for Eleanor. He knew the lay of things when he saw Tom Bird on the third day cutting calves for vaccination in the corrals of Double Diamond number two. He walked right through cows and calves and offered his hand. Bird dismounted before he took the hand.

"I came here to press my suit," Hap Means said. "Instead, I give you my permission."

"A thing much appreciated," Tom Bird said and mounted again and went back to work.

9

It was fall when Hap Means came again to Bannock. He came to see why Tom and Eleanor weren't married. As before, he whiled several days before he saw either of them. Eleanor was supposed to be returning from San Francisco on the day of his arrival but had detoured to the Denver racetrack to watch Bird's horse run. Hap was relegated to Sally's hospitality that was stellar except where his curiosity was concerned; she offered only the simple observation that having a fiance was perhaps the best of what followed and that Tom and Eleanor were old enough to perceive that.

Hap was playing cribbage with Sally on her deck in the morning sun while Bob Honstead quoted the Omaha beef prices from the newspaper when the pickup and trailer came up the hill. They all went outside to greet the two and the talk was short since Bird was determined to keep Henry and Tyree in the truck. "The young have so much boundless energy," Eleanor explained. And Bird said, "Should have hauled the durn kids in the trailer!" He had left the horse on shares with a trainer and just now thought what a comfort it might have been for restless boys and weary travelers to have used that empty trailer.

Hap followed the pickup and trailer to Bird's place in his car. The boys bounded out and wrestled in the gravel for the last pop in the cooler while Tom unhitched the trailer. Eleanor went inside to "use the facilities" and came back out to face the first of Hap's queries. She said she didn't know why they weren't married and if he asked the next logical question she would slap his face for being dishonorable. Bird came up and said he would drive her home as she probably needed to shed road-dust and kid-burrs, and to Hap said he was as antsy as the boys and wanted to make a tough fishing trip to the North Fork, and would Hap be willing even though they would have to hike and wouldn't be back until long after dark. Hap told him to gather gear while he drove Eleanor home, and on the road the first question Hap asked Eleanor is why there were two homes.

Eleanor was looking out the window at the yellowing grass, pleased to be with her friend yet tired enough that the pleasure was one of contentment not excitement. Hap heard it in her voice. "He's settled and I'm settled and we don't know what to do. Nor are we in a hurry to find out." Now she was looking out at Double Diamond pasture and perked up. "I'm in love. It's a miracle to me. I threw poison spray on those feelings for many years, and so did Tom, and it's a miracle they grow so well. I'll rest today and he'll come by sometime tomorrow, maybe for only five minutes, depending on his work, and I'll be happy."

She pointed to the fork in the road that led to her house and was asleep by the time Hap steered under the sawn Ponderosa trunks with the hanging sign that read Double Diamond inside a perimeter of the thirty or so burned-black brands the ranch had sometime owned. Eleanor woke up to thank him for the lift and to tell him to come by tomorrow and by all means to go fishing with Tom.

It was a long drive through the mountains and Hap found the fishing cowboy as taciturn as his fiancee. Sometimes he would steal a glance at Bird and wonder the why of his loss, but he was of a nature to accept things and plan ahead. The visit with Eleanor was tomorrow and after that he would go away from here. He now found fishing agreeable. Tom said this place was one he had to visit once a year and the time was prime besides running out.

When they stopped they were looking at steep country and Bird pointed to the notch where they would cross the steep white ridge to get to the North Fork, a route across three gullies that were hardly traversed by game trails, it so inhospitable. "I plan to wade wet," Bird said, digging in a duffel bag. "Do you want sneakers?"

They made the last ascent over rock and white-granule sand on hands and knees. They were sweating and dirty when they reached the spine and looked down the long sheer descent to the North Fork, steep as a playground slide, through white scree and frosted undergrowth unlit by a sun past noon.

"This is upright country," said Hap Means. "You got any water?"

"I don't," said Bird. "It gives me motivation to go on down."

Hap shook a cellophane bag and made a pile of sweetened grain in his palm. "Trail mix," said Hap, shaking some out into Bird's palm.

"Yep," said Bird, chewing. "Tastes like trail." They rested until Bird said, "Let's start down at that big red rock up ahead, where there's some brush to stop our slide."

To reach that swath of brush they walked a ridge spine like the edge of a spear blade. They teetered in gusts of wind, in this place where only birds and bugs belonged. Then the descent: coasting and quick shuffles and heel-braking and rockslides and buttslides and grabbing for limbs and grabbing at quadricep cramps, fetching up at a battlement of boulders a vertical thirty feet over the translucent green river.

Bird picked out a handful of flies—an olive-bodied elk hair caddis, a hare's-ear nymph, a cinnamon-and-black ant—and tucked them into Hap's shirt pocket. "Try the ant first," he said and descended the boulders and crossed the river while rigging his rod. In the marbled green water below a white spraying run his line paused and he ripped and was onto a fat fourteen-inch wild fish. After releasing the fish, he looked for Hap to remind him that ant was first, but Hap was moving upstream, an etiquette and wisdom noted begrudgingly by Bird.

After catching two smaller fish, Bird moved downstream, warily avoiding a sliver of sand grass where he had seen the rattlesnake with Eleanor months before, the day after the Grange dance...

Then the river had been high and murky, and Eleanor was sitting on the battlement of rocks above him when he heard the sound. A grasshopper's *tick-tick-tick* flight might momentarily alarm, as might the wind-rattle of seeding vetch, but the unmistakable *buzzzz* of a rattler touches one's ears like electricity. From her rock perch Eleanor saw Tom spring six lateral feet into the river.

He eyed the bank. The bronze and brown diamondback rattler moved slowly through the grass, thick, thick as a man's wrist, moving slow as a tube of motor oil. Bird fished stones from the river and bombarded the big snake until he was triumphant with dinner.

The sectioned snake writhed on the griddle. Eleanor had her hands in her hip pockets as she peered at the spiraling snake. "I have to eat a moving target," she said.

"They say it's like chicken," Bird said.

"Chicken doesn't spin," said Eleanor. She had a new concern. "You mean you've never eaten snake?"

"One time. A little water snake. But I was mighty hungry." He made a cook's poke. The snake was spinning slower, and evenly, like a rotisserie.

The snake stilled and they ate a bite.. It tasted like frog, which was supposed to taste like chicken. Frogs don't taste like chicken. Rockchucks don't taste like chicken. The jays known as camp-robbers don't taste like chicken. Trail mix doesn't taste like chicken. Bird tried to catch fish for dinner but couldn't in the brown water. They walked upstream in the twilight for a last try at dinner and on a grassy terrace eased down to the earth to make love, Tom's coat beneath them. Eleanor was beautiful, naked and milk-white, on the green grass. The terrace still had slope and Eleanor said the earth moved and Bird thought that wonderful until she pointed pragmatically uphill to his coat several body lengths above them.

Almost sundown Bird came back to the departure point, where Hap Means was cleaning two nice trout, which like the two Bird kept for dinner had gullets gorged with cinnamon ants. They packed their gear and attacked the slope. Yellow-jackets orbited the killed fish they held by the gills in one hand above the dirt while the other three limbs scrambled in a gait God never assigned any creature from His book of gaits. The good fishing had become a memory. On the ridge they rested, in view of the truck down the hill and across a meadow where a man on a swather was mowing a poor abandoned homestead for its few ton of hay. High above the meadow, but below their vantage point, a red-tail hawk held like a kite against the wind while being harassed by a pair of blackbirds. The smaller birds swooped at the hawk's back, and made bluff rushes, for no apparent purpose. The hawk was looking for voles in the exposed hay, nesting was over, and anyway these were not the frantic air attacks on egg-thieving magpies, but a leisurely harassment that made the hawk change tracks. It was just what small fast birds did to big hawks, to while the time.

Hap brushed off dirt from the sun-wrinkled fish. "That night you ran off from the dance you came here, didn't you? I saw a big piece of her dress hanging on a fir tree forty feet up. What went on here?"

"Wind," said Bird.

The dropping sun sent its shadow across the valley floor. The hawk and the farmer headed home. Bird let Hap's delectable imagination hold, but actually the dress had been spread to dry and then forgotten when they packed to go out.

"If you two fall apart," said Hap, "I guess she'll know where to turn. In the meantime, I guess I'll find me some young thing who likes grizzled faces and a mature stock holding, which is altogether more seemly conduct than this other thing, and certainly better for business. Having a pretty thing on your arm shows you got the horsepower to swing some deals."

Dusk was coming fast in this steep country. Nighthawks were flying over the cottonwoods below, scarfing bugs. Bird said, "Have you ever worked for a living?"

"Yep. And I ain't forgot what it's like."

This made Bird contemplate work. It was a simple formula: step to the task. Far simpler than the work Hap faced in acquiring his pretty young hood ornament. Eleanor to Hap had been the antithesis of that busy-ness. She was contentment waving bye-bye, and Hap had become resigned to the next goddamned tomorrow. Bird had a suspicion that the magnanimity of winners came to no account, but he stood and offered a hand and said, "Thanks for coming."

Hap shook hands and loaded up. "We're like family," Hap said. "We don't much like one another but we have to make the best of it." When they hit the flat, Hap said, "There's a young lady I know with an inattentive husband and it just makes me tired thinking of it. Taking her to the people shows and getting the right gifts and the fistfight with the hubby. Eleanor would have been a whole bunch nicer." He sounded abject.

"You're just tired," Bird said. "You'll buck up."

Bird pulled into his place long after dark. He chased Tyree and Henry to bed, so Hap could get some sleep on the couch, and then drove to Number Two to check out the grain bins. He knuckled up the side of the tin on the first bin to find the depth and found it full. He didn't need to check the other two because he came upon the last combine hopper of barley dumped on the gravel. So they were all full. Not a bad yield for a dryland afterthought. The yearlings could gorge on this cheap feed and slice off some of the finishing. He needed a feedlot to complete the picture. Lop off all of those getting a cut. That would be a turn for Ramey, except she had been morose lately. Probably she had hit a snag in up-to-no-good. But he had to admit Jason Abo as partner had done swell. He had taken over the hay and the barley. After the ranch sale, no equipment was left, so it was all done custom, and this Abo handled, pretending to boss swathers and balers and stackers and combiners while writing big fat checks.

The partnership meeting the next day began with Bob Honstead wailing about the redline plummet of feeder prices. Bird interrupted to say they all could work a pencil, and seventy cents would be their ruin, and one alternative was to hold onto the steers and convert Number Two to a feedlot; the old horse corrals would serve, and they could bring in corn on the rail line before the rails were torn up, now that the mill was gone. They didn't have enough hay to winter the herd but they had preserved some grass, enough to get by even without grain and corn, probably. Lastly, maybe Ramey could spin off some of that betting money to pay the mortgage interest and they ought to have heavy steers in the spring when the price was better.

The partners were drinking orange juice on Sally's deck, intent on Bird's scenario. Indeed, their pencils all worked, and they had all balanced the tough margin of the year against the potential value of the ranch and its grass. Bird said, "I know this cow ranch can produce twenty percent—but with money costing ten, and prices sliding ten, we have a tough show." The partners' mood swung to tough it out. Yes, the Double Diamond would be saved. And then they turned to Ramey.

She was dressed in a black dress like an evening gown, a slinky thing in the hot September sun, and when she stood now she teetered over the hot tub, proof that the flask that had come courteously from Jason Abo's pocket had not been mineral water like the two of them claimed. Her hair was looped over one shoulder, bound by a turquoise clip. She looked into her hands enfolding a pink and white geranium.

"It takes all the guts I have to tell you this—"

Sally rose to interrupt. "Ramey, you tell your father first."

For the first time in a long time, Ramey obeyed.

The principals waited on the deck, drinking juice, piqued by the sound of Bob's 1957 Chevy taking the hill curves at a centrifugal tease.

Ramey returned and spoke with a dead formality: "I made five million yen in the first day on derivatives. Nearly a million dollars the next. I lost all that and more. I didn't touch the Double Diamond, but you don't have the scratch I last said you had. The shameful part is Mom doesn't have the scratch she used to have. Let's beat the IRS out of being an estate partner, I said. That was smart, but I chunked it away. Dad is peeved that the reading of his will won't have the weight it used to. He always figured I'd squander it, so that ain't changed. But you heard him peel out of here." Heretofore she had been speaking into her clasped hands but now she tossed the geranium in the air and spoke with a lilting tone. "I am hired on as a nanny." She spun to find Tom in a lawn chair, his rough brown hands on his knees, a working stiff who had stood up to time and loss. "Uncle Tom, you can guess who for. God, I don't know whether to laugh or howl or cry." She crossed the deck to her uncle's chair. "I can see why you don't like me," she said in a low voice. "I can't see why you love me." Tom stood and she stepped into his arms and bawled.

The others looked away. Abo had been in a meeting once where a vice-president blubbered for several minutes and then started throwing ice cubes from the water pitcher at everyone, necessitating a quick adjournment and a hallway agreement that showing Wally the gate was clearly a sound move. So he, at least, was not surprised when Ramey shifted gears again and sang brightly to the ensemble, "So I'm outta here!" She had the bright step of a soldier going home as she walked across the deck into the house.

"Juice, anyone?" Sally said.

Jason Abo raised his glass, thinking the exit of this powermaid turned nanny was also a sound move, a move toward solvency for those left on the deck. He eyed Bird over his shoulder. That clever man on a ranch was having women fall into his arms lately. If all the pumped weights and lap miles failed to stave off age, he needed to start picking up some pointers. That thought made a blip on the moral radar he had been constructing since the near crisis of the freckle-chested woman with the acrobat boyfriend. His next thought—how he might have waltzed into Ramey's embrace with applications of simple kindness—splashed on his moral screen like an *alert!* Now he looked at Joan, his brain switching from radar to telepathy. *I'm working on it!*

As Sally went by her brother with the tray, she said to him, "Predictable, yes? But you've been a comfort to her. It's nice to know she still has feelings."

Bird nodded. He never wanted to see Ramey again. Her spectacular losses on a Double Diamond subsidiary would show. Never mind that they came against some earlier wins. The record would show momentum. A solvent ranch had become spectacularly assetted and was now on a slide so well-known to the banks which were always muscled into first position and did their civic duty to call in before tradesmen and suppliers got stuck any worse. Getting a grass season in arrears was not likely. Winter these cattle, he thought with a grim conviction. He proposed this to the partners. Ship enough this fall to satisfy some interest, and take advantage of the spring prices. That would get them a year. If interest fell a tad and beef prices rose a tad..."Two ifs is one too many," Bird concluded. "But what else can we do?"

"I'll tell you what we can do." It was Abo, on his feet, gathering attention. "We can get Tom's ass out of this. If there's a failure, we'll waltz out of here and start a fire with the partnership papers. He'll lose his place. We shouldn't have given it to the bank to hold in the first place." His throat was dry and he fetched his bottle and gestured around in an offer, calling it Russian mineral water, suitable for their juice. "So the rest of us need to buy it back and take

Tom's note. I've seen enough of this business in a short time to recognize unequal participation."

"I can't let you do that," Bird said.

"I'm calling for a vote, Tom."

"Listen to me first."

They were interrupted as Tyree and Henry came shouting up from the cottonwood gulch below, Tyree waving a garter snake. Joan shooed them back into the gulch.

Bird resumed: "First, no bank will agree to release it except at an inflated value. They'll see a leaky ship and will reassign at something far above the original figure."

"I can deal with those buggers hiding behind mythical examiners," Abo countered. "They get reasonable once you kidnap their children. Trust me."

"I do," Bird said. "And I appreciate this thing." He took Abo's flask and poured some into Eleanor's juice, a concoction she liked. Then he faced the group. "The second thing I have to say is if our *ifs* don't happen, my place is still gone unless I go begging to the noteholders. So it's not even a thing to discuss and there will be no vote."

The people rubbed their chins and gazed at the sky. This meeting had brought clarity but no happiness. Optimism was an old duty of Western women, and Sally and Joan stood to the task. The cattle were fat, anyone could see, and if a feedlot could put that last bit of grease on a New York cut, dripping chins everywhere would be nodding for more meat. A can't-lose scenario, the first Sally or Joan had ever seen. Joan suggested they move this group to the Bonanza Lanes for more celebratory fun. Jason Abo would rather watch paint dry than bowl, but his earlier moral slip impelled him to swing behind his wife's idea, and the group did convene at the bowling alley, where Bird and Eleanor were informed they had to rent shoes to replace their boots, and in tandem said no thanks and together rolled all the nearby balls down a lane like slow mammoth buckshot and exited laughing and apologizing to the clerk for the mess they'd made.

When they woke up, snow was falling.

The big flakes fell softly in the still air like parachutes, and when the last snow cloud drifted east, unveiling the sun, the pasture grass was sticking through a web of brilliant white. Tom Bird grilled hotcakes and looked out the kitchen window at a pair of tawny fist-sized burrowing owls on the gateposts. If you've looked into the eyes of these somewhat diurnal owls from a few feet, you've seen fierce little suns, and Tom fancied that the pair of owls on the posts burned off the snow with their gaze while he and Eleanor ate breakfast. When the snow was a thin lacing, the little owls went back to their homes in a pile of rock drug from the field, and Tom and Eleanor loaded up the gray yearling. Tom was taking the colt to the Omaha sale.

"You oughta wait a couple of hours," Eleanor said, looking at the worn pickup tires. "The pass is likely to have some snow."

"I do have a few errands first. Snow don't bother me so long as it don't measure up to '87." Eleanor looked at him quizzically but he didn't explain. When he was young on the Wyoming plains, people still talked of that stock-killing winter as though it was the inception of history. Even the grain farmer who homesteaded on the heels of the prices of the Boer War and the Great War might link his failure to prove up to the terrible toll of '87. "Well, time to strap on my driving ass."

"Don't see how you do it, all that long driving."

"I can't say I like it. But it's the only way to get from here to there." The yearling was stamping and whinnying in the trailer, a restlessness that would ease once they were on the road, away from the sounds and smells of home. Bird was pretty much the same, and this lingering was hard. He took Eleanor in his arms. "I'm taking Hap Means to the airstrip. Want me to tell him anything?"

"'Goodbye.' That'll work."

"I've almost come to like that scamp."

"'Come back soon,' then."

Bird slid behind the wheel and started the engine, letting the oil warm. "Eleanor, you've traveled in circles that I am not familiar with. It's okay if you keep traveling them."

She just smiled. He drove to town. The little gravel spur road to Bobby Coles' trailer was a tight turnaround, with the junked cars and formation of burn barrels. Bobby, out feeding his rabbits as Bird drove up, reached into a hutch and pulled out a stiff white carcass and tragically held it up for the fishing cowboy to see. "It seems I'll starve out one way or t'other. Least, I got fed there in that durn jail." He was disposed to listen to Bird's explanation of some preliminary work to turn Two into a feedlot and happily accepted the job. "Say, Tom, you got any extra money?"

"Sure. I was just going to throw the extra out the window." Bobby's hopeful little jump spoiled Tom's take on "extra" money, and he handed over a twenty. Besides, a man going to work needed some food in him. "You can get somebody to help you. Even Worthless, if it comes to that."

"Tom, I do appreciate this. What with the mill closing, I'm just a-scratching."

"Skip being grateful and work as you know how to do."

They shook hands and Bobby Coles' parting words were, "I won't eat a sick rabbit," but Bird had long known a warren of these Coles and was sure this sturdy speech would lose in negotiation with the belly. He drove to the old Knutsen hotel, a relic almost barbarous in its amenities but once had been the epitome of comfort in the heyday of the mill, when Eleanor's father had bankrolled the granite edifice to host lumber buyers. The exterior stone was still monumental, but the interior was a scabbed-up mess of low ceilings, crammed bathrooms, squeaking floors, and unreliable electricity. Hap trotted out the oak door with his garment bag and threw it in the truck bed.

"Holiday Inn more my type," Hap said. "Eleanor booked me here. Was that instruction or a joke?" He lit up a cigar, gift of a cowboy who remembered the redlight province of the third floor and was chumming out cigars in hopes of getting updated. "That one of my boy's progeny in the trailer?" Hap asked as they drove south to the airstrip. "Eleanor's colt woke everyone up. But the second crop is middling. Kentucky is quick to turn. My stud that the world slavered over is now officially second-rate. My Messiah is now an oh-well-maybe. Christ, this race business is fickle." Tom Bird hung around while Hap fueled and filled out his flight plan in the cinderblock shed. Hap looked at the orange wind socks. Bird wanted to hear more about the Kentucky attitude. Instead he heard Hap's boarding farewell: "I don't believe I'll ever be back here. Thanks for the fishing. Eleanor's breasts must sag like hell but I bet they feel a good cushion against your own pot belly." Bird was studying this umbrage when Hap continued, trance-like, "It feels like I never tasted lobster, but only heard about it."

Tom Bird felt like he'd accomplished a prodigious day's work when Hap Means' airplane disappeared over the batholith peaks and mountain goats.

The school year for Joan began with this meeting with a mother whose son was in her sophomore biology class: "What is your philosophy about masturbation?" the pretty yellow-haired woman asked.

They were three, sitting in student desks, like bumper cars going head on at the fair. "I really don't have a philosophy, per se," Joan said.

"Just do it?" the woman said belligerently.

"That is a commercial slogan, very ingenious. I reiterate: no philosophy. Probably I'm slipshod in not having developed one."

"You ruined the disaster auction," the pretty yellow-haired woman pointed out. They were close to blows.

Loyal Gary, the principal, was the third party present, and now he crowed, "What's a disaster auction without a disaster?" He deadpanned around like he'd seen Jack Benny do with a bad joke.

Joan inched her desk forward and said, "I recommend your boy be home schooled."

Standing in the hall after the meeting, loyal Gary asked Joan if she might see her way to be more tactful.

"That bitch had an agenda," Joan said, "and it included belittling me."

"This school won't run smoothly if you're always mean to people."

"If I'm dirty and mean, I'll draw all the fire. In a year or two you can demote me to the classroom and come off saintly."

The principal looked as blue as his mortician's suit. "Are you going to be mean to me, too? Pretty Boy—er, your new husband has changed you."

"I'm more fond of him than you, so think before you speak."

She was not sharp in this remark but her backbone had the steel of new conviction. Summers off to teachers were like crop rotation, reinvigorating. Joan's rebirth came from ten weeks of political brooding.

For a decade she had foreseen a barbarous time, with dossiers on everyone and greedheads prevailing at every level. Yet it wasn't so. America hadn't climbed into enlightenment, but neither had she gone to the devil. Every third decade the nation rebounded and took stock of ethics and the future. And the young, as ever, were the catalysts. "I was born to disagree" was not one philosophe's destiny but everyman's. Joan saw this cycle, punk rock and nose rings and gangsta rap notwithstanding. And she saw herself now as an elder, following the tradition of *simpatico* elders who lent to the young their hearts and sometimes their guile, and on lucky occasion their wisdom. Elders needed to preserve the ways of the people, and that required the most serious reflection. Elders needed to say to the young, We are dust and this is yours; and our knowledge of the world, which is new to you, tells us thus about your tomorrows. And Joan the Elder, over the summer, saw herself as a terrible abdicator. She was a teacher!

Her classroom became a collage. She continued to teach biology, but literature and history were ever handy. After a day of putting X and Y genes in a tic-tac-toe grid, students learned of Nietzche and genocide. Next came the proof, intuited by most, that tic-tac-toe was a winless game, consigned to the cat. On the following day, the topic was cats: a blessing for what they did to rodents and a curse for gamebirds. (Shotgunning became a major cause of feline death in the ensuing bird season.) The next day's learning was the toll silt from logging extracted from all spawning fishes of the rocky streams, and the last day of the week explored what dams did to the anadromous salmon and steelhead. In this besieged logging town, the week ended with uproar against this subversive teacher. For a second time, Joan was on the agenda of the Monday board meeting. On the heels of a mostly insignificant slam against logging, she had explained how the nutritionally-meager rocky streams had *demanded* the salmon's peculiar ways of living short-term in the birthing stream and coming back, ocean-fat and refusing to take nutrition, to feed the stream with their decomposing bodies. Niche evolution, at its most obvious. That lesson became known around town as the day Mrs. Collins-Abo told the kids evolution was fact not theory, and anyone who thought differently had adobe for brains. What Joan actually said was somewhat different.

It had been a trying day with Chuck, a steady nemesis. A frail boy with a large toothy head, Chuck voiced every thought; he never understood directions; he was in and out of his seat; when she booted him to the hall, he came back like a yo-yo with innocent questions; he called her sir; his routine through the classroom door was to shout "I'm very studious today, Sir!" but of course he wasn't and would mope his way to the hall before long. Other students, while working, routinely said, "Shut up, Chuck," but he so willingly and blithely withstood the torment of other students he was never beaten up, though he was the kid everyone could beat up. He was in Junior ROTC. He called himself Charles Von Schnelling the Third, when his name was Chuck Snell.

On that day of exploring the marvel of salmon somebody tolled the word *problem* loud enough to rouse Chuck from his singular interest at picking lint from his pressed green uniform, and he shot up a fist and blurted, "Never fear— Von Schnelling's here!"

"Chuck," sighed Joan, "you're such a—" She groped for the word. *Hindrance*, that was it. But before she could say it, Chuck muttered a single syllable with a long *e*. "What?" she asked.

"The word is dweeb, sir," Chuck said pleasantly.

Joan liked his honesty, but all in all it was best for the class for Chuck to either go back to picking lint from his uniform or retire to the hall. Chuck did the latter. But "emergency situation, sir!" moments arose, such as when Chuck needed a rubber band, then an averaging of his grade, then a pass to the history teacher where he needed to know his grade, then a trip to the bathroom—and finally an eavesdropping dramatic entrance, "Evolution is a theory, sir! You've got to say that in the public schools."

"I don't have to say anything, you dweeb." She didn't need tact with Chuck; he was indestructible. Then she explained to the other students, the best of whom, as a rule, went through church doors on a Sunday. "Take the Bible metaphorically. I do. Accept its own evolution of translations and additions and probable editing. Jesus of Nazareth walked the earth. But the world was not created ten thousand years ago. Start with that *fact* and you'll do all right."

After class she knelt by a secretary and typed in a transfer for Chuck to another teacher on the Schoolmaster computer program. This sudden act became known around town as a brazen persecution of a Christian. Chuck was memorialized as the boy-who-challenged-the-teacher. Marie Chayevsky, the Polish ex-singer in a chicken suit, promised to see the boy canonized, for finally God had looked down on the plain between Germany and Russia and was pleased, and a Pole at the Vatican was the first of many miracles to come. The uproar had to find audience with the school board, even though a member as fervent as Marie interviewed Chuck Snell and emerged from the process commenting to his fellow board members, "God, that little maggot." When the incident was fully ablaze in the Monday meeting, Art Snell, Chuck's dad, got himself recognized with a wrecked-seaman's desperate semaphore wave of the hand, stood and said, "I apologize for my boy. He thinks Mrs. Collins is the best teacher he ever had."

Harvey Wells, the electrician on the board, had encouraged Joan to stay home when the Christian persecution came up on the agenda, and after the meeting drove to the Abo house to tell her that the board as a whole wanted her not to be discouraged by these three "incidents." She might consider being more circumspect, however, at least for a while.

"That makes four incidents," Joan said.

Tom Bird rigged his rod at a sliver of meadow on the Sur Fork. His coffee pot began to boil on the campfire and he set the pot on the dirt outside the fire ring and dumped in the coffee. After he filled the pockets of his vest with the right fly boxes, he poured a cup of cold water from the river into the pot to settle the grounds. Then he smoked and drank a cup. This part of the river, above the reservoir, was a freestone stream, which roared with May and June flood, and harbored few fish in the summer months; mostly, people fished the hatchery truck. A few miles upstream, the river was broken, had boulders and cascades and pools and bugs. Bird would save that sure fishery for the late forenoon. He would start with this bad water. Once in this water he'd hooked a rainbow that rolled onto the nymph with its tail laid flat like a canoe paddle; when hooked it shivered upstream past Pablo who said, "Jesus! Five pounds!" and when it ran past Cindy she said, "Seven!" and Jack yelled, "Goddamn it, nine!" Jack was the last one to see the fish before it bulled into the roots of a fallen pine and broke off, which kept the fish as big as he said. Bird had seen at the take a nice three-pounder, and so this water of sparse feed was fertile in extraordinary ways. Had one more companion been there to witness, it would have grown to be the biggest trout he had ever hooked.

He waded the braided fingers to their reuniting turbulence and lobbed stone flies to that long-ago lair. Nothing hit. He waded upstream and as he approached the bridge he came upon hatchery fish. They didn't hang close to the bottom, but spurted forward and subsided to rest mid-depth in the lee shelter of a rock, then writhed again in a spurt into fast water and wafted back to a lee. Their backs were too black and they were swimming too hard and too close to the surface. While Bird enticed one sojourner to follow a renegade stripped artlessly to his waders, he saw a bigger trout, colored like green on sand, slip from the undulating moss-tails of a bank current into the sunlit main current, then vanish in a lazy sink to the stones below. He could not catch this fish or the black writhing ones. Fishing to the latter was like playing miniature golf, a stupid damn exercise when the ball wouldn't go down, and stupid when the visible river

182

prisoners might for hours bump a fly without taking—unless it were tipped with corn, which might make them wrestle like pirhanas.

Tom Bird didn't have any corn. He drank a cup of coffee and drove upstream to the better broken water. Husks of stoneflies were on the brushy banks. Some caddis flies were taking wing when he stepped into the river, and then there came a surge of caddis like pink clinging fog, a hundred river yards of this caddis blizzard, and Bird grounded his rod and smoked. He watched a watersnake clinging with its lower half to a submerged rock, its head and upper half skimming right and left on the current, delicately moving with and against the water. Presently, the snake extended too far and was swept off the rock. The pale yellow of its underside was exposed in a slow roll before it regained its composure and slithered to the bank. Tom thought of human swimmers and human craft, paddle-driven or propellor-torqued, and the difference between these churners of water and the aquatic organisms—the snake, the moss, the fish, the water itself, which all moved by wave. He began to reinvent the vessel.

The caddis on the wing were like a froth on the water, and no trout rose. Bird slumped to the truck. That evening he waved to Sally and Tyree passing on the road as he drove on to the Macgregor place where he unloaded salt blocks in the new skiff of snow. Magpies rose languidly from the creek willows and settled on the ground. They were egg-eaters, scourge of gamebirds and only marginally redeemed by cleaning up roadkill.

Magpies—unlike Tom Bird—deserved their slander.

He had come from the Ak-Sar-Ben thoroughbred sale in Omaha where he had delivered the yearling filly out of a common mare. On the long drive back he'd chewed on his slander. Of course the filly didn't look good. She was bony and had a splattered clay color charitably called gray by the Jockey Club. But Bird knew she would grow to her genes, and precociousness was a small part of a horse. However, her faults were accentuated next to the steroid-treated gargantuans of the other hip numbers. In such sleek muscled company, her ribs and hip bones stood out like x-rays. She looked too poor to pull a wagon. She looked like something abandoned along the trail. The auctioneer tolled a steady theme of neglect during the interludes of calling, implying that some nurture by a real horseman might salvage the carcass. Bird sipped a drink in the alley between the bleachers and thought he could be no less shamed to march across the sawdust to the auctioneer's stand and grab that silly ass and neglect him intensely for a minute or so.

Anson Montgomery interceded and halloed him there in the bleacher alley. Anson was a lean Britisher with gray sideburns and a big Adam's apple, a farrier turned pinhooker and agent. Bird met him many years ago in Colorado when Anson lifted a horse's foot, cleaned out the mud with a pick, scraped each side of the frog, took a sliver of toe off with the nippers, made a few strokes with the rasp, dropped the leg and inquired, "Who butchered this animal?" It cost Bird two twenty-dollar bills to receive this judgement about what had seemed a routine trimming a week before. But it gave him respect for British exactitude. Now he shook hands with Anson, who asked how many horses he was selling.

"How many pounds, you mean. I sell by the pound, apparently."

Anson waved to someone in the stands. "Mr. Bird, have you made plans for your mares? I'm repping for Tuscon Light. Only one freshman sire has more stakes horses."

"That right?" Bird growled. "Could you tell me where I might find that sire?"

"That color," Anson sympathized.

"The horse will outrun those tranquilized steroid-monsters when he sizes up," Bird said. He was facing the arena, thinking *That's right, auctioneer, keep pulling on that water pitcher and you may have to leave to take a piss.*

"That color," Anson repeated. "I understand you own the Double Diamond. Congratulations." Anson with a flash of rolled sale catalogue made a bid on a son of Mr. Prospector with a splayed hind foot. "My countrymen, idle sons of the aristocracy, owned the cow lands of your West, as an amusement. Then Labor got elected, and the Empire was lost, and here I am reclaiming our English bloodhorses for my Arab clients." He flashed the catalogue and was irritated when the spotter failed to see and he had to repeat the gesture. "He's got a long shoulder and springy ribs and a regal manner," he noted of the colt, "which cannot be said of any of my queen's get or their matings." His next bid won the horse and he left Tom with another handshake and a rueful remark. "That colt I just bought might be a runner of some consequence. Hind splays don't matter. But it would ruin my reputation to try to peddle that splay-footed horse. I think your disaster with your mud-colored horse infiltrated my judgement and led me on a foray into logic. Some village has been deprived of an idiot. On the eighth day God invented luck and made a scramble of everything."

Bird finished salting at Two Trees. He pulled out the.22 from behind the truck seat and plunked at a magpie. He missed. What was he to tell Eleanor about the sale? He did not want any bad thing to touch his time with her. He had spent some road hours pondering the Britisher's remark about luck. It was a dismaying thought. Good luck could only portend trouble. And while bad luck had its comforts in hope and willful endurance, it was still bad luck.

BOOK THREE

Cotton Ward

186

1

The valley pheasants had a terrible time all winter. Snow came early and stayed. After the hunting season several birds would come stealing in at dusk to the Abo place, running in short cautious spurts over the snow, alert to opened house or barn door as they approached the mangers with their dross of grain. Hungry winter howled and then there were two dozen, and three, and four dozen flying in at dusk like attack planes, and then that many were roosting in the big yard cottonwood through the night and into midday, heedless of humans. One night a hundred or more exploded from the tree when Tyree brought Lucky, his new German shorthair yearling, for an introduction. Thereafter the numbers in the tree dwindled. The boy and his dog found feathers in the snow, flesh and bone devoured by coyotes. When the feeding operation stopped on Two, the remaining pheasants left for some other spare diet. Some survived, as always. But for a week after the spring growth the boy could not find a pheasant for his dog to point.

On the eighth day the dog went birdy on Willow Creek and trailed to a point in a bottom of tall yellow grass. The boy saw the grass slit. The dog moved with stealthy obsession, as though a string was attached from the slitting grass to the dog's snout. The string shortened. Then the boy realized the bird was stopped, inert beneath the dog's muzzle. The point was as pure and rigid as Tom had described. Tyree approached slowly, like the dog. He saw it: a Chinese rooster made of Chinese fireworks, eyeball to eyeball with the dog. He crept forward and eased both hands in a scoop beneath the bird's breast. He slowly raised it. At the moment eye contact between dog and bird was broken, the rooster erupted, raking his hands with its spurs and the wings beating in his face. The dog leaped and snared a tail feather. Tyree put that tail feather in his cigar box at home and sometimes took it out to hold while he read the hunting dog books Joan had bought.

He took along a sling shot on subsequent hunts. Quail scent kept the dog earnest and busy, but often it took all day to find a pheasant, and then Tyree's stone missed or merely bruised. Books he'd read had men, even boys, killing birds with a slingshot, but he couldn't do it, couldn't see how it could be done.

And then it was done. A rock hit a flushing rooster's wing and broke it. The cock hit the ground running and the dog was in pursuit. They made a long run on the pasture's slope, the cock darting and the dog wheeling to rebound onto the scent. Then the dog bounded above the grass to see the bird and in a moment had it. She did not savage the bird but lay down with it beneath her paws, panting. When Tyree fetched it and wrung its neck, the dog leaped and tore the breast hide. Tyree remembered Tom's admonition to insist that the dog do what it knows how to do. He slugged Lucky's ribs and she yelped and slunk away. Then he put the bird on the ground and talked to the dog. After a few trials, Lucky picked up the rooster and brought it to him and sat. Walking home, Tyree wished he could tell Henry of this remarkable business. But that was a convoluted impossibility. He knew the dog had replaced Henry.

It had been Christmas eve when he overheard Jason tell Joan, "Henry's father is out of jail and wants his boy back. To teach him a trade, I guess." Tyree and Henry were sorting the gifts beneath the tree and could hear the adults in the kitchen. "Worthless has a pointer hardly more than a pup," said Jason. "Let's get the boy a dog. Maybe it'll replace Henry."

He could hardly bear the dog when it slunk across the floor the next day, but in a few night their separate crying became a joint crying, and then the crying ceased.

Light seeped orange over the west mountains and thin clouds hung like pink streamers when Tyree brought his pheasant home. Jason Abo praised the mighty hunter and said they would have to make dinner of the bird another day. "I'm running a 10K in the morning," Jason said. "I need pasta." He had taken to running since the bad snow. "And the place we're moving to will have more pheasants. It will be a good place for a dog." Jason finished putting new laces on his running shoes and plucked a tail feather for his cap. "When you're getting run out of town, straighten your hat and pretend you're leading the parade."

2

Winter first got Tom Bird when he and Eleanor had been fishing in November on Green River below the big dam. It was a steep walk into the gorge and very cold. The river came from the bottom of the reservoir and was fifty degrees, but bank ice formed beyond the tailrace and hindered wading and casting. Bird coached Eleanor to roll cast and fished on downstream. The wet line froze in the rod guides, and he had to put the guides in his mouth to melt the ice. Eventually he caught two trout and a whitefish. When he walked back to Eleanor, he saw a nice fish working, and he told Eleanor to cast up and walk toward him at current speed, and be prepared. The trout rose and grabbed the tellico and swung down and then felt the hook and shot out of the water and bounced as though the water were a trampoline. The good trout kept jumping after it had broken off. Bird saw that Eleanor's guides had frozen tight. That was a good fish she could have caught with a working rod.

They drove home in a ground blizzard, over mesmerizing snakes of snow. That drifting blizzard and cold aftermath killed almost two hundred thousand cattle in North Dakota. It is a strange sad fact of crops or livestock that another's misfortune is your own salvation. A rising tide does not lift all boats. A Kansas wheat-farmer might save his house and land and status and marriage if the Austrailian crop fails. So it was now with cows. By the time Tom Bird and Eleanor were home, cattle prices were spiking up, and their herd was still doing fine on grass poking through a skiff of snow, while the Midwest suffered drifts that separated cows from hay and water and killed them.

Their first look at home was where a drunk dairy farmer had driven off the road and laid down a hundred feet of wire fence on Bird's home place. A feeble attempt had been made at propping up the fence. Bird's horses were still in the pasture. Bird sent Eleanor on home and grabbed his tools and went to repair the break. He had to reset poles, splice wire and stretch it. Eleanor had offered to help, but he was glad he had sent her home. It was a one-man job. Two would have to work together for days to achieve any decent coordination. Most ranch work was a one-man job. He hadn't thought of it before, but it was true. Maybe that was why he had been content to be alone. But he wasn't alone now. He had Eleanor. He had Tyree. Tyree was not his child, but he was close enough. Maybe Tyree would disappoint him, as Ramey had. But maybe that was bad figuring. The girl Ramey still swayed giggling in his arms. She still ran across the yard to him and swung in the tire swing and held his hand as they carried gopher traps down the ditchbank. The good things that had happened to him still lived. He only had to think of them. Still, it was good to have new good things. A man couldn't choose his thinking all the time. It would be a good trick, though. It would be useful. Maybe that's what those lamas in Tibet did. He would like to see the Himalayas. Probably they would disappoint him. A little mountain above the treeline was a fine thing to gaze upon, but too much rock and glacier would be only a thing to see and not a place to live. He had chosen good country. And he had found Eleanor. He would like to be with her now, drinking coffee in her kitchen while she read the newspaper, rather than untangling the ropes of the wire-stretcher in the dark. They were no longer young and there was a comfort that maybe wasn't as wonderful as the delirium of youth. He had missed that part. He knew he had missed that part. He had always loved her and had always taken care of her, and she had always been near, but it would have been wonderful to hold her when he was young. He could finish this job and drive to Three and hold her now. But she was tired and would be sleeping. He would hold her in the morning and make blueberry pancakes. He had a box of mix. Some people scoffed at the boxes, but he had not known a cook who could do as well as someone with a box and a pan of water. They weren't delirious youngsters. Maybe if he had fallen in love with a stranger, like that Jesus-freak Rose, maybe it would be like being young. He and Eleanor had too much traffic in their heads. They could only be happy, not delirious. He owned the Double Diamond, but he didn't, also. It would be a useful trick, all right, choosing what to think about.

After stretching the bottom strand, he lay down the fencing pliers and staples and sat on a stump. In the moonless night the clumps of wild rosebush looked like horses drifting toward the gap. As he shifted his gaze they appeared anew. He watched and listened. The dark blots were truly rosebush. From the dairyman Jimmy's place bawled upset cows. Though the cows were a mile away, the discordant sound carried in the still air and unsettled him like a burr.

"Come on, Jimmy, sober up and milk your goddamn cows."

His ire was partly directed at an otherwise decent man's drunkenness, partly at dumb egocentric gumptionless cattle, some at the cold, some at the blind finger-fumbling black night, some at his misplaced gloves and bleeding hands— but mostly at the near country and vast cosmos where he alone knew that some things should be done before thinking about them.

He could feel the air going colder as he stretched the next strand.

A few days later he was watching a television show with Eleanor which showed a cougar chasing and killing a bighorn sheep. The film was cut awkwardly and Bird leaned forward from his comfortable seat and said, "That kill is fake."

Eleanor said, "Tom, haven't you watched television before?"

"That cougar was let out of a cage. There's the sheep on the ridge, then the cougar running up the hill after him—that's the only time they're seen together—

then the sheep running, cougar running, back and forth, sheep and cougar, and then the cougar is daintily laying on a carcass."

"I took my father to see Hitchcock's The Birds. He said it scared the pants off him, even though he kept telling himself seagulls don't do that."

Bobby Coles knocked at the door. He stepped inside cradling his fine Ithaca double-barrel and commanded his bird dog to sit and stay on the porch. He brought the news that ducks for the last few nights had been flocking in to the Crooked River for gravel. Bobby, by way of asking permission, wondered if Tom might like to go. Tom did. Migrating birds found a brief seasonal clove of food and open water in the high country. These mallards from the Canadian prairies came at once and didn't stay long.

As Bobby promised, the ducks came at late dusk. They were fat northern birds, with bright orange feet. The shooting was fast in the last hold of light. Bird found it hard to pick out the drakes.

"Are we after hours?" he said.

Bobby got out his penlight to look at his watch, but the batteries were dead. "I don't think so," he said.

The eastern sky was black; the western sky still had a backdrop of gray for the black whistling wings. Bird fired and flame leaped out of the barrel.

"Are you sure we aren't after hours?"

"Naw," Bobby said as he swung up, tracked whistling wings, saw movement, and fired. "I can still hear them."

His dog quartered out and brought back a drake.

They dressed the birds under the headlights. Bobby Coles plucked his, while Bird skinned out the breasts.

Bobby said, "That bitch I gave Worthless—well, I just don't trust him to do right by her. And he ain't paid me."

"Not me, Bobby. I wouldn't teach her well, either."

"When Worthless was fifteen or thereabouts, he killed a neighbor's pig because some kids told him the pig was pregnant."

Bird thought about this. "I'll ask Jason and Joan," he said. "A boy can always use a dog."

Tom stopped at Two to give some ducks to Joan and to mention the dog. While he did the fine cleaning in the sink, Jason spoke of the surge of feeder steers. Moreover, heifers were rising, here on the brink of winter. People were again building herds. That was a good sign. Henry and Tyree were in the living room playing a video game on the television. Tom could not draw their attention from the game to say a proper hello. The game dead-ended but their fingers went *tap tap tap* as they launched into a new game.

"Kiddie coke," explained Abo.

191

3

Abo answered the phone. A recorded voice said, *This is a special computer survey conducted by the Aspen Institute. Please answer the questions. You are under no obligation—*

"Let me get this straight," said Abo.

—and you will win a valuable prize.

"You're a machine and you done just called me up."

Do you own a home?

4

Joan showed slides of medieval paintings to her biology class. Her intent was to show their failure of perspective. Then she diagrammed the Paola experiment that taught the world to see. Without science, ran her lesson, we cannot even do a simple thing like see. Prodigious silence lingered until a student said the Virgin Mary looked more prosperous in the early painting.

Joan bought Thanksgiving groceries at Sales and sat in her car in the parking lot, thinking of prosperous Mary and Her doomed son. Joan's own child, Ricky, had died of spinal meningitis—one morning he had a headache, and the following evening his aches were gones, and hers exploded. Three years ago she had connived to buy a pie from a Nazi Betty Crocker in this store, and had succeeded and regained life. Meningitis and Nazis would forswear her believing in pious giving of thanks, but she was grateful for the duties of providing a table and, to that extent, rang the bell for banal prosperity. Let us eat.

On the Saturday after Thanksgiving, a Bannock man hung himself in the Bannock jail. He had been arrested for battery against his wife who had given him nine children. The jail staff had taken his belt and pocketknife and put them in a plastic bag. They were eating takeout chicken while he used his undershirt to make a noose.

Bobby Coles counted the deceased as a friend. They had been together on smoke-jumping crews. One summer they went to Alaska and jumped over a thick forest, a solid canopy. The jumpers thought someone had made a grievous mistake. But the trees were dwarfs, eight feet tall. Bobby packed his chute and loaded a.44 magnum. His friend told him to file off the front sight. Bobby asked why. His friend replied, So it don't hurt so bad when Griz shoves it up your ass.

That was the story Bobby told during the procession into the church, which was a procession of stories about this Marine, policeman, volunteer coach, hunter and back-slapper, drywall contractor, also a very devout Mormon, an elder, one of the Seventy.

Inside the church better Mormons excused the man's transgression. A suicide was hellbound, of course, *unless* he had "bad chemicals in the brain." *Bad chemicals in the brain* was the refrain spoken by the bishop and the eulogizing brother and the sermonizing uncle, who was a forester and said he spoke as a scientist The dead man had a glimmer of hope, because he was so rotten. The wife was rotten, too, but she could be forgiven, for though she had forced the battery she had not forced the suicide. The three speakers heartily agreed on the glory of the church in this occasion of praying for the soul of a maybe. Most of the folks in the pews were moved to throw the worthless fuck in the coffin into the pond outside and get home to dinner.

Afterwards, on the church grass, Worthless Coles said, "We'd hang men who spoke of our kin that way."

Coles had it right, Tom Bird thought. However, he prevented Worthless from offering his services to the widow at this moment.

5

Then it was not the brink of winter. It was winter. Cold came before the snow, and frost speared deep into the unprotected ground during twelve days of clear skies and still arctic air. With enough clothes and ample pantry, Bird did not mind the cold. What it did to machines—our other halves—was frightful. Pipes and pumps froze and car batteries waned and electrical circuit breakers popped. At twenty-nine below, essentials became known: water and food to all critters. During the subzero span, Bird progressed through the freezing of the underground outside lines, the gelling of his furnace oil and subsequent freezing of inside taps, then the frozen stoppage of the lowest outlet at the well, and finally the creek itself frozen. The space heaters of his neighbors and the rental place in town were in use, so he strung light bulbs on extension cords in hopes of keeping pipes from bursting.

With an axe he cut a swath of ice-blocks across the creek. The trickle he exhumed quickly froze. He built a fire and heated galvanized cans full of ice-chunks to water the horses. The chore took all day and when the last horse walked back to the hay, a gloaming twilight was settling on the silver brush-lines of hoarfrost. Now he thought: what about me? He went to feed with Eleanor. Then he checked the water on the three Double Diamond places and put in 100-watt bulbs to replace the sixties in the well-houses. It was a race against frost that was approaching three feet deep. A single frost-free faucet was watering eight hundred bred heifers at the airstrip house.

The snowfall in the morning was a welcome sight, a blanket to stop the frost. It started heavy but by mid-morning was a thin snow borne by cold wind, drifting. On a morning television show the weatherman pointed to dipping lines on a national map and did a mock shiver. He then pointed to sunny Florida and made a joke.

Bird drove to Two to talk with Jason Abo. They stood in the lots by their pickups. As they spoke the lee of the tires drifted up to the hubs.

Bird said, "Let's open the gates to the creek bottoms and herd what we can in our trucks to the gates. It will make a feeding mess, and later a sorting mess. I hate to make such a mess on account of a clown on television, but I think we ought to."

Abo had to shout, it seemed. "Ain't it too cold to snow?"

"It sure is. And it's snowing. If you agree—"

"I agree."

"You take south from here. You fueled up?" Bird involuntarily did the weatherman's crossed-arm hunch and shiver. "Don't force any drifts. Rescue might be long in coming. You want me to sketch out the gates?"

Abo shook his head.

Bird said, "Open all you can get to, even into the haystacks. They're good windbreaks."

"Tom, tell me seriously. Are we in trouble?"

"Nah, just that silly ass weatherman. And some mean ass weather."

Bird drove all day. Drifts stopped him. It was like driving a maze. He would guess the contour to the next gate, be blocked by a drift...calculate his momentum to storm through it or retreat to make a new guess. He worried about Abo, who did not have his knowledge of ditches and rock fields. He worried about the ten cars of corn for the finishing lot that were sitting in Bannock. It would be a while before the snowplows would come his way.

When he met Abo back at Two, it was twilight. They had got most of the gates open. Abo said Bruin and Salt creeks were icing bad. They parted with weary congratulations to one another that took this form: *There was a bad spot or two.*

The second day was the worst, twenty-two degrees below zero with a steady gale, a chill factor calculated at eighty below by the radio man who said travelers were stranded by the hundreds, in Bannock and elsewhere. Tom Bird stepped outside and could not stand or breathe or see. He doubted it was snowing, being so cold; snowflakes were hustling by too fast to be visible; it was a strange slanting fog, gray and formless and cold so intense it burned. He bundled up and made a second effort to reach his pickup and start it. It fired up. He stuffed a blanket in the gap between the grill and radiator, and retreated to the house with frost-stung face and ears and hands. He gathered up clothing and blankets and food, and carried them to the pickup. No horse could face that wind. He knew he had to cut the fence to allow the Greenhurst cows to get up into the Forest Service timber, but he didn't know how. The lee fenceline was a mile from the road. That flat pasture would be too drifted for a truck, even if chained all around. He put on the chains in increments between dashes back into the house. His fleece-lined gloves were not good enough, and his hands ached when warm. This was weather a body should just sit out. Ignore the world for two days and then crawl out of the hole to make a new acquaintance. Hell, if those cows were only buffalo. They only needed to be buffalo once a decade, and this was that time. Buffalo could look out for themselves. Cattle needed a man to look out for them. He cut up a blanket to wrap his face like a mummy, drank a cup of hot chocolate, and went out.

To stay on the road, he had to travel in compound, slower than a walk. He could not see the depths of the drifts, but felt them, in the sink and spin of the tires. He expected one to prove too deep, in fact might have counted on it happening soon so that he could walk home safely in a tire track and hole up having tried. But he kept moving, navigating by the dim alleyway of trees. Then he was on the flats and the trees were gone. He tracked a line of fenceposts or the left; one section was completely drifted over, and for a time he merely guessed at the road, feeling for when a front tire began to drop off it. He had only a rough idea where he was.

He felt the swale and stopped. This was it. He drove a little farther to be sure. One mile east was the fence. If he could cut that fence, the cattle could get into the brush and trees and survive. Already some cows would be aborting. Two more days they would be dehydrating and death would be wholesale. These, to be given a chance for two more days, had to escape the wind. Bird had not expected to get to this point. And now he felt afraid. He knew he could travel using the north-by-northwest wind as a guide for direction and he could count his steps for distance, and so the thing could be done, and that plausibility made him afraid, for he would have to do it.

There was no point in carrying blankets or food or candles. If he lost direction, he would be a corpse. He tied twelve-inch pieces of baling twine to his belt and wrists. They were his weathervanes. He stood outside the pickup and keyed in to the windward push on his body and the angles of the twine. He told himself he would go one hundred yards and then judge whether it was prudent to go on. That decision allowed him to overcome his fear and pain in this shocking cold. One hundred yards, a bit of misery, backtrack to his truck.

Wind and cold and snow erased the land, but he made this first leg and scuffed around in the snow and right away found a pile of old corral wood. So his compass was true and his distance also, and he simply went on. If attention was paid and the wind stayed constant, the salvation of these cows was plausible.

He removed his gloves to open a fresh pack of cigarettes, but his fingers were stone. He lifted the mummy stocking and used his teeth to tear open the cellophane and foil. With his teeth he lifted out one cigarette and spit it out. One cigarette for each hundred yards, he planned. All he had to do was go one hundred yards at a time, paying attention to the wind and counting steps and remembering there were twenty cigarettes in a pack.

Fifteen cigarettes were gone from the pack when he came upon the first carcass. Then there were several. He had been trudging for a long time by reptilian instinct, his fear abandoned because death loomed puny against this awesome misery of cold. It was strange to find himself in possession yet of a mind as he examined the dead cattle. They had died of suffocation, ice filling their nostrils and their mouths frozen shut. A strip of woolen blanket would have saved them.

The last cigarette he kept, to smoke before he died. He was matter-of-fact. He had come too far. He had veered. He might be anywhere. The wind had stepped up audibly, into a scream, and maybe it had shifted. He stepped in a big drift and it blew away like smoke; the big drift just vanished, leaving bare ground. He could not hope to burrow into a drift, for the shell would blow away or the cavity fill. The wind was telling all the stories now.

He backtrailed. Shortly his footprints could not be discerned. He set his mind again to the twine. There was no point in figuring distance. He would make the road or not.

Then he came upon dead cattle. One was a Lazarus and stood. Then he was at the edge of a silent herd. He vectored toward the slant of their heads, moving through the phantoms until he came to the wire. His hand wouldn't grip and he dropped the cutters. He held the cutters in his two palms and awkwardly pushed the handles together. The top wire popped like a guitar string. He worked down. No hurry now, he told himself. There was a lot of wire to cut and the ends had to be wrapped around the posts. He knew he hadn't the coordination to pull the staples. This was a job that mustn't discourage him.

He became more adroit at cutting. Pawing through the snow to find the wire was the worst. The wire whipped about when he yanked it from the snow, but he was so wrapped he had only to shield his eyes. He moved down the line of mute, listless cattle. After cutting the fourth section he swung back to push the cows through the breaks, but they were unyielding, stolid as fenceposts, suffocating in the gale of ice. Presently he heard one low, and then several, and there was a general stirring, and phantom cattle passed him moving resolutely with the wind, some even trotting, rambunctious ones amid the forlorn. There were more Lazaruses, though plenty remained on the snow, plenty beneath it. A coyote stood up from between two carcasses as Bird approached and circled back to recapture the windbreak as the man passed. Bird stood over a prone cow with blinking eyes and attempted to kick her up. He dug in her mouth and snared her tongue and yanked, but she wouldn't beller or move. It hit him that this was the end of the Double Diamond.

The cows, the live ones, were moving. That was all he could do. The wind in his face made a better compass, though it stole his breath. He settled into a rhythm of a swimmer, three steps and turning his head to breathe. He entered a netherworld of three-steps, breathe, face the wind. An eon or an instant later he noted with detached surprise that he was looking at his truck.

In the cab, out of the wind, he began to itch all over.

The third day of the blizzard was not so bad.

On the fourth day the sun came dazzling, and the air was still, and it was forty-two below. Snowplows worked all day to clear the road to Bruin. In places the road was banked high like a toboggan run. Bird was able to get about some. With binoculars he looked at the Greenhurst pasture and saw carcasses and snow-mounds and estimated five hundred dead out of the eleven hundred that had been there. The survivors were in the timber dehydrating. The Map Rock pasture with the Dubois yearlings was empty. They had crossed a drifted-over fence and were into the Sur Fork canyon, probably. Eleanor had got assurance that the National Guard would be making helicopter dumps of hay if the good weather held, and that her stranded Sur Fork herd would be on the list. There were other missing herds, gone over drifted fences, herds of two and three hundred. He and Baumgarten and Abo, working from trucks, brought several of those back to feed and water, and the rest they would get on horses the next day. They made plans and Tom Bird bunked with Eleanor that night and was numb from what he had seen that day.

The sun rose bright and rang in the still air. It was ten degrees, almost pleasant, as they saddled at Two. They would ride in pairs: Jason and Tyree, Baumgarten and Henry, Bobby Coles and Eleanor, Worthless and Joan, Bird and Sally. Bob Honstead would wait for the fleet of snowmachine volunteers that were coming out from Bannock. Bird gave detailed instructions and told no one to improvise. It was to be accepted that maybe the jobs assigned could not be done, and all should be turned back to the valley by three o'clock, cows or no.

The first bunch that Bird and Sally found were belly deep in a ravine of second-growth fir. Their ribs showed dehydration. Sally broke trail while Bird lined out the bunch, his horse floundering. Some of the cows seemed to be blind. When they were all moving, he rode up the ridge and dug beneath the snow with his hands until he found the ring of stones of a campfire that some hunters had made in October. He loaded his pockets with charcoal, painted his cheekbones, and rode ahead to give the treatment to Sally.

Worthless and Joan became snowblind. They had the flat northern pasture to ride and the sun reflected off the unbroken snow and burned their eyes. They first felt a slight irritation of the eyes, and then it was sand in the eyes, and then pea-gravel. They came in with their eyes closed in the company of twelve heifers. Fifty or so were behind them, somewhere.

The riders in the timber did not suffer snowblindness, but they had a hard time breaking trail to bring the herds out. A cow in Eleanor's bunch lay down on the march and labored to expel a still-born calf; prolapsed, she would lie five weeks in that spot, swinging an angry head when hay and water were carried to her, a statistic of the dead count until she stood and lived.

Baumgarten and Henry couldn't find the bunch they were after. The trail was clear enough. Three hundred cows had drifted over the fence on a huge mound that in traveling single file they had tramped down like a hallway. Over the mound the trail became a narrow lane which angled up the first ridge and began to disperse and then was gone. The jockey and the boy methodically worked the hillside and the bottom of a rocky draw and then roamed in farther casts, without finding a cow. They crossed another ridge and now had a wider fan of country to search, a country of steep draws and thick dark growth. Sunlight slipped through the trees infrequently. The snow fell off the branches down their necks. Henry wore a slicker and rubber boots. His feet were numb-cold, but they were dry. Baumgarten was wearing a leather boot and was beginning to feel scared about his good foot. His pants were mostly damp. His bandana was wet, and water had soaked through his down vest and shirt onto his chest where he had not kept his leather jacket buttoned. He periodically got off to walk to warm up. When a wind kicked up late afternoon, he grew too cold to continue.

"How you doin', Henry?" Baumgarten asked.

"Fine," said the boy. He was cold.

"Let's skedaddle home. It's too late to go over the other side. These cattle can stand the night better than I can."

When they got back on top of the ridge, the valley was obscured. Behind them the Cayuse Canyon was clear, but ahead it was gray. Baumgarten studied what remained of his view for a line back to the truck. He had only a brief look at the ridge yet to cross before it was enveloped by a gray mass which seemed to be rising up from the earth like a line of dark geysers rather than snow falling from the sky.

The snow was borne into them on a sharp wind, small flakes, a driving screen that was absolute at ten yards. The bent trees moaned. The jockey and the boy huddled over the horses' necks. The horses cheated against facing the wind. Baumgarten, leading, decided they were traversing too much. He was wet and cold and thought that they might strike their forenoon trail on the traversing route. He was using his heels constantly, like a sport on a spoiled dude horse. Then he decided to go back to the ridgetop and get the line again, and this time hold it against the horses' cheating. He called to Henry to follow. Without snow blowing into his face, backtracking was easy for a time. Then snow blew heavy enough to obscure the ground, and the jockey was leaning low out of the saddle to see the ground, and the tracks were filling, and the light was fading. The ridgeline had no definition. He came to some alders and wondered. He was looking for a tree by a wedge of alders with a natural stack of rocks at the funnel end. These alders were not that wedge.

They were riding down again. He could not be sure of it for a while. Then he was. The wind was at their backs, so they were heading the wrong way.

He turned and called, "How you doing, Henry?"

"Fine," said the muffled voice of the hunched boy in his slicker.

Baumgarten reined back into the wind.

The horses climbed and sidehilled and descended. They repeated and reversed the sequence. Baumgarten had flat lost the cardinal points, along with all sense of distance.

Night came and still the snow came.

Henry stood in a windbreak of skinny lodgepole pine while Baumgarten cut the horses' throats. The boy's hands and feet hurt and he was hunched in his slicker, moving minutely to get his back to the wind while the horses fell.

Baumgarten labored, splitting the hide. Plunging his hands into the entrails felt wonderful. He warmed his hands, then resolutely set to eviscerating two horses. It was long, hard. He couldn't get the windpipes. Finally he called Henry and rebuked him for his queasiness and ushered him into the cavity of a horse.

The smell was strong and Henry's cheek was sticky where it lay against the ribs, but he was warm and he slept, meaning to live.

The snow machines buzzed the dawn. Their coming woke Baumgarten. He could hear several, revving and slacking. He had slept in short increments, mostly, but the snow machines had pulled him from dream. He wriggled free. He was alive. Beneath an overcast sky, he saw where he was. He knelt in the snow and cocked an ear this and thus toward the engine noise. He hurled a red saddle blanket aloft three times before it stuck in the branches of a tree.

Henry's horse had been dropped with a lee brisket, and the snow had drifted to make a snow cave. Baumgarten pulled the boy out like a birthing. The two cleansed themselves of blood while awaiting the machines.

The first to arrive was driven by Julio Delotorriente, paralyzed from the waist down, with Tom Bird clinging behind.

Bird had been out all night. He had ridden one fat horse and led a fat packhorse with tent and bedding and fuel and food. The two horses were now tied three miles away. He had sunburned eyeballs which, because they hadn't been given rest, were rasping. He flicked his eyelids open briefly to see the yellow slicker and dark face of Henry. He waded forward through the snow to grab the boy's arm. "Are you all right?" he asked.

The boy said he was. Baumgarten was there, too. Bird raised and lowered his eyelids to take in the rest.

Julio said, "Tom, did the horses die, or did they butcher them?"

Bird faced Baumgarten. "Why'd you think to do such a thing? Did you read about it?"

"You weren't there, Tom."

The other snow machines arrived singularly. Bird tried to shoo the first rescuers away with the survivors, but the machines gathered, and their riders wondered *Why hadn't they given the horses their heads?*

"You all weren't there," Baumgarten proclaimed. He gathered tack to tote to the machines.

No more blizzards came, but it stayed cold for ten days. The National Guard dropped hay. Farmers in Iowa donated hay, which didn't change things. But it was appreciated, one farmer to another. Most of the Double Diamond cattle were found. Dehydration did the most sinister work. Some would not drink when trailed to water, and death continued to diminish a herd for three days after it was saved. Many aborted. Too many aborted, so many they aborted the Double Diamond.

6

The men and woman of the Double Diamond scrambled to save the calves. Jason Abo observed they should all be receiving wages from the bank, since all they were accomplishing was minimizing the hit to the bank; and they all knew this, but they worked anyway, even to salvaging bone-meal value of the carcasses. The last train to roll from Bannock before the tracks were lifted in 1992 was a train of frozen cows stacked and lashed on twelve flatbeds, to be rendered into fertilizer.

Henry's father, on his drive to Bannock, had met this slow-chugging train. Being free was eerie, the woods were eerie, this train of death downright spooky. He hurried along until he was fidgeting in the ranch yard, declining the invitation to dinner. He was prison strong. His muscles wanted to jump out of his skin and fly over the trees to the good warm asphalt of San Diego. Lifting and eating and reading the Bible, is how Mr. Ortiz had paid his debt to society. Smiling and multiple thank-you's was how he paid his debt to this white couple with the little boy. He did not fail to see the sad, lingering soul-shake of the two boys. Driving away, he took the Bible off the dash and set it on his lap. Somewhere within was the good wisdom to erase Henry's sadness.

7

In late March, Tom Bird was sitting on the stoop of his house surrounded by headstalls and halters and reins coiled on the steps and draped from yard rocks. He had been oiling and patching since noon. Yesterday he had done the saddles and Deckers, all the latigos and cinches and martingales and breechings; the day before that, all the panniers and hobbles and lariats and rope. It was unbelievable what the barn had disgorged. And he was fixing to get skinny.

A car pulled in. Bird could smell Al before he saw him. His eyes really hadn't got right. He had not been in to the Alforcas since the first blizzard, in December.

"For sale," Bird said, gesturing broadly.

"I don't like horses," Al said, mounting the steps. "I only live here because there isn't traffic."

Bird finished tying a sash cord around a bosal to make hackamore reins and a longe rope. He went inside to bring out crackers and smoked goose. He came back and looked at his harvest of tack. The boxes of tools in the pickup were just things. The tack was stories. He was hauling it all to Bobby Coles. Bobby would sell what he could to individuals and consign the rest to suitable auctions. Having Bobby in possession of his wealth was akin to dumping it in the river, but he did want the good things used.

They ate and drank coffee.

"Winter is long," Al said.

"Seems long," Bird said.

One of the horses looked wrong. His two-year-old, Little Man, was standing on the wrong side of the fence down by the creek. Tom got the binoculars. He saw coils of wire, the horse beyond, a glint of red on snow. This he narrated to Al, who understood and buttoned his coat to leave.

"Eleanor's moved into the Holiday Inn."

"Yes."

"I always say I don't give advice."

"That's a habit to be much admired."

"This is good goose," Al said.

"It's the Chinese sauce."

"Of course," Al said. He got busy eating until the plate was empty.

Then Bird said, "Before I leave I would like to sled the bones of those we couldn't salvage to the Cayuse River. They would be good for the *ph* content of the water, good for mayflies and caddisflies and stoneflies." He went into the house to get his vet bag from the refrigerator and trailed Al to his car. "Also, would like to go back East and fish those limestone streams, just to see what they're like. Those are two plans. I'm studying on others."

"If there's anything—"

"—you can do, I will tell you the moment I think of it."

Tom waved goodbye and hiked to the creek with his vet bag. Little Man was criss-crossed with wire cuts across the chest and front legs. Some of the cuts were clean red lines with the distinct marks of the barbs, as though stitched. In other cuts the hide hung loose and blood flowed. A plate-sized patch of hide dangled from his brisket.

"Little Man," said Tom Bird, "you are a mess."

He applied sulfa powder and injected 50 cc's of penicillin and drove to town to convey to the bank the sorry state of this critter and made a trade.

Two months later, astride scarred Little Man, Bird led his pack mare beneath the crossbar of the O-X. On the mare were his possessions. On top was tied a basketball hoop. Bird rode on up the lane and turned to look at the dim outline of Two Teats eighty miles and two river drainages away. He had ridden out of the mountains. This was hill country, coulees and chukar and cheat grass; water trucks had to be filled from wells to water stock in metal tanks. The O-X was owned by Texans, adulterated by a dude service and hunting privileges and piecemeal development, but still mostly a ranch where cows paid the bills. There were several trailer houses and the old headquarters bunkhouse. The foreman of the O-X came out of a trailer house to greet Bird.

"Glad to have you aboard," said the foreman. "We'll put up that hoop right away, Mr. Bird."

Printed in the United States
1501

9 780759 626157